AF527254

Critical Guide to Literature in English

CRITICAL GUIDE TO LITERATURE IN ENGLISH

Ritupurna Tripathy

SWASTIK

SWASTIK PUBLICATIONS

DELHI–110094 (INDIA)

SWASTIK PUBLICATIONS
31 Gali No. 1, A Block, Pocket 5, CRP Water Tank,
Sonia Vihar, Delhi-110094
Cell: 9968482939, 9899462604
e-mail: swastik_books@yahoo.com

Critical Guide to Literature in English

© Reserved

First Published 2012

ISBN:- 978-93-81084-18-2

[No Part of this book may be reproduced in any form by photocopying or by any electronic or mechanical means, including, information storage or retrieval systems, without permission in writting from publisher of this book.]

PRINTED IN INDIA

Published by Indra Mani Pandey for Swastik Publications, Delhi and Printed at Asian Offset Press, Delhi-53

PREFACE

English literature is the literature written in the English language, including literature composed in English by writers not necessarily from England; for example, Robert Burns was Scottish, James Joyce was Irish, Joseph Conrad was born in Poland, Dylan Thomas was Welsh, Edgar Allan Poe was American, V. S. Naipaul was born in Trinidad, and Vladimir Nabokov was Russian, but all are considered important writers in the history of English literature. In other words, English literature is as diverse as the varieties and dialects of English spoken around the world.

This book embodying a series of appreciations of the great English writers, should helpful in the college teaching of literature. The contents have been selected and arranged to present a chronological and almost continuous account of English literature from its beginning in the age of Elizabeth down to Modern Literature. Original quotations and critical commentaries are given to maintain the gravity of the text. All major works of leading writers are aptly discussed with extensive criticism. Shakespearean characterization to Romanticism is characteristically dealt with.

Classical Miltonic literature is worth reading and an extensive survey on Victorian literature has been illustrated with modern perceptions of recent critics. Hope this book will help the students and teachers of different Indian Universities in a very fruitful manner.

Author

CONTENTS

Preface V

1. The Age of Elizabeth 1
2. Spenser 22
3. Shakspeare 32
4. The Characters of Shakspeare's Plays 44
5. Milton 87
6. Pope 101
7. The English Novelists 112
8. Character of Mr. Burke, 1807 125
9. Mr. Coleridge 150
10. Mr. Southey 158
11. Sir Walter Scott 162
12. Lord Byron 169
13. 18th Century in Literature 200
14. Romanticism 242
15. Victorian Literature 250
16. Modern Literature 256

Bibliography 261

1

The Age of Elizabeth

The earlier half of Elizabeth's reign, also, though not lacking in literary effort, produced no work of permanent importance. After the religious convulsions of half a century time was required for the development of the internal quiet and confidence from which a great literature could spring. At length, however, the hour grew ripe and there came the greatest outburst of creative energy in the whole history of English literature. Under Elizabeth's wise guidance the prosperity and enthusiasm of the nation had risen to the highest pitch, and London in particular was overflowing with vigorous life. A special stimulus of the most intense kind came from the struggle with Spain.

After a generation of half-piratical depredations by the English seadogs against the Spanish treasure fleets and the Spanish settlements in America, King Philip, exasperated beyond all patience and urged on by a bigot's zeal for the Catholic Church, began deliberately to prepare the Great Armada, which was to crush at one blow the insolence, the independence, and the religion of England. There followed several long years of breathless suspense; then in 1588 the Armada sailed and was utterly overwhelmed in one of the most complete disasters of the world's history. Thereupon the released energy of England broke out exultantly into still more impetuous achievement in almost every line of activity. The great literary period is taken by common consent to begin with the publication of Spenser's 'Shepherd's Calendar' in 1579, and to end in some sense at the death of Elizabeth in 1603, though in the drama, at least, it really continues many years longer.

Several general characteristics of Elizabethan literature and writers should be indicated at the outset.

1. The period has the great variety of almost unlimited creative force; it includes works of many kinds in both

verse and prose, and ranges in spirit from the loftiest Platonic idealism or the most delightful romance to the level of very repulsive realism.

2. It was mainly dominated, however, by the spirit of romance.
3. It was full also of the spirit of dramatic action, as befitted an age whose restless enterprise was eagerly extending itself to every quarter of the globe.
4. In style it often exhibits romantic luxuriance, which sometimes takes the form of elaborate affectations of which the favourite 'conceit' is only the most apparent.
5. It was in part a period of experimentation, when the proper material and limits of literary forms were being determined, oftentimes by means of false starts and grandiose failures. In particular, many efforts were made to give prolonged poetical treatment to many subjects essentially prosaic, for example to systems of theological or scientific thought, or to the geography of all England.
6. It continued to be largely influenced by the literature of Italy, and to a less degree by those of France and Spain.
7. The literary spirit was all-pervasive, and the authors were men (not yet women) of almost every class, from distinguished courtiers, like Ralegh and Sidney, to the company of hack writers, who starved in garrets and hung about the outskirts of the bustling taverns.

Prose Fiction

The period saw the beginning, among other things, of English prose fiction of something like the later modern type. First appeared a series of collections of short tales chiefly translated from Italian authors, to which tales the Italian name 'novella' (novel) was applied. Most of the separate tales are crude or amateurish and have only historical interest, though as a class they furnished the plots for many Elizabethan dramas, including several of Shakespeare's. The most important collection was Painter's 'Palace of Pleasure,' in 1566. The earliest original, or partly original, English prose fictions to appear were handbooks of morals and manners in story form, and here the beginning was made by John Lyly, who is also of some importance in the history of the Elizabethan drama. In 1578 Lyly, at the age of twenty-five, came from Oxford to London, full of the enthusiasm of Renaissance learning, and evidently determined to fix himself as a new and dazzling star in the literary sky. In this ambition he achieved a remarkable and immediate success, by the publication of a little book entitled 'Euphues and His Anatomie of Wit.' 'Euphues' means 'the well-bred man,' and though there is a slight action, the work is mainly a series of moralising disquisitions (mostly rearranged from Sir Thomas North's translation of 'The Dial of Princes' of the Spaniard Guevara) on love, religion, and conduct.

Most influential, however, for the time-being, was Lyly's style, which is the most conspicuous English example of the later Renaissance craze, then rampant throughout Western Europe, for refining and beautifying the art of prose expression in a mincingly affected fashion. Witty, clever, and sparkling at all costs, Lyly takes especial pains to balance his sentences and clauses antithetically, phrase against phrase and often word against word, sometimes emphasising the balance also by an exaggerated use of alliteration and assonance. A representative sentence is this:

> Although there be none so ignorant that doth not know, neither any so impudent that will not confesse, friendship to be the jewell of humaine joye; yet whosoever shall see this amitie grounded upon a little affection, will soone conjecture that it shall be dissolved upon a light occasion.'

Others of Lyly's affectations are rhetorical questions, hosts of allusions to classical history, and literature, and an unfailing succession of similes from all the recondite knowledge that he can command, especially from the fantastic collection of fables which, coming down through the Middle Ages from the Roman writer Pliny, went at that time by the name of natural history and which we have already encountered in the medieval Bestiaries. Preposterous by any reasonable standard, Lyly's style, 'Euphuism,' precisely hit the Court taste of his age and became for a decade its most approved conversational dialect.

In literature the imitations of 'Euphues' which flourished for a while gave way to a series of romances inaugurated by the 'Arcadia' of Sir Philip Sidney. Sidney's brilliant position for a few years as the noblest representative of chivalrous ideals in the intriguing Court of Elizabeth is a matter of common fame, as is his death in 1586 at the age of thirty-two during the siege of Zutphen in Holland. He wrote 'Arcadia' for the amusement of his sister, the Countess of Pembroke, during a period of enforced retirement beginning in 1580, but the book was not published until ten years later. It is a pastoral romance, in the general style of Italian and Spanish romances of the earlier part of the century.

The pastoral is the most artificial literary form in modern fiction. It may be said to have begun in the third century B. C. with the perfectly sincere poems of the Greek Theocritus, who gives genuine expression to the life of actual Sicilian shepherds. But with successive Latin, Medieval, and Renaissance writers in verse and prose the country characters and setting had become mere disguises, sometimes allegorical, for the expression of the very far from simple sentiments of the upper classes, and sometimes for their partly genuine longing, the outgrowth of sophisticated weariness and ennui, for rural naturalness. Sidney's very complicated tale of adventures in love and war, much longer than any of its successors, is by no means free from artificiality, but it finely mirrors his own knightly spirit and remains a permanent English classic. Among his followers were some of the better hack-writers of the time, who were also among the minor dramatists and poets, especially Robert Greene and Thomas Lodge. Lodge's 'Rosalynde,' also much influenced by Lyly, is in itself a pretty story and is noteworthy as the original of Shakespeare's 'As You Like It.'

Lastly, in the concluding decade of the sixteenth century, came a series of realistic stories depicting chiefly, in more or less farcical spirit, the life of the poorer classes. They belonged mostly to that class of realistic fiction which is called picaresque, from the Spanish word 'picaro,' a rogue, because it began in Spain with the 'Lazarillo de Tormes' of Diego de Mendoza, in 1553, and because its heroes are knavish serving-boys or similar characters whose unprincipled tricks and exploits formed the substance of the stories. In Elizabethan England it produced nothing of individual note.

The age of Elizabeth was distinguished, beyond, perhaps, any other in english history, by a number of great men, famous in different ways, and whose names have come down to us with unblemished honours; statesmen, warriors, divines, scholars, poets, and philosophers, Raleigh, Drake, Coke, Hooker, and higher and more sounding still, and still more frequent in our mouths, Shakspeare, Spenser, Sidney, Bacon, Jonson, Beaumont and Fletcher, men whom fame has eternised in her long and lasting scroll, and who, by their words and acts, were benefactors of their country, and ornaments of human nature.

Their attainments of different kinds bore the same general stamp, and it was sterling: what they did, had the mark of their age and country upon it. Perhaps the genius of Great Britain (if I may so speak without offence or flattery), never shone out fuller or brighter, or looked more like itself, than at this period. Our writers and great men had something in them that savoured of the soil from which they grew: they were not French, they were not Dutch, or German, or Greek, or Latin; they were truly English.

They did not look out of themselves to see what they should be; they sought for truth and nature, and found it in themselves. There was no tinsel, and but little art; they were not the spoiled children of affectation and refinement, but a bold, vigorous, independent race of thinkers, with prodigious strength and energy, with none but natural grace, and heartfelt unobtrusive delicacy. They were not at all sophisticated. The mind of their country was great in them, and it prevailed. With their learning and unexampled acquirement, they did not forget that they were men: with all their endeavours after excellence, they did not lay aside the strong original bent and character of their minds. What they performed was chiefly nature's handy work; and time has claimed it for his own.

To these, however, might be added others not less learned, nor with a scarce less happy vein, but less fortunate in the event, who, though as renowned in their day, have sunk into "mere oblivion," and of whom the only record (but that the noblest) is to be found in their works. Their works and their names, "poor, poor dumb names," are all that remains of such men as Webster, Deckar, Marston, Marlow, Chapman, Heywood, Middleton, and Rowley! "How lov'd, how honour'd once, avails, them not:" though they were the friend and fellow labourers of Shakspeare, sharing his fame and fortune, with him, the rivals of Jonson, and the masters of Beaumont and Fletcher's well sung woes!

They went out one by one unnoticed, like evening lights; or were swallowed up in the headlong torrent of puritanic zeal which succeeded, and swept away everything in its unsparing course, throwing up the wrecks of taste and genius at random, and at long fitful intervals, amidst the painted gew–gaws and foreign frippery of the reign of Charles II and from which we are only now recovering the scattered fragments and broken images to erect a temple to true Fame! How long, before it will be completed?

If I can do anything to rescue some of these writers from hopeless obscurity, and to do them right, without prejudice to well deserved reputation, I shall have succeeded in what I chiefly propose. I shall not attempt, indeed, to adjust the spelling, or restore the pointing, as if the genius of poetry lay hid in errors of the press, but leaving these weightier matters of criticism to those who are more able and willing to bear the burden, try to bring out their real beauties to the eager sight, "draw the curtain of Time, and shew the picture of Genius," restraining my own admiration within reasonable bounds! . . .

We affect to wonder at Shakspeare, and one or two more of that period, as solitary instances upon record; whereas it is our own dearth of information that makes the waste; for there is no time more populous of intellect, or more prolific of intellectual wealth, than the one we are speaking of. Shakspeare did not look upon himself in this light, as a sort of monster of poetical genius, or on his contemporaries as "less than smallest dwarfs," when he speaks with true, not false modesty, of himself and them, and of his wayward thoughts, "desiring this man's art, and that man's scope." We fancy that there were no such men, that could either add to or take anything away from him, but such there were. He indeed overlooks and commands the admiration of posterity, but he does it from the tableland of the age in which he lived.

He towered above his fellows, "in shape and gesture proudly eminent;" but he was one of a race of giants, the tallest, the strongest, the most graceful, and beautiful of them; but it was a common and a noble brood. He was not something sacred and aloof from the vulgar herd of men, but shook hands with nature and the circumstances of the time, and is distinguished from his immediate contemporaries, not in kind, but in degree and greater variety of excellence. He did not form a class or species by himself, but belonged to a class or species. His age was necessary to him; nor could he have been wrenched from his place in the edifice of which he was so conspicuous a part, without equal injury to himself and it. Mr. Wordsworth says of Milton, that "his soul was like a star, and dwelt apart." This cannot be said with any propriety of Shakspeare, who certainly moved in a constellation of bright luminaries, and "drew after him a third part of the heavens." If we allow, for argurnent's sake (or for truthes, which is better), that he was in himself equal to all his competitors put together; yet there was more dramatic excellence in that age than in the whole of the period that has elapsed since.

If his contemporaries, with their united strength, would hardly make one Shakspeare, certain it is that all his successors would not make half a one. With the exception of a single writer, Otway, and of a single play of his (Venice Preserved), there is nobody in tragedy and dramatic poetry (I do not here speak of comedy) to be compared to the great men of the age of Shakspeare, and immediately after. They are a mighty phalanx of kindred spirits closing him round, moving in the same orbit, and impelled by the same causes in their whirling and eccentric career.

They had the same faults and the same excellences; the same strength and depth and richness, the same truth of character, passion, imagination, thought and language, thrown, heaped, massed together without careful polishing or exact method, but poured out in unconcerned profusion from the lap of nature and genius in boundless and unrivalled magnificence. The sweetness of Deckar, the thought of Marston, the gravity of Chapman, the grace of Fletcher and his young–eyed wit, Jonson's learned sock, the flowing vein of Middleton, Heywood's ease, the pathos of Webster, and Marlow's deep designs, add a double lustre to the sweetness, thought, gravity, grace, wit, artless nature, copiousness, ease, pathos, and sublime conceptions of Shakspeare's Muse.

They are indeed the scale by which we can best ascend to the true knowledge and love of him. Our admiration of them does not lessen our relish for him: but, on the contrary, increases and confirms it. For such an extraordinary combination and development of fancy and genius many causes may be assigned; and we may seek for the chief of them in religion, in politics, in the circumstances of the time, the recent diffusion of letters, in local situation, and in the character of the men who adorned that period, and availed themselves so nobly of the advantages placed within their reach.

I shall here attempt to give a general sketch of these causes, and of the manner in which they operated to mould and stamp the poetry of the country at the period of which I have to treat; independently of incidental and fortuitous causes, for which there is no accounting, but which, after all, have often the greatest share in determining the most important results.

The first cause I shall mention, as contributing to this general effect, was the Reformation, which had just then taken place. This event gave a mighty impulse and increased activity to thought and inquiry, and agitated the inert mass of accumulated prejudices throughout Europe. The effect of the concussion was general; but the shock was greatest in this country.

It toppled down the full–grown, intolerable abuses of centuries at a blow; heaved the ground from under the feet of bigotted faith and slavish obedience; and the roar and dashing of opinions, loosened from their accustomed hold, might be heard like the noise of an angry sea, and has never yet subsided. Germany first broke the spell of misbegotten fear, and gave the watch–word; but England joined the shout, and echoed it back with her island voice, from her thousand cliffs and craggy shores, in a longer and a louder strain. With that cry, the genius of Great Britain rose, and threw down the gauntlet to the nations. There was a mighty fermentation: the waters were out; public opinion was in a state of projection.

Liberty was held out to all to think and speak the truth. Men's brains were busy; their spirits stirring; their hearts full; and their hands not idle. Their eyes were opened to expect the greatest things, and their ears burned with curiosity and zeal to know the truth, that the truth might make them free. The death blow which had been struck at scarlet vice and bloated hypocrisy, loosened their tongues, and made the talismans and love tokens of Popish superstition, with which she had beguiled her followers and committed abominations with the people, fall harmless from their necks.

The translation of the Bible was the chief engine in the great work. It threw open, by a secret spring, the rich treasures of religion and morality, which had been there locked up as in a shrine. It revealed the visions of the prophets, 'and conveyed the lessons of inspired teachers (such they were thought) to the meanest of the people. It gave them a common interest in the common cause.

Their hearts burnt within them as they read. It gave a mind to the people, by giving them common subjects of thought and feeling. It cemented their union of character and sentiment: it created endless diversity and collision of opinion. They found objects to employ their faculties, and a motive in the magnitude of the consequences attached to them, to exert the utmost eagerness in the pursuit of truth, and the most daring intrepidity in maintaining it.

Religious controversy sharpens the understanding by the subtlety and remoteness of the topics it discusses, and braces the will by their infinite importance. We perceive in the history of this period a nervous masculine intellect. No levity, no feebleness, no indifference; or if there were, it is a relaxation from the intense activity which gives a tone to its general character. But there is a gravity approaching to piety; a seriousness of impression, a conscientious severity of argument, an habitual fervour and enthusiasm in their mode of handling almost every subject. The debates of the schoolmen were sharp and subtle enough; but they wanted interest and grandeur, and were besides confined to a few: they did not affect the general mass of the community. But the Bible was thrown open to all ranks and conditions "to run and read," with its wonderful table of contents from Genesis to the Revelations.

Every village in England would present the scene so well described in Burns's Cotter's Saturday Night. I cannot think that all this variety and weight of knowledge could be thrown in all at once upon the mind of a people, and not make some impression upon it, the traces of which might be discerned in the manners and literature of the age. For to leave more disputable points, and take only the historical parts of the Old Testament, or the moral sentiments of the New, there is nothing like them in the power of exciting awe and admiration, or of rivetting sympathy.

We see what Milton has made of the account of the Creation, from the manner in which he has treated it, imbued and impregnated with the spirit of the time of which we speak: Or what is there equal (in that romantic interest and patriarchal simplicity which goes to the heart of a country, and rouses it, as it were, from its lair in wastes and wildernesses) equal to the story of Joseph and his Brethren, of Rachael and Laban, of Jacob's Dream, of Ruth and Boaz, the descriptions in the Book of Job, the deliverance of the Jews out of Egypt, or the account of their captivity and return from Babylon? There is in all these parts of the Scripture, and numberless more of the same kind, to pass over the Orphic hymns of David, the prophetic denunciations of Isaiah, or the gorgeous visions of Ezekiel, an originality, a vastness of conception, a depth and tenderness of feeling, and a touching simplicity in the mode of narration, which he who does not feel, need be made of no "penetrable stuff." There is something in the character of Christ too (leaving religious faith quite out of the question) of more sweetness and majesty, and more likely to work a change in the mind of man, by the contemplation of its idea alone, than any to be found in history, whether actual or feigned.

This character is that of a sublime humanity, such as was never seen on earth before, nor since. This shone manifestly both in his words and actions. We see it in his washing the

Disciples' feet the night before his death, that unspeakable instance of humility and love, above all art, all meanness, and all pride, and in the leave he took of them on that occasion, "My peace I give unto you, that peace which the world cannot give, give I unto you;" and in his last commandment, that "they should love one another."

Who can read the account of his behaviour on the cross, when turning to his mother he said, "Woman, behold thy son," and to the Disciple John, "Behold thy mother," and "from that hour that Disciple took her to his own home," without having his heart smote within him! We see it in his treatment of the woman taken in adultery, and in his excuse for the woman who poured precious ointment on his garment as an offering of devotion and love, which is here all in all. His religion was the religion of the heart.

We see it in his discourse with the Disciples as they walked together towards Emmaus, when their hearts burned within them; in his sermon from the Mount, in his parable of the good Samaritan, and in that of the Prodigal Son, in every act and word of his life, a grace, a mildness, a dignity and love, a patience and wisdom worthy of the Son of God. His whole life and being were imbued, steeped in this word, charity; it was the spring, the well–head from which every thought and feeling gushed into act; and it was this that breathed a mild glory from his face in that last agony upon the cross, "when the meek Saviour bowed his head and died," praying for his enemies.

He was the first true teacher of morality; for he alone conceived the idea of a pure humanity. He redeemed man from the worship of that idol, self, and instructed him by precept and example to love his neighbour as himself, to forgive our enemies, to do good to those that curse us and despitefully use us. He taught the love of good for the sake of good, without regard to personal or sinister views, and made the affections of the heart the sole seat of morality, instead of the pride of the understanding or the sternness of the will. In answering the question, "who is our neighbour?" as one who stands in need of our assistance, and whose wounds we can bind up, he has done more to humanise the thoughts and tame the unruly passions, than all who have tried to reform and benefit mankind. The very idea of abstract benevolence, of the desire to do good because another wants our services, and of regarding the human race as one family, the offspring of one common parent, is hardly to be found in any other code or system. It was "to the Jews a stumbling block, and to the Greeks foolishness." The Greeks and Romans never thought of considering others, but as they were Greeks or Romans, as they were bound to them by certain positive ties, or, on the other hand, as separated from them by fiercer antipathies.

Their virtues were the virtues of political machines, their vices were the vices of demons, ready to inflict or to endure pain with obdurate and remorseless inflexibility of purpose. But in the Christian religion, "we perceive a softness coming over the heart of a nation, and the iron scales that fence and harden it, melt and drop off." It becomes malleable, capable of pity, of forgiveness, of relaxing in its claims, and remitting its power. We strike it, and it does not hurt us: it is not steel or marble, but flesh and blood, clay tempered with tears, and "soft as sinews of the newborn babe."

The gospel was first preached to the poor, for it consulted their wants and interests, not its own pride and arrogance. It first promulgated the equality of mankind in the community of duties and benefits. It denounced the iniquities of the chief Priests and Pharisees, and declared itself at variance with principalities and powers for it sympathises not with the oppressor, but the oppressed. It first abolished slavery, for it did not consider the power of the will to inflict injury, as clothing it with a right to do so. Its law is good, not power. It at the same time tended to wean the mind from the grossness of sense, and a particle of its divine flame was lent to brighten and purify the lamp of love!

There have been persons who, being sceptics as to the divine mission of Christ, have taken an unaccountable prejudice to his doctrines, and have been disposed to deny the merit of his character; but this was not the feeling of the great men in the age of Elizabeth (whatever might be their belief) one of whom says of him, with a boldness equal to its piety:

"The best of men That e'er wore earth about him was a sufferer; A soft, meek, patient, humble, tranquil spirit; The first true gentleman that ever breathed." This was old honest Deckar, and the lines ought to embalm his memory to every one who has a sense either of religion, or philosophy, or humanity, or true genius.

Nor can I help thinking, that we may discern the traces of the influence exerted by religious faith in the spirit of the poetry of the age of Elizabeth, in the means of exciting terror and pity, in the delineation of the passions of grief, remorse, love, sympathy, the sense of shame, in the fond desires, the longings after immortality, in the heaven of hope, and the abyss of despair it lays open to us. The literature of this age then, I would say, was strongly influenced (among other causes), first by the spirit of Christianity, and secondly by the spirit of Protestantism. The effects of the Reformation on politics and philosophy may be seen in the writings and history of the next and of the following ages.

They are still at work, and will continue to be so. The effects on the poetry of the time were chiefly confined to the moulding of the character, and giving a powerful impulse to the intellect of the country. The immediate use or application that was made of religion to subjects of imagination and fiction was not (from an obvious ground of separation) so direct or frequent, as that which was made of the classical and romantic literature.

For much about the same time, the rich and fascinating stores of the Greek and Roman mythology, and those of the romantic poetry of Spain and Italy, were eagerly explored by the curious, and thrown open in translations to the admiring gaze of the vulgar. This last circumstance could hardly have afforded so much advantage to the poets of that day, who were themselves, in fact, the translators, as it shews the general curiosity and increasing interest in such subjects, as a prevailing feature of the times.

There were translations of Tasso by Fairfax, and of Ariosto by Harrington, of Homer and Hesiod by Chapman, and of Virgil long before, and Ovid soon after; there was Sir Thomas Northes translation of Plutarch, of which Shakspeare has made such admirable use in his Coriolanus and Julius Caesar; and Ben Jonson's tragedies of Catiline and Sejanus may themselves be considered as almost literal translations into verse, of Tacitus, Sallust, and Cicero's Orations in his consulship.

Boccacio, the divine Boccacio, Petrarch, Dante, the satirist Aretine, Machiavel, Castiglione, and others, were familiar to our writers, and they make occasional mention of some few French authors, as Ronsard and Du Bartas; for the French literature had not at this stage arrived at its Augustan period, and it was the imitation of their literature a century afterwards, when it had arrived at its greatest height (itself copied from the Greek and Latin), that enfeebled and impoverished our own.

But of the time that we are considering, it might be said, without much extravagance, that every breath that blew, that every wave that rolled to our shores, brought with it some accession to our knowledge, which was engrafted on the national genius. In fact, all the disposeable materials that had been accumulating for a long period of time, either in our own, or in foreign countries, were now brought together, and required nothing more than to be wrought up, polished, or arranged in striking forms, for ornament and use. To this every inducement prompted, the novelty of the acquisition of knowledge in many cases, the emulation of foreign wits, and of immortal works, the want and the expectation of such works among ourselves, the opportunity and encouragement afforded for their production by leisure and affluence; and, above all, the insatiable desire of the mind to beget its own image, and to construct out of itself, and for the delight and admiration of the world and posterity, that excellence of which the idea exists hitherto only in its own breast, and the impression of which it would make as universal as the eye of heaven, the benefit as common as the air we breathe. The first impulse of genius is to create what never existed before: the contemplation of that, which is so created, is sufficient to satisfy the demands of taste; and it is the habitual study and imitation of the original models that takes away the power, and even wish to do the like.

Taste limps after genius, and from copying the artificial models, we lose sight of the living principle of nature. It is the effort we make, and the impulse we acquire, in overcoming the first obstacles, that projects us forward; it is the necessity for exertion that makes us conscious of our strength; but this necessity and this impulse once removed, the tide of fancy and enthusiasm, which is at first a running stream, soon settles and crusts into the standing pool of dulness, criticism, and virtu.

What also gave an unusual impetus to the mind of man at this period, was the discovery of the New World, and the reading of voyages and travels. Green islands and golden sands seemed to arise, as by enchantment, out of the bosom of the watery waste, and invite the cupidity, or wing the imagination of the dreaming speculator. Fairy land was realised in new and unknown worlds. "Fortunate fields and groves and flowery vales, thrice happy isles," were found floating "like those Hesperian gardens famed of old," beyond Atlantic seas, as dropt from the zenith. The people, the soil, the clime, every thing gave unlimited scope to the curiosity of the traveller and reader. Other manners might be said to enlarge the bounds of knowledge, and new mines of wealth were tumbled at our feet. It is from a voyage to the Straits of Magellan that Shakspeare has taken the hint of Prospero's Enchanted Island, and of the savage Caliban with his god Setebos. Spenser seems to have had the same feeling in his mind in the production of his Faery Queen, and vindicates his poetic fiction on this very ground of analogy.

Right well I wore, most mighty sovereign, That all this famous antique history of some the abundance of an idle brain Will judged be, and painted forgery, Rather than matter of just memory: Since none that breatheth living air, doth know Where is that happy land of faery Which I so much do vaunt, but no where show, But vouch antiquities, which nobody can know.

But let that man with better sense avise, That of the world least part to us is read: And daily how through hardy enterprise Many great regions are discovered, Which to late age were never mentioned. Who ever heard of the Indian Peru? Or who in venturous vessel measured The Amazons' huge river, now found true? Or fruitfullest Virginia who did ever view?

Yet all these were when no man did them know, Yet have from wisest ages hidden been: And later times things more unknown shall show. Why then should witless man so much misween That nothing is but that which he hath seen? What if within the moon's fair shining sphere, What if in every other star unseen, Of other worlds he happily should hear, He wonder would much more; yet such to some appear.

Fancy's air–drawn pictures after history's waking dream shewed like clouds over mountains; and from the romance of real life to the idlest fiction, the transition seemed easy. Shakspeare, as well as others of his time, availed himself of the old Chronicles, and of the traditions or fabulous inventions contained in them in such ample measure, and which had not yet been appropriated to the purposes of poetry or the drama. The stage was a new thing; and those who had to supply its demands laid their hands upon whatever came within their reach: they were not particular as to the means, so that they gained the end. Lear is founded upon an old ballad; Othello on an Italian novel; Hamlet on a Danish, and Macbeth on a Scotch tradition; one of which is to be found in Saxo–Grammaticus, and the last in Hollingshed. The Ghost–scenes and the Witches in each, are authenticated in the old Gothic history. There was also this connecting link between the poetry of this age and the supernatural traditions of a former one, that the belief in them was still extant, and in full force and visible operation among the vulgar (to say no more) in the time of our authors.

The appalling and wild chimeras of superstition and ignorance, "those bodiless creations that ecstacy is very cunning in," were inwoven with existing manners and opinions, and all their effects on the passions of terror or pity might be gathered from common and actual observation might be discerned in the workings of the face, the expressions of the tongue, the writhings of a troubled conscience. "Your face, my Thane, is as a book where men may read strange matters." Midnight and secret murders too, from the imperfect state of the police, were more common; and the ferocious and brutal manners that would stamp the brow of the hardened ruffian or hired assassin, more incorrigible and undisguised.

The portraits of Tyrrel and Forrest were, no doubt, done from the life. We find that the ravages of the plague, the destructive rage of fire, the poisoned chalice, lean famine, the serpent's mortal sting, and the fury of wild beasts, were the common topics of their poetry, as they were common occurrences in more remote periods of history. They were the strong ingredients thrown into the cauldron of tragedy, to make it "thick and slab." Man's life was (as it appears to me) more full of traps and pit–falls; of hair–breadth accidents by flood and field; more way–laid by sudden and startling evils; it trod on the brink of hope and fear; stumbled upon fate unawares; while the imagination, close behind it, caught at and clung to the shape of danger, or "snatched a wild and fearful joy" from its escape. The accidents of nature were less provided against; the excesses of the passions and of lawless power were less regulated, and produced more strange and desperate catastrophes. The tales of Boccacio are founded on the great pestilence of Florence, Fletcher the poet died of the plague, and Marlow was stabbed in a tavern quarrel. The strict authority of parents, the inequality of ranks, or the hereditary feuds between different families, made more unhappy loves or matches.

"The course of true love never did run even."

Again, the heroic and martial spirit which breathes in our elder writers, was yet in considerable activity in the reign of Elizabeth. "The age of chivalry was not then quite gone, nor the glory of Europe extinguished for ever." Jousts and tournaments were still common with the nobility in England and in foreign countries: Sir Philip Sidney was particularly distinguished for his proficiency in these exercises (and indeed fell a martyr to his ambition as a soldier)—and the gentle Surrey was still more famous, on the same account, just before him. It is true, the general use of fire–arms gradually superseded the necessity of skill in the sword, or bravery in the person: and as a symptom of the rapid degeneracy in this respect, we find Sir John Suckling soon after boasting of himself as one—

"Who prized black eyes, and a lucky hit At bowls, above all the trophies of wit."

It was comparatively an age of peace,

"Like strength reposing on his own right arm;"

but the sound of civil combat might still be heard in the distance, the spear glittered to the eye of memory, or the clashing of armour struck on the imagination of the ardent and the young. They were borderers on the savage state, on the times of war and bigotry, though in the lap of arts, of luxury, and knowledge. They stood on the shore and saw the billows rolling after the storm: "they heard the tumult, and were still." The manners and out of door amusements were more tinctured with a spirit of adventure and romance. The war with wild beasts was more strenuously kept up in country sports. I do not think we could get from sedentary poets, who had never mingled in the vicissitudes, the dangers, or excitements of the chase, such descriptions of hunting and other athletic games, as are to be found in Shakspeare Midsummer Night's Dream or Fletcher Noble Kinsmen.

With respect to the good cheer and hospitable living of those times, I cannot agree with an ingenious and agreeable writer of the present day, that it was general or frequent. The very stress laid upon certain holidays and festivals, shews that they did not keep up the same Saturnalian licence and open house all the year round. They reserved themselves for great occasions, and made the best amends they could, for a year of abstinence and toil by a week of merriment and convivial indulgence.

Persons in middle life at this day, who can afford a good dinner every day, do not look forward to it as any particular subject of exultation: the poor peasant, who can only contrive to treat himself to a joint of meat on a Sunday, considers it as an event in the week. So, in the old Cambridge comedy of the Return from Parnassus, we find this indignant description of the progress of luxury in those days, put into the mouth of one of the speakers. "Why is't not strange to see a ragged clerke, Some stammell weaver, or some butcher's sonne, That scrubb'd a late within a sleeveless gowne, When the commencement, like a morrice dance, Hath put a bell or two about his legges, Created him a sweet cleane gentleman:

How then he 'gins to follow fashions. He whose thin sire dwelt in a smokye roofe, Must make tobacco, and must wear a locke. His thirsty dad drinkes in a wooden bowle, But his sweet self is served in silver plate. His hungry sire will scrape you twenty legges, For one good Christmas meal on new year's day, But his mawe must be capon cramm'd each day."

Act III. Scene 2

This does not look as if in those days "it snowed of meat and drink," as a matter of course throughout the year!–The distinctions of dress, the badges of different professions, the very signs of the shops, which we have set aside for written inscriptions over the doors, were, as Mr. Lamb observes, a sort of visible language to the imagination, and hints for thought. Like the costume of different foreign nations, they had an immediate striking and picturesque effect, giving scope to the fancy. The surface of society was embossed with hieroglyphics, and poetrv existed "in art and compliment extern." The poetry of former times might be directly taken from real life, as our poetry is taken from the poetry of former times. Finally, the face of nature, which was the same glorious object then that it is now, was open to them; and coming first they gathered her fairest flowers to live for ever in their verse: the movements of the human heart were not hid from them, for they had the same passions as we, only less disguised, and less subject to controul. Deckar has given an admirable description of a mad–house in one of his plays.

But it might be perhaps objected, that it was only a literal account taken from Bedlam at that time; and it might be answered, that the old poets took the same method of describing the passions and fancies of men whom they met at large, which forms the point of communion between us: for the title of the old play, "A Mad World, my Masters," is hardly yet obsolete; and we are pretty much the same Bedlam still, perhaps a little better managed, like the real one, and with more care and humanity shewn to the patients!

Lastly, to conclude this account; what gave a unity and common direction to all these causes, was the natural genius of the country, which was strong in these writers in proportion to their strength. We are a nation of islanders, and we cannot help it; nor mend ourselves if we would. We are something in ourselves, nothing when we try to ape others. Music and painting are not our forte: for what we have done in that way has been little, and that borrowed from others with great difficulty. But we may boast of our poets and philosophers. That's something. We have had strong heads and sound hearts among us. Thrown on one side of the world, and left to bustle for ourselves, we have fought out many a battle for truth and freedom. That is our natural style; and it were to be wished we had in no instance departed from it.

Our situation has given us a certain cast of thought and character; and our liberty has enabled us to make the most of it. We are of a stiff clay, not moulded into every fashion, with stubborn joints not easily bent. We are slow to think, and therefore impressions do not work upon us till they act in masses. We are not forward to express our feelings, and therefore they do not come from us till they force their way in the most impetuous eloquence.

Our language is, as it were, to begin anew, and we make use of the most singular and boldest combinations to explain ourselves. Our wit comes from us, "like birdlime, brains and all." We pay too little attention to form and method, leave our works in an unfinished state, but still the materials we work in are solid and of nature's mint; we do not deal in counterfeits: We both under and over–do, but we keep an eye to the prominent features, the main chance.

We are more for weight than show; care only about what interests ourselves, instead of trying to impose upon others by plausible appearances, and are obstinate and intractable in not conforming to common rules, by which many arrive at their ends with half the real waste of thought and trouble. We neglect all but the principal object, gather our force to make a great blow, bring it down, and relapse into sluggishness and indifference again.

Materiam stipcrabat opus, cannot be said of us. We may be accused of grossness, but not of flimsiness; of extravagance, but not of affectation; of want of art and refinement, but not of a want of truth and nature. Our literature, in a word, is Gothic and grotesque; unequal and irregular; not cast in a previous mould, nor of one uniform texture, but of great weight in the whole, and of incomparable value in the best parts. It aims at an excess of beauty or power, hits or misses, and is either very good indeed, or absolutely good for nothing. This character applies in particular to our literature in the age of Elizabeth, which is its best period, before the introduction of a rage for

French rules and French models; for whatever may be the value of our own original style of composition, there can be neither offence nor presumption in saying, that it is af least better than our second–hand imitations of others.

Our understanding (such as it is, and must remain to be good for anything) is not a thoroughfare for common places, smooth as the palm of one's hand, but full of knotty points and jutting excrescences, rough, uneven, overgrown with brambles; and I like this aspect of the mind (as some one said of the country), where nature keeps a good deal of the soil in her own hands. Perhaps the genius of our poetry has more of Pan than of Apollo; "but Pan is a God, Apollo is no more!

2

Spenser

Spenser flourished in the reign of Queen Elizabeth, and was sent with Sir John Davies into Ireland, of which he has left behind him some tender recollections in his description of the bog of Allan, and a record in an ably written paper, containing observations on the state of that country and the means of improving it, which remain in full force to the present day. Spenser died at an obscure inn in London, it is supposed in distressed circumstances. The treatment he received from Burleigh is well known. Spenser, as well as Chaucer, was engaged in active life; but the genius of his poetry was not active: it is inspired by the love of ease, and relaxation from all the cares and business of life. Of all the poets, he is the most poetical. Though much later than Chaucer, his obligations to preceding writers were less. He has in some measure borrowed the plan of his poem (as a number of distinct narratives) from Ariosto; but he has engrafted upon it an exuberance of fancy, and an endless voluptuousness of sentiment, which are not to be found in the Italian writer.

Farther, Spenser is even more of an inventor in the subject matter. There is an originality, richness, and variety in his allegorical personages and fictions, which almost vies with the splendor of the ancient mythology. If Ariosto transports us into the regions of romance, Spenser's poetry is all fairy–land. In Ariosto, we walk upon the ground, in a company, gay, fantastic, and adventurous enough.

In Spenser, we wander in another world, among ideal being. The poet takes and lays us in the lap of a lovelier nature, by the sound of softer streams, among greener hills and fairer valleys. He paints nature, not as we find it, but as we expected to find it; and fulfils the delightful promise of our youth. He waves his wand of enchantment and at once embodies airy beings, and throws a delicious veil over all actual objects. The two world of reality and of fiction are poised on the wings of his imagination. His ideas, indeed, seem more distinct than his perceptions.

He is the painter of abstractions, and describes them with dazzling minuteness. In the Mask of Cupid he makes the God of Love "clap on high his coloured winges twain;" and it is said of Gluttony in the Proccssion of the Passions,

"In green vine leaves he was right fitly clad."

At times he becomes picturesque from his intense love of beauty; as where he compares Prince Arthur's crest to the appearance of the almond tree:

> "Upon the top of all his lofty crest, A bunch of hairs discolour'd diversely With sprinkled pearl and gold full richly diest Did shake and seem'd to daunce for jollity; Like to an almond tree ymounted high On top of green Selenis all alone, With blossoms brave bedecked daintily; Her tender locks do tremble every one At every little breath that under heav'n is blown."

The love of beauty, however, and not of truth, is the moving principle of his mind; and he is guided in his fantastic delineations by no rule but the impulse of an inexhaustible imagination. He luxuriates equally in scenes of Eastern magnificence; or the still solitude of a hermit's cell in the extremes of sensuality or refinement.

In reading the Faery Queen, you see a little withered old man by a wood–side opening a wicket, a giant, and a dwarf lagging far behind, a damsel in a boat upon an enchanted lake, wood–nymphs, and satyrs; and all of a sudden you are transported into a lofty palace, with tapers burning, amidst knights and ladies, with dance and revelry, and song, "and mask, and antique pageantry." What can be more solitary, more shut up in itself, than his description of the house of Sleep, to which Archimago sends for a dream:

"And more to lull him in his slumber soft A trickling stream from high rock tumbling down, And ever–drizzling rain upon the loft, Mix'd with a murmuring wind, much like the sound Of swarming Bees, did cast him in a swound. No other noise, nor people's troublous cries That still are wont t' annoy the walled town Might there be heard; but careless Quiet lies

Wrapt in eternal silence, far from enemies."

It is as if "the honey–heavy dew of slumber" had settled on his pen in writing these lines. How different in the subject (and yet how like in beauty) is the following description of the Bower of Bliss:

> "Eftsoones they heard a most melodious sound of all that mote delight a dainty ear; Such as at once might not on living ground, Save in this Paradise, be heard elsewhere: Right hard it was for wight which did it hear, To tell what manner musicke that mote be; For all that pleasing is to living eare Was there consorted in one harmonee: Birds, voices, instruments, windes, waters, all agree. The joyous birdes shrouded in chearefull shade Their notes unto the voice attempred sweet: The angelical soft trembling voices made To the instruments divine respondence meet. The silver sounding instruments did meet With the base murmur of the water's fall; The water's fall with difference discreet, Now soft, now loud, unto the wind did call; The gentle warbling wind low answered to all."

The remainder of the passage has all that voluptuous pathos, and languid brilliancy of fancy, in which this writer excelled:

> "The whiles some one did chaunt this lovely lay; Ah! see, whoso fayre thing dost fain to see, In springing flower the image of thy day! Ah! see the virgin rose, how sweetly she Doth first peep forth with bashful modesty, That fairer seems the less ye see her may! Lo! see soon after, how more bold and free Her bared bosom she doth broad display; Lo! see soon after, how she fades and falls away! So passeth in the passing of a day Of mortal life the leaf, the bud, the flower; Ne more doth flourish after first decay, That erst was sought to deck both bed and bower Of many a lady and many a paramour! Gather therefore the rose whilst yet is prime, For soon comes age that will her pride deflower; Gather the rose of love whilst yet is time, Whilst loving thou mayst loved be with equal crime."

He ceased; and then gan all the quire of birds Their divers notes to attune unto his lay, As in approvance of his pleasing wordes. The constant pair heard all that he did say, Yet swerved not, but kept their forward way Through many covert groves and thickets close, In which they creeping did at last display. That wanton lady with her lover loose, Whose sleepy head she in her lap did soft dispose.

Upon a bed of roses she was laid As faint through heat, or dight to pleasant sin; And was arrayed or rather disarrayed, All in a veil of silk and silver thin, That hid no whit her alabaster skin, But rather shewed more white, if more might be: More subtle web Arachne cannot spin; Nor the fine nets, which oft we woven see of scorched dew, do not in the air more lightly flee.

Her snowy breast was bare to greedy spoil of hungry eyes which n'ote therewith be fill'd. And yet through languor of her late sweet toil Few drops more clear than nectar forth distill'd, That like pure Orient perles adown it trill'd; And her fair eyes sweet smiling in delight Moisten'd their fiery beams, with which she thrill'd Frail hearts, yet quenched not; like starry light, Which sparkling on the silent waves does seem more bright."

The finest things in Spenser are, the character of Una, in the first book; the House of Pride; the Cave of Mammon, and the Cave of Despair; the account of Memory, of whom it is said, among other things—

The wars he well remember'd of King Nine, of old Assaracus and Inachus divine; the description of Belphoebe; the story of Florimel and the Witch's son; the Gardens of Adonis, and the Bower of Bliss; the Mask of Cupid; and Colin Clout's vision, in the last book. But some people will say that all this may be very fine, but that they cannot understand it on account of the allegory. They are afraid of the allegory, as if they thought it would bite them: they look at it as a child looks at a painted dragon, and think it will strangle them in its shining folds. This is very idle. If they do not meddle with the allegory, the allegory will not meddle with them. Without minding it at all, the whole is as plain as a pike–staff. It might as well be pretended that we cannot see Poussin's pictures for the allegory, as that the allegory prevents us from understanding Spenser. For instance, when Britomart, seated amidst the young warriors, lets fall her hair and discovers her sex, is it necessary to know the part she plays in the allegory, to understand the beauty, of the following stanza?

"And eke that stranger knight amongst the rest, Was for like need enforcd to disarray. Tho when as vailed was her lofty crest, Her golden locks that were in trammels gay Upbounden, did themselves adown display, And raught unto her heels like sunny beams, That in a cloud their light did long time stay; Their vapoor faded, shew their golden gleams, And through the persant air shoot forth their azure streams."

Or is there any mystery in what is said of Belphoebe, that her hair was sprinkled with flowers and blossoms which had been entangled in it as she fled through the woods? Or is it necessary to have a more distinct idea of Proteus, than that which is given of him in his boat, with the frighted Florimel at his feet, while "—the cold icicles from his rough beard Dropped adown upon her snowy breast!"

Or is it not a sufficient account of one of the sea–gods that pass by them, to say—

> "That was Arion crowned:—So went he playing on the watery plain." Or to take the Procession of the Passions that draw the coach of Pride, in which the figures of Idleness, of Gluttony, of Lechery, of Avarice, of Envy, and of Wrath speak, one should think, plain enough for themselves; such as this of Guttony:

"And by his side rode loathsome Gluttony, Deformed creature, on a filthy swine; His belly was up blown with luxury; And eke with fatness swollen were his eyne; And like a crane his neck was long and fine, With which he swallowed up excessive feast, For want whereof poor people oft did pine. In green vine leaves he was right fitly clad; For other clothes he could not wear for heat; And on his head an ivy garland had, From under which fast trickled down the sweat: Still as he rode, he somewhat still did eat, And in his hand did bear a bousing can, Of which he supt so oft, that on his seat His drunken corse he scarce upholden can; In shape and life more like a monster than a man."

Or this of Lechery: "And next to him rode lustfull Lechery Upon a bearded goat, whose rugged hair And whaly eyes (the sign of jealousy) Was like the person's self whom he did bear Who rough and black, and filthy did appear. Unseemly man to please fair lady's eye: Yet he of ladies oft was loved dear, When fairer faces were bid standen by: O! who does know the bent of woman's fantsay? In a green gown he clothed was full fair, Which underneath did hide his filthiness; And in his hand a burning heart he bare, Full of vain follies and new fangleness; For he was false and fraught with fickleness; And learned had to love with secret looks; And well could dance; and sing with ruefulness; And fortunes tell; and read in loving books; And thousand other ways to bait his fleshly hooks.

Inconstant man that loved all he saw, And lusted after all that he did love; Ne would his looser life be tied to law; But joyed weak women's hearts to tempt and prove, If from their loyal loves he might them move."

This is pretty plain–spoken. Mr. Southey says of Spenser: "Yet not more sweet Than pure was he, and not more pure than wise; High priest of all the Muses' mysteries!"

On the contrary, no one was more apt to pry into mysteries which do not strictly belong to the Muses.

Of the same kind with the Procession of the Passions, as little obscure, and still more beautiful, is the Mask of Cupid, with his train of votaries: The first was Fancy, like a lovely boy of rare aspect, and beauty without peer;

His garment neither was of silk nor say, But painted plumes in goodly order dight, Like as the sun–burnt Indians do array, Their tawny bodies in their proudest plight; As those same plumes so seem'd he vain and light, That by his gait might easily appear; For still he far'd as dancing in delight, And in his hand a windy fan did bear, That in the idle air he mov'd still here and there.

And him beside march'd amorous Desire, Who seem'd of riper years than the other swain, Yet was that other swain this elder's sire, And gave him being, common to them twain: His garment was disguised very vain, And his embroidered bonnet sat awry; 'Twixt both his hands few sparks he close did strain, Which still he blew, and kindled busily, That soon they life conceiv'd and forth in flames did fly. Next after him went Doubt, who was yclad In a discolour'd coat of strange disguise,

That at his back a broad capuccio had, And sleeves dependant Albanese–wise; He lookt askew with his mistrustful eyes, And nicely trod, as thorns lay in his way, Or that the floor to shrink he did avise; And on a broken reed he still did stay, His feeble steps, which shrunk when hard thereon he lay.

With him went Daunger, clothed in ragged weed, Made of bear's skin, that him more dreadful made; Yet his own face was dreadfull, ne did need Strange horror to deform his grisly shade; A net in the one hand, and a rusty blade, In the other was; this Mischiefe, that Mishap; With the one his foes he threat'ned to invade, With the other he his friends meant to enwrap; For whom he could not kill he practiz'd to entrap.

Next him was Fear, all arm'd from top to toe, Yet thought himself not safe enough thereby, But fear'd each shadow moving to and fro; And his own arms when glittering he did spy Or clashing heard, he fast away did fly, As ashes pale of hue, and winged heel'd; And evermore on Daunger fixt his eye, 'Gainst whom he always bent a brazen shield, Which his right hand unarmed fearfully did wield. With him went Hope in rank, a handsome maid, Of chearfull look and lovely to behold; In silken samite she was light array'd, And her fair locks were woven up in gcld; She always smil'd, and in her hand did hold An holy water sprinkle dipt in dew, With which she sprinkled favours manifold On whom she list, and did great liking shew, Great liking unto many, but true love to few.

Next after them, the winged God himself Came riding on a lion ravenous, Taught to obey the menage of that elfe That man and beast with power imperious Subdueth to his kingdom tyrannous: His blindfold eyes he bade awhile unbind, That his proud spoil of that same dolorous Fair dame he might behold in perfect kind; Which seen, he much rejoiced in his cruel mind.

Of which full proud, himself uprearing high, He looked round about with stern disdain, And did survey his goodly company; And marshalling the evil–ordered train, With that the darts which his right hand did strain, Full dreadfully he shook, that all did quake, And clapt on high his colour'd winges twain, That all his any it afraid did make: Tho, blinding him again, his way he forth did take. The description of Hope, in this series of historical portraits, is one of the most beautiful in

Spenser: and the triumph of Cupid at the mischief he has made, is worthy of the malicious urchin deity. In reading these descriptions, one can hardly avoid being reminded of Rubens's allegorical pictures; but the account of Satyrane taming the lion's whelps and lugging the bear's cubs along in his arms while yet an infant, whom his mother so naturally advises to "go seek some other play–fellows," has even more of this high picturesque character. Nobody but Rubens could have painted the fancy of Spenser; and he could not have given the sentiment, the airy dream that hovers over it!

With all this, Spenser neither makes us laugh nor weep. The only jest in his poem is an allegorical play upon words, where he describes Malbecco as escaping in the herd of goats, "by the help of his fayre horns on hight." But he has been unjustly charged with a want of passion and of strength. He has both in an immense degree. He has not indeed the pathos of immediate action or suffering, which is more properly the dramatic; but he has all the pathos of sentiment and romance— all that belongs to distant objects of terror, and uncertain, imaginary distress. His strength, in like manner, is not strength of will or action, of bone and muscle, nor is it coarse and palpable but it assumes a character of vastness and sublimity seen through the same visionary medium, and blended with the appalling associations of preternatural agency. We need only turn, in proof of this, to the Cave of Despair, or the Cave of Mammon, or to the account of the change of Malbecco into Jealousy. The following stanzas, in the description of the Cave of Mammon, the grisly house of Plutus, are unrivalled for the portentous massiness of the forms, the splendid chiaro–scuro, and shadowy horror.

That house's form within was rude and strong, Like an huge cave hewn out of rocky clift, From whose rough vault the ragged breaches hung, Embossed with massy gold of glorious gift, And with rich metal loaded every rift, That heavy ruin they did seem to threat: And over them Arachne high did lift Her cunning web, and spread her subtle net, Enwrapped in foul smoke, and clouds more black than jet.

Both roof and floor, and walls were all of gold, but overgrown with dust and old decay, And hid in darkness that none could behold, The hue thereof: for view of cheerful day, Did never in that house itself display, But a faint shadow of uncertain light; Such as a lamp whose light doth fade away; Or as the moon clothed with cloudy night Does shew to him that walks in fear and sad affright. And over all sad Horror with grim hue Did always soar, beating his iron wings; And after him owls and night–ravens flew, The hateful messengers of heavy things, Of death and dolour telling sad tidings; While sad Celleno, sitting on a clift, A song of bale and bitter sorrow sings, That heart of flint asunder could have rift; Which having ended, after him she flieth swift.

The Cave of Despair is described with equal gloominess and power of fancy; and the fine moral declamation of the owner of it, on the evils of life, almost makes one in love with death. In the story of Malbecco, who is haunted by jealousy, and in vain strives to run away from his own thoughts.

"High over hill and over dale he flies" , the truth of human passion and the preternatural ending are equally striking. It is not fair to compare Spenser with Shakspeare, in point of interest. A fairer comparison would be with Comus; and the result would not be unfavourable to Spenser. There is only one work of the same allegorical kind, which has more interest than Spenser (with scarcely less imagination): and that is the Pilgrim's Progress. The three first books of the Faery Queen are very superior to the three last. One would think that Pope, who used to ask if any one had ever read the Faery Queen through, had only dipped into these last. The only things in them equal to the former, are the account of Talus, the Iron Man, and the delightful episode of Pastorella. The language of Spenser is full, and copious, to overflowing: it is less pure and idiomatic than Chaucer's, and is enriched and adorned with phrases borrowed from the different languages of Europe, both ancient and modern. He was, probably, seduced into a certain license of expression by the difficulty of filling up the moulds of his complicated rhymed stanza from the limited resources of his native language. This stanza, with alternate and repeatedly recurring rhymes, is borrowed from the Italians. It is peculiarly fitted to their language, which abounds in similar vowel terminations, and is as little adapted to ours, from the stubborn, unaccommodating resistance which the consonant endings of the northern languages make to this sort of endless sing-song.

Not that I would, on that account, part with the stanza of Spenser. We are, perhaps, indebted to this very necessity of finding out new forms of expression, and to the occasional faults to which it led, for a poetical language rich and varied and magnificent beyond all former, and almost all later example. His versification is, at once, the most smooth and the most sounding in the language.

It is a labyrinth of sweet sounds, "in many a winding bout of linked sweetness long drawn out" that would cloy by their very sweetness, but that the ear is constantly relieved and enchanted by their continued variety of modulation dwelling on the pauses of the action, or flowing on in a fuller tide of harmony with the movement of the sentiment. It has not the bold dramatic transitions of Shakspeare's blank verse, nor the high–raised tone of Milton's; but it is the perfection of melting harmony, dissolving the soul in pleasure, or holding it captive in the chains of suspense. Spenser was the poet of our waking dreams; and he has invented not only a language, but a music of his own for them. The undulations are infinite, like those of the waves of the sea: but the effect is still the same, lulling the senses into a deep oblivion of the jarring noises of the world, from which we have no wish to be ever recalled.

3

Shakspeare

The four greatest names in English poetry, are almost the four first we come to Chaucer, Spenser, Shakspeare, and Milton. There are no others that can really be put in competition with these. The two last have had justice done them by the voice of common fame. Their names are blazoned in the very firmament of reputation; while the two first, (though "the fault has been more in their stars than in themselves that they are underlings") either never emerged far above the horizon, or were too soon involved in the obscurity of time. The three first of these are excluded from Dr. Johnson's Lives of the Poets (Shakspeare indeed is so from the dramatic form of his compositions): and the fourth, Milton, is admitted with a reluctant and churlish welcome. In comparing these four writers together, it might be said that Chaucer excels as the poet of manners, or of real life; Spenser, as the poet of romance; Shakspeare, as the poet of nature (in the largest use of the term): and Milton, as the poet of morality. Chaucer most frequently describes things as they are; Spenser, as we wish them to be; Shakspeare, as they would be; and Milton as they ought to be.

As poets, and as great poets, imagination, that is, the power of feigning things according to nature, was common to them all: but the principle or moving power, to which this faculty was most subservient in Chaucer, was habit, or inveterate prejudice; in Spenser, novelty, and the love of the marvellous; in Shakspeare, it was the force of passion, combined with every variety of possible circumstances; and in Milton, only with the highest. The characteristic of Chaucer is intensity; of Spenser, remoteness; of Milton, elevation; of Shakspeare, everything. It has been said by some critic, that Shakspeare was distinguished from the other dramatic writers of his day only by his wit; that they had all his other qualities but that; that one writer had as much sense, another as much fancy, another as much knowledge of character, another the same depth of passion, and another as great a power of language. This statement is not true; nor is the inference from it well founded, even if it were. This person does not seem to have been aware that, upon his own shewing, the great distinction of Shakspeare's genius was its virtually including the genius of all the great men of his age, and not his differing from them in one accidental particular. But to have done with such minute and literal trifling.

The striking peculiarity of Shakspeare's mind was its generic quality, its power of communication with all other minds so that it contained a universe of thought and feeling within itself, and had no one peculiar bias, or exclusive excellence more than another. He was just like any other man, but that he was like all other men. He was the least of an egotist that it was possible to be. He was nothing in himself; but he was all that others were, or that they could become. He not only had in himself the germs of every faculty and feeling, but he could follow them by anticipation, intuitively, into all their conceivable ramifications, through every change of fortune or conflict of passion, or turn of thought. He had "a mind reflecting ages past," and present: all the people that ever lived are there. There was no respect of persons with him. His genius shone equally on the evil and on the good, on the wise and the foolish, the monarch and the beggar: "All corners of the earth, kings, queens, and states, maids, matrons, nay, the secrets of the grave," are hardly hid from his searching glance. He was like the genius of humanity, changing places with all of us at pleasure, and playing with our purposes as with his own.

He turned the globe round for his amusement, and surveyed the generations of men, and the individuals as they passed, with their different concerns, passions, follies, vices, virtues, actions, and motives as well those that they knew, as those which they did not know, or acknowledge to themselves. The dreams of childhood, the ravings of despair, were the toys of his fancy. Airy beings waited at his call, and came at his bidding. Harmless fairies "nodded to him, and did him curtesies:" and the night hag bestrode the blast at the command of "his so potent art."

The world of spirits lay open to him, like the world of real men and women: and there is the same truth in his delineations of the one as of the other; for if the preternatural characters he describes could be supposed to exist, they would speak, and feel, and act, as he makes them. He had only to think of any thing in order to become that thing, with all the circumstances belonging to it. When he conceived of a character whether real or imaginary, he not only entered into all its thoughts and feelings, but seemed instantly, and as if by touching a secret spring, to be surrounded with all the same objects, "subject to the same skyey influences," the same local, outward, and unforeseen accidents which would occur in reality.

Thus the character of Caliban not only stands before us with a language and manners of its own, but the scenery and situation of the enchanted island he inhabits, the traditions of the place, its strange noises, its hidden recesses, "his frequent haunts and ancient neighbourhood," are given with a miraculous truth of nature, and with all the familiarity of an old recollection. The whole "coheres semblably together" in time, place, and circumstance. In reading this author, you do not merely learn what his characters say, you see their persons. By something expressed or understood, you are at no loss to decypher their peculiar physiognomy, the meaning of a look, the grouping, the byeplay, as we might see it on the stage.

A word, an epithet paints a whole scene, or throws us back whole years in the history of the person represented. So (as it has been ingeniously remarked) when Prospero describes himself as left alone in the boat with his daughter, the epithet which he applies to her, "Me and thy crying self," flings the imagination instantly back from the grown woman to the helpless condition of infancy, and places the first and most trying scene of his misfortunes before us, with all that he must have suffered in the interval.

How well the silent anguish of Macduff is conveyed to the reader, by the friendly expostulation of Malcolm—What! man, ne'er pull your hat upon your brows!" Again, Hamlet, in the scene with Rosencrans and Guildenstern, somewhat abruptly concludes his fine soliloquy on life by saying, "Man delights not me, nor woman neither, though by your smiling you seem to say so." Which is explained by their answer –My lord, we had no such stuff in our thoughts. But we smiled to think, if you delight not in man, what lenten entertainment the players shall receive from you, whom we met on the way:—as if while Hamlet was making this speech, his two old schoolfellows from Wittenberg had been really standing by, and he had seen them smiling by stealth, at the idea of the players crossing their minds.

It is not "a combination and a form" of words, a set speech or two, a preconcerted theory of a character, that will do this: but all the persons concerned must have been present in the poet's imagination, as at a kind of rehearsal; and whatever would have passed through their minds on the occasion, and have been observed by others, passed through his, and is made known to the reader. I may add in passing, that Shakspeare always gives the best directions for the costume and carriage of his heroes. Thus, to take one example, Ophelia gives the following account of Hamlet; and as Ophelia had seen Hamlet, I should think her word ought to be taken against that of any modern authority.

Ophelia. My lord, as I was reading in my closet, Prince Hamlet, with his doublet all unbrac'd, No hat upon his head, his stockings loose, Ungartred, and down–gyved to his ancle, Pale as his shirt, his knees knocking each other, And with a look so piteous, As if he had been sent from hell To speak of horrors, thus he comes before me.

Polonius. Mad for thy love!

Oph. My lord, I do not know,But truly I do fear it.Pol. What said he?

Oph. He took me by the wrist and held me hard. Then goes he to the length of all his arm; And with his other hand thus o'er his brow, He falls to such perusal of my face, As he would draw it: long staid he so; At last, a little shaking of my arm, And thrice his head thus waving up and down, He rais'd a sigh so piteous and profound, As it did seem to shatter all his bulk, And end his being. That done, he lets me go, And with his head over his shoulder turn'd, He seem'd to find his way without his eyes; For out of doors he went without their help, And to the last bended their light on me.

Act II. Scene I

How after this airy, fantastic idea of irregular grace and bewildered melancholy any one can play Hamlet, as we have seen it played, with strut, and stare, and antic right as at a kind of rehearsal; and whatever would have passed through their minds on the occasion, and have been observed by others, passed through his, and is made known to the reader. I may add in passing, that Shakspeare always gives the best directions for the costume and carriage of his heroes. Thus, to take one example, Ophelia gives the following account of Hamlet; and as Ophelia had seen Hamlet, I should think her word ought to be taken against that of any modern authority.

How after this airy, fantastic idea of irregular grace and bewildered melancholy any one can play Hamlet, as we have seen it played, with strut, and stare, and antic right character he wishes to represent, and to pass from one to another, like the same soul successively animating different bodies. By an art like that of the ventriloquist, he throws his imagination out of himself, and makes every word appear to proceed from the mouth of the person in whose name it is given. His plays alone are properly expressions of the passions, not descriptions of them. His characters are real beings of flesh and blood; they speak like men, not like authors. One might suppose that he had stood by at the time, and overheard what passed.

As in our dreams we hold conversations with ourselves, make remarks, or communicate intelligence, and have no idea of the answer which we shall receive, and which we ourselves make, till we hear it: so the dialogues in Shakspeare are carried on without any consciousness of what is to follow, without any appearance of preparation or premeditation. The gusts of passion come and go like sounds of music borne on the wind. Nothing is made out by formal inference and analogy, by climax and antithesis: all comes, or seems to come, immediately from nature. Each object and circumstance exists in his mind, as it would have existed in reality: each several train of thought and feeling goes on of itself, without confusion or effort. In the world of his imagination, every thing has a life, a place, and being of its own! Chaucer's characters are sufficiently distinct from one another, but they are too little varied in themselves, too much like identical propositions. They are consistent, but uniform; we get no new idea of them from first to last; they are not placed in different lights, nor are their subordinate traits brought out in new situations; they are like portraits or physiognomical studies, with the distinguishing features marked with inconceivable truth and precision, but that preserve the same unaltered air and attitude. Shakspeare's are historical figures, equally true and correct, but put into action, where every nerve and muscle is displayed in the struggle with others, with all the effect of collision and contrast, with every variety of light and shade. Chaucer's characters are narrative, Shakspeare's dramatic, Milton's epic.

That is, Chaucer told only as much of his story as he pleased, as was required for a particular purpose. He answered for his characters himself. In Shakspeare they are introduced upon the stage, are liable to be asked all sorts of questions, and are forced to answer for themselves. In Chaucer we perceive a fixed essence of character. In Shakspeare there is a continual composition and decomposition of its elements, a fermentation of every particle in the whole mass, by its alternate affinity or antipathy to other principles which are brought in contact with it. Till the experiment is tried, we do not know the result, the turn which the character will take in its new circumstances. Milton took only a few simple principles of character, and raised them to the utmost conceivable grandeur, and refined them from every base alloy. His imagination, "nigh sphered in Heaven," claimed kindred only with what he saw from that height, and could raise to the same elevation with itself. He sat retired, and kept his state alone, "playing with wisdom;" while Shakspeare mingled with the crowd, and played the host, "to make society the sweeter welcome."

The passion in Shakspeare is of the same nature as his delineation of character. It is not some one habitual feeling or sentiment preying upon itself, growing out of itself, and moulding every thing to itself; it is passion modified by passion, by all the other feelings to which the individual is liable, and to which others are liable with him; subject to all the fluctuations of caprice and accident; calling into play all the resources of the understanding and all the energies of the will;

irritated by obstacles or yielding to them; rising from small beginnings to its utmost height; now drunk with hope, now stung to madness, now sunk in despair, now blown to air with a breath, now raging like a torrent. The human soul is made the sport of fortune, the prey of adversity: it is stretched on the wheel of destiny, in restless ecstacy. The passions are in a state of projection. Years are melted down to moments, and every instant teems with fate. We know the results, we see the process. Thus after Iago has been boasting to himself of the effect of his poisonous suggestions on the mind of Othello, "which, with a little act upon the blood, will work like mines of sulphur," he adds: "Look where he comes! not poppy, nor mandragora, Nor all the drowsy syrups of the East, Shall ever medicine thee to that sweet sleep Which thou ow'dst yesterday."

And he enters at this moment, like the crested serpent, crowned with his wrongs and raging for revenge! The whole depends upon the turn of a thought. A word, a look, blows the spark of jealousy into a flame; and the explosion is immediate and terrible as a volcano. The dialogues in Lear, in Macbeth, that between Brutus and Cassius, and nearly all those in Shakspeare, where the interest is wrought up to its highest pitch, afford examples of this dramatic fluctuation of passion.

The interest in Chaucer is quite different; it is like the course of a river, strong, and full, and increasing. In Shakspeare, on the contrary, it is like the sea, agitated this way and that, and loud–lashed by furious storms; while in the still pauses of the blast, we distinguish only the cries of despair or the silence of death! Milton, on the other hand, takes the imaginative part of passion that which remains after the event, which the mind reposes on when all is over, which looks upon circumstances from the remotest elevation of thought and fancy, and abstracts them from the world of action to that of contemplation. The objects of dramatic poetry affect us by sympathy, by their nearness to ourselves, as they take us by surprise, or force us upon action, "while rage with rage doth sympathise:" the objects of epic poetry affect us through the medium of the imagination, by magnitude and distance, by their permanence and universality. The one fill us with terror and pity, the other with admiration and delight. There are certain objects that strike the imagination, and inspire awe in the very idea of them, independently of any dramatic interest, that is, of any connection with the vicissitudes of human life.

For instance, we cannot think of the pyramids of Egypt, of a Gothic ruin, or an old Roman encampment, without a certain emotion, a sense of power and sublimity coming over the mind. The heavenly bodies that hang over our heads wherever we go, and "in their untroubled element shall shine when we are laid in dust, and all our cares forgotten," affect us in the same way. Thus Satan's address to the Sun has an epic, not a dramatic interest; for though the second person in the dialogue makes no answer and feels no concern, yet the eye of that vast luminary is upon him, like the eye of heaven, and seems conscious of what he says, like an universal presence.

Dramatic poetry and epic, in their perfection, indeed, approximate to and strengthen one another. Dramatic poetry borrows aid from the dignity of persons and things, as the heroic does from human passion, but in theory they are distinct. When Richard II calls for the looking glass to contemplate his faded majesty in it, and bursts into that affecting exclamation: "Oh, that I were a mockery king of snow, to melt away before the sun of Bolingbroke," we have here the utmost force of human passion, combined with the ideas of regal splendour and fallen power. When Milton says of Satan: "His form had not yet lost All her original brightness, nor appear'd Less than archangel ruin'd, and the excess of glory obscur'd;" the mixture of beauty, of grandeur, and pathos, from the sense of irreparable loss, of never ending, unavailing regret, is perfect.

The great fault of a modern school of poetry is, that it is an experiment to reduce poetry to a mere effusion of natural sensibility; or what is worse, to divest it both of imaginary splendour and human passion, to surround the meanest objects with the morbid feelings and devouring egotism of the writers' own minds. Milton and Shakspeare did not so understand poetry. They gave a more liberal interpretation both to nature and art. They did not do all they could to get rid of the one and the other, to fill up the dreary void with the Moods of their own Minds. They owe their power over the human mind to their having had a deeper sense than others of what was grand in the objects of nature, or affecting in the events of human life. But to the men I speak of there is nothing interesting, nothing heroical, but themselves. To them the fall of gods or of great men is the same. They do not enter into the feeling. They cannot understand the terms. They are even debarred from the last poor, paltry consolation of an unmanly triumph over fallen greatness; for their minds reject, with a convulsive effort and intolerable loathing, the very idea that there ever was, or was thought to be, any thing superior to themselves. All that has ever excited the attention or admiration of the world they look upon with the most perfect indifference; and they are surprised to find that the world repays their indifference with scorn. "With what measure they mete, it has been meted to them again."

Shakspeare's imagination is of the same plastic kind as his conception of character or passion. "It glances from heaven to earth, from earth to heaven." Its movement is rapid and devious. It unites the most opposite extremes; or, as Puck says, in boasting of his own feats, "puts a girdle round about the earth in forty minutes." He seems always hurrying from his subject, even while describing it; but the stroke, like the lightning's, is sure as it is sudden. He takes the widest possible range, but from that very range he has his choice of the greatest variety and aptitude of materials. He brings together images the most alike, but placed at the greatest distance from each other; that is, found in circumstances of the greatest dissimilitude. From the remoteness of his combinations, and the celerity with which they are effected, they coalesce the more indissolubly together. The more the thoughts are strangers to each other, and the longer they have been kept asunder, the more intimate does their union seem to become. Their felicity is equal to their force. Their likeness is made more dazzling by their novelty. They startle, and take the fancy prisoner in the same instant. I will mention one or two which are very striking, and not much known, out of Troilus and Cressida. Eneas says to Agamemnon,

"I ask that I may waken reverence, And on the cheek be ready with a blush Modest as morning, when she coldly eyes The youthful Phoebus."

Ulysses urging Achilles to shew himself in the field, says— "No man is the lord of any thing, Till he communicate his parts to others: Nor doth he of himself know them for aught, Till he behold them formed in the applause, Where they're extended! which like an arch reverberates, The voice again, or like a gate of steel, Fronting the sun, receives and renders back, Its figure and its heat."

Patroclus gives the indolent warrior the same advice.

"Rouse yourself; and the weak wanton Cupid Shall from your neck unloose his amorous fold, And like a dew-drop from the lion's mane Be shook to air."

Shakspeare's language and versification are like the rest of him. He has a magic power over words: they come winged at his bidding; and seem to know their places. They are struck out at a heat, on the spur of the occasion, and have all the truth and vividness which arise from an actual impression of the objects. His epithets and single phrases are like sparkles, thrown off from an imagination, fired by the whirling rapidity of its own motion. His language is hieroglyphical. It translates thoughts into visible images. It abounds in sudden transitions and elliptical expressions. This is the source of his mixed metaphors, which are only abbreviated forms of speech. These, however, give no pain from long custom. They have, in fact, become idioms in the language. They are the building, and not the scaffolding to thought. We take the meaning and effect of a wellknown passage entire, and no more stop to scan and spell out the particular words and phrases, than the syllables of which they are composed. In trying to recollect any other author, one sometimes stumbles, in case of failure, on a word as good. In Shakspeare, any other word but the true one, is sure to be wrong. If any body, for instance, could not recollect the words of the following description,

"Light thickens, And the crow makes wing to the rooky wood," he would be greatly at a loss to substitute others for them equally expressive of the feeling. These remarks, however, are strictly applicable only to the impassioned parts of Shakspeare's language, which flowed from the warmth and originality of his imagination, and were his own. The language used for prose conversation and ordinary business is sometimes technical, and involved in the affectation of the time. Compare, for example, Othello's apology to the senate, relating "his whole course of love," with some of the preceding parts relating to his appointment, and the official dispatches from Cyprus. In this respect, "the business of the state does him offence." His versification is no less powerful, sweet, and varied. It has every occasional excellence, of sullen intricacy, crabbed and perplexed, or of the smoothest and loftiest expansion from the ease and familiarity of measured conversation to the lyrical sounds "Of ditties highly penned, Sung by a fair queen in a summer's bower,With ravishing division to her lute."

It is the only blank verse in the language, except Milton's, that for itself is readable. It is not stately and uniformly swelling like his, but varied and broken by the inequalities of the ground it has to pass over in its uncertain course, "And so by many winding nooks it strays, With willing sport to the wild ocean."

It remains to speak of the faults of Shakspeare. They are not so many or so great as they have been represented; what there are, are chiefly owing to the following causes. The universality of his genius was, perhaps, a disadvantage to his single works; the variety of his resources sometimes diverting him from applying them to the most effectual purposes. He might be said to combine the powers of Aeschylus and Aristophanes, of Dante and Rabelais, in his own mind. If he had been only half what he was, he would perhaps have appeared greater. The natural ease and indifference of his temper made him sometimes less scrupulous than he might have been. He is relaxed and careless in critical places; he is in earnest throughout only in Timon, Macbeth, and Lear.

Again, he had no models of acknowledged excellence constantly in view to stimulate his efforts, and by all that appears, no love of fame. He wrote for the "great vulgar and the small," in his time, not for posterity. If Queen Elizabeth and the maids of honour laughed heartily at his worst jokes, and the catcalls in the gallery were silent at his best passages, he went home satisfied, and slept the next night well. He did not trouble himself about Voltaire's criticisms. He was willing to take advantage of the ignorance of the age in many things; and if his plays pleased others, not to quarrel with them himself. His very facility of production would make him set less value on his own excellences, and not care to distinguish nicely between what he did well or ill. His blunders in chronology and geography do not amount to above half a dozen, and they are offences against chronology and geography, not against poetry. As to the unities, he was right in setting them at defiance. He was fonder of puns than became so great a man. His barbarisms were those of his age. His genius was his own. He had no objection to float down with the stream of common taste and opinion: he rose above it by his own buoyancy, and an impulse which he could not keep under, in spite of himself or others, and "his delights did shew most dolphin like."

He had an equal genius for comedy and tragedy; and his tragedies are better than his comedies, because tragedy is better than comedy. His female characters, which have been found fault with as insipid, are the finest in the world. Lastly, Shakspeare was the least of a coxcomb of any one that ever lived, and much of a gentleman.

4

The Characters of Shakspeare's Plays

CYMBELINE

Cymbeline is one of the most delightful of Shakspeare historical plays. It may be considered as a dramatic romance, in which the most striking parts of the story are thrown into the form of a dialogue, and the intermediate circumstances are explained by the different speakers, as occasion renders necessary. The action is less concentrated in consequence; but the interest becomes more aerial and refined from the principle of perspective introduced into the subject by the imaginary changes of scene, as well as by the length of time it occupies.

The reading of this play is like going a journey with some uncertain object at the end of it, and in which the suspense is kept up and heightened by the long intervals between each action. Though the events are scattered over such an extent of surface, and relate to such a variety of characters, yet the links which bind the different interests of the story together are never entirely broken. The most straggling and seemingly casual incidents are contrived in such a manner as to lead at last to the most complete developement of the catastrophe. The ease and conscious unconcern with which this is effected only makes the skill more wonderful.

The business of the plot evidently thickens in the last act: the story moves forward with increasing rapidity at every step; its various ramifications are drawn from the most distant points to the same centre; the principal characters are brought together, and placed in very critical situations; and the fate of almost every person in the drama is made to depend on the solution of a single circumstance the answer of Iachimo to the question of Imogen respecting the obtaining of the ring from Posthumus. Dr. Johnson is of opinion that Shakspeare was generally inattentive to the winding up of his plots. We think the contrary is true; and we might cite in proof of this remark not only the present play, but the conclusion of Lear, of Romeo and Juliet, of Macbeth, of Othello, even of Hamlet, and of other plays of less moment, in which the last act is crowded with decisive events brought about by natural and striking means.

The pathos in Cymbeline is not violent or tragical, but of the most pleasing and amiable kind. A certain tender gloom overspreads the whole. Posthumus is the ostensible hero of the piece, but its greatest charm is the character of Imogen. Posthumus is only interesting from the interest she takes in him; and she is only interesting herself from her tenderness and constancy to her husband. It is the peculiar excellence of Shakspeare's heroines, that they seem to exist only in their attachment to others.

They are pure abstractions of the affections. We think as little of their persons as they do themselves, because we are let into the secrets of their hearts, which are more important. We are too much interested in their affairs to stop to look at their faces, except by stealth and at intervals. No one ever hit the true perfection of the female character, the sense of weakness leaning on the strength of its affection's for support, so well as Shakspeare no one ever so well painted natural tenderness free from affectation and disguise no one else ever so well shewed how delicacy and timidity, when driven to extremity, grow romantic and extravagant; for the romance of his heroines (in which they abound) is only an excess of the habitual prejudices of their sex, scrupulous of being false to their vows, truant to their affections, and taught by the force of feeling when to forego the forms of propriety for the essence of it. His women were in this respect exquisite logicians; for there is nothing so logical as passion.

They knew their own minds exactly; and only followed up a favourite purpose, which they had sworn to with their tongues, and which was engraven on their hearts, into its untoward consequences. They were the prettiest little set of martyrs and confessors on record. Cibber, in speaking of the early English stage, accounts for the want of prominence and theatrical display in Shakspeare's female characters from the circumstance, that women in those days were not allowed to play the parts of women, which made it necessary to keep them a good deal in the background. Does not this state of manners itself, which prevented their exhibiting themselves in public, and confined them to the relations and charities of domestic life, afford a truer explanation of the matter? His women are certainly very unlike stage heroines; the reverse of tragedy queens.

We have almost as great an affection for Imogen as she had for Posthumus; and she deserves it better. Of all Shakspeare's women she is perhaps the most tender and the most artless. Her incredulity in the opening scene with Iachimo, as to her husband's infidelity, is much the same as Desdemona's backwardness to believe Othello's jealousy. Her answer to the most distressing part of the picture is only, "My lord, I fear, has forgot Britain." Her readiness to pardon Iachimo's false imputations and his designs against herself, is a good lesson to prudes; and may shew that where there is a real attachment to virtue, it has no need to bolster itself up with an outrageous or affected antipathy to vice. The scene in which Pisanio gives Imogen his master's letter, accusing her of incontinency on the treacherous suggestions of Iachimo, is as touching as it is possible for anything to be:

Pisanio: What cheer, Madam?

Imogen: False to his bed! What is it to be false? To lie in watch there, and to think on him? To weep 'twixt clock and clock? If sleep charge nature, To break it with a fearful dream of him, And cry myself awake? That's false to's bed, is it?

Pisanio: Alas, good lady!

Imogen: I false? thy conscience witness, Iachimo, Thou didst accuse him of incontinency, Thou then look'dst like a villain: now methinks, Thy favour's good enough. Some Jay of Italy, Whose mother was her painting, hath betray'd him: Poor I am stale, a garment out of fashion, And for I am richer than to hang by the walls, I must be ript; to pieces with me. Oh, Men's vows are women's traitors. All good seeming By thy revolt, oh husband, shall be thought Put on for villainy: not born where't grows, But worn a bait for ladies.

Pisanio: Good Madam, hear me

Imogen: Talk thy tongue weary, speak: I have heard I am a strumpet, and mine ear, Therein false struck, can take no greater wound, Nor tent to bottom that.

When Pisanio, who had been charged to kill his mistress, puts her in a way to live, she says,

"Why, good fellow, What shall I do the while? Where bide? How live? Or in my life what comfort, when I am Dead to my husband?"

Yet when he advises her to disguise herself in boy's clothes, and suggests "a course pretty and full in view," by which she may "happily be near the residence of Posthumus," she exclaims,

"Oh, for such means, Though peril to my modesty, not death on't, I would adventure."

And when Pisanio, enlarging on the consequences, tells her she must change—

"Fear and niceness, The handmaids of all women, or more truly, Woman its pretty self, into a waggish courage, Ready in gibes, quick answer'd, saucy, and As quarrellous as the weazel"—

she interrupts him hastily:

"Nay, be brief; I see into thy end, and am almost A man already."

In her journey thus disguised to Milford–Haven, she loses her guide and her way; and unbosoming her complaints, says beautifully:

"My dear lord, Thou art one of the false ones; now I think on thee, My hunger's gone; but even before, I was At point to sink for food."

She afterwards finds, as she thinks, the dead body of Posthumus, and engages herself as a foot boy to serve a Roman officer, when she has done all due obsequies to him whom she calls her former master–

"And when With wild wood–leaves and weeds I ha' strew'd his grave, And on it said a century of pray'rs, Such as I can, twice o'er, I'll weep and sigh, And leaving so his service, follow you, So please you entertain me."

Now this is the very religion of love. She all along relies little on her personal charms, which she fears may have been eclipsed by some painted Jay of Italy; she relies on her merit, and her merit is in the depth of her love, her truth and constancy. Our admiration of her beauty is excited with as little consciousness as possible-on her part. There are two delicious descriptions given of her, one when she is asleep, and one when she is supposed dead. Arviragus thus addresses her--

"With fairest flowers, While summer lasts, and I live here, Fidele, I'll sweeten thy sad grave; thou shalt not lack The flow'r that's like thy face, pale primrose, nor The azur'd hare–bell, like thy veins, no, nor The leaf of eglantine, which not to slander, Out sweeten'd not thy breath."

The yellow Iachimo gives another thus, when he steals into her bedchamber: "Cytherea, How bravely thou becom'st thy bed! Fresh lily, And whiter than the sheets! That I might touch, But kiss, one kiss, Tis her breathing that Perfumes the chamber thus: the flame o' the taper Bows toward her, and would under peep her lids , To see the enclosed lights now canopied Under the windows, white and azure, laced With blue of Heav'ns own tinct, on her left breast A mole cinque spotted, like the crimson drops I' the bottom of a cowslip."

There is a moral sense in the proud beauty of this last image, a rich surfeit of the fancy, as that well–known passage beginning, "Me of my lawful pleasure she restrained, and prayed me oft forbearance," sets a keener edge upon it by the inimitable picture of modesty and selfdenial.

The character of Cloten, the conceited, booby lord, and rejected lover of Imogen, though not very agreeable in itself, and at present obsolete, is drawn with much humour and quaint extravagance. The description which Imogen gives of his unwelcome addresses to her "Whose love suit hath been to me as fearfull as a siege", is enough to cure the most ridiculous lover of his folly. It is remarkable that though Cloten makes so poor a figure in love, he is described as assuming an air of consequence as the Queen's son in a council of state, and with all the absurdity of his person and manners, is not without shrewdness in his observations. So true is it that folly is as often owing to a want of proper sentiments as to a want of understanding! The exclamation of the ancient critic, Oh Menander and Nature, which of you copied from the other!

would not be misapplied to Shakspeare. The other characters in this play are represented with great truth and accuracy, and as it happens in most of the author's works, there is not only the utmost keeping in each separate character; but in the casting of the different parts, and their relation to one another, there is an affinity and harmony, like what we may observe in the gradations of colour in a picture. The striking and powerful contrasts in which Shakspeare abounds could not escape observation; but the use he makes of the principle of analogy to reconcile the greatest diversities of character and to maintain a continuity of feeling throughout, has not been sufficiently attended to.

In Cymbeline, for instance, the principal interest arises out of the unalterable fidelity of Imogen to her husband under the most trying circumstances. Now the other parts of the picture are filled up with subordinate examples of the same feeling, variously modified by different situations, and applied to the purposes of virtue or vice. The plot is aided by the amorous importunities of Cloten, by the persevering determination of Iachimo to conceal the defeat of his project by a darin itself, and at present obsolete, is drawn with much humour and quaint extravagance.

The description which Imogen gives of his unwelcome addresses to her "Whose love–suit hath been to me as fearfull as a siege", is enough to cure the most ridiculous lover of his folly. It is remarkable that though Cloten makes so poor a figure in love, he is described as assuming an air of consequence as the Queen's son in a council of state, and with all the absurdity of his person and manners, is not without shrewdness in his observations. So true is it that folly is as often owing to a want of proper sentiments as to a want of understanding! The exclamation of the ancient critic, Oh Menander and Nature, which of you copied from the other! would not be misapplied to Shakspeare.

The other characters in this play are represented with great truth and accuracy, and as it happens in most of the author's works, there is not only the utmost keeping in each separate character; but in the casting of the different parts, and their relation to one another, there is an affinity and harmony, like what we may observe in the gradations of colour in a picture. The striking and powerful contrasts in which Shakspeare abounds could not escape observation; but the use he makes of the principle of analogy to reconcile the greatest diversities of character and to maintain a continuity of feeling throughout, has not been sufficiently attended to.

In Cymbeline, for instance, the principal interest arises out of the unalterable fidelity of Imogen to her husband under the most trying circumstances. Now the other parts of the picture are filled up with subordinate examples of the same feeling, variously modified by different situations, and applied to the purposes of virtue or vice. The plot is aided by the amorous importunities of Cloten, by the persevering determination of Iachimo to conceal the defeat of his project by a darin itself, and at present obsolete, is drawn with much humour and quaint extravagance.

The description which Imogen gives of his unwelcome addresses to her, "Whose love suit hath been to me as fearfull as a siege" is enough to cure the most ridiculous lover of his folly. It is remarkable that though Cloten makes so poor a figure in love, he is described as assuming an air of consequence as the Queen's son in a council of state, and with all the absurdity of his person and manners, is not without shrewdness in his observations. So true is it that folly is as often owing to a want of proper sentiments as to a want of understanding! The exclamation of the ancient critic, Oh Menander and Nature, which of you copied from the other! would not be misapplied to Shakspeare.

The other characters in this play are represented with great truth and accuracy, and as it happens in most of the author's works, there is not only the utmost keeping in each separate character; but in the casting of the different parts, and their relation to one another, there is an affinity and harmony, like what we may observe in the gradations of colour in a picture.

The striking and powerful contrasts in which Shakspeare abounds could not escape observation; but the use he makes of the principle of analogy to reconcile the greatest diversities of character and to maintain a continuity of feeling throughout, has not been sufficiently attended to. In Cymbeline, for instance, the principal interest arises out of the unalterable fidelity of Imogen to her husband under the most trying circumstances. Now the other parts of the picture are filled up with subordinate examples of the same feeling, variously modified by different situations, and applied to the purposes of virtue or vice. The plot is aided by the amorous importunities of Cloten, by the persevering determination of Iachimo to conceal the defeat of his project by a darin.

That have a sharper known; well corresponding With your stiff age: but unto us it is A cell of ignorance; travelling a-bed, A prison for a debtor, that not dares To stride a limit.

Arviragus. What should we speak of When we are old as you? When we shall hear The rain and wind beat dark December! How, In this our pinching cave, shall we discourse The freesing hours away? We have seen nothing. We are beastly; subtle as the fox for prey, Like warlike as the wolf for what we eat: Our valour is to chase what flies; our cage We make a quire, as doth the prison'd bird, And sing our bondage freely.

The answer of Bellarius to this expostulation is hardly satisfactory; for nothing can be an answer to hope, or the passion of the mind for unknown good, but experience. The forest of Arden in As you like it can alone compare with the mountain scenes in Cymbeline: yet how different the contemplative quiet of the one from the enterprising boldness and precarious mode of subsistence in the other! Shakspeare not only lets us into the minds of his characters, but gives a tone and colour to the scenes he describes from the feelings of their supposed inhabitants.

He at the same time preserves the utmost propriety of action and passion, and gives all their local accompaniments. If he was equal to the greatest things, he was not above an attention to the smallest. Thus the gallant sportsmen in Cymbeline have to encounter the abrupt declivities of hill and valley: Touchstone and Audrey jog along a level path. The deer in Cymbeline are only regarded as objects of prey, "The game's a foot," *etc.* with Jaques they are fine subjects to moralise upon at leisure, "under the shade of melancholy boughs."

We cannot take leave of this play, which is a favourite with us, without noticing some occasional touches of natural piety and morality. We may allude here to the opening of the scene in which Bellarius instructs the young princes to pay their orisons to heaven: See, boys! this gate Instructs you how t' adore the Heav'ns; and bows you, To morning's holy office.

Guiderius. Hail, Heav'n!

Arviragus. Hail, Heav'n!

Bellarius. Now for our mountain–sport, up to yon hill.

What a grace and unaffected spirit of piety breathes in this passage! In like manner, one of the brothers says to the other, when about to perform the funeral rites to Fidele,

"Nay, Cadwall, we must lay his head to the east; My Father hath a reason for't" —

—as if some allusion to the doctrines of the Christian faith had been casually dropped in conversation by the old man, and had been no farther inquired into.

Shakspeare's morality is introduced in the same simple, unobtrusive manner. Imogen will not let her companions stay away from the chase to attend her when sick, and gives her reason for it –

"Stick to your journal course; the breach of custom Is breach of all!" When the Queen attempts to disguise her motives for procuring the poison from Cornelius, by saying she means to try its effects on "creatures not worth the hanging," his answer conveys at once a tacit reproof of her hypocrisy, and a useful lesson of humanity—

—"Your Highness Shall from this practice but make hard your heart."

MACBETH

"The poet's eye in a fine frenzy rolling Doth glance from heaven to earth, from earth to heaven; And as imagination bodies forth, The forms of things unknown, the poet's pen Turns them to shape, and gives to airy nothing A local habitation and a name."

Macbeth and Lear, Othello and Hamlet, are usually reckoned Shakspeare's four principal tragedies. Lear stands first for the profound intensity of the passion; Macbeth for the wildness of the imagination and the rapidity of the action; Othello for the progressive interest and powerful alternations of feeling: Hamlet for the refined development of thought and sentiment. If the force of genius shewn in each of these works is astonishing, their variety is not less so. They are like different creations of the same mind, not one of which has the slightest reference to the rest.

This distinctness and originality is indeed the necessary consequence of truth and nature. Shakspeare's genius alone appeared to possess the resources of nature. He is "your only tragedy maker." His plays have the force of things upon the mind. What he represents is brought home to the bosom as a part of our experience, implanted in the memory as if we had known the places, persons, and things of which he treats. Macbetch is like a record of a preternatural and tragical event.

It has the rugged severity of an old chronicle with all that the imagination of the poet can engraft upon traditional belief. The castle of Macbeth, round which "the air smells wooingly," and where "the temple haunting martlet builds," has a real subsistence in the mind; the Weird Sisters meet us in person on "the blasted heath;" the "air drawn dagger" moves slowly before our eyes; the "gracious Dun–can," can," the "blood boultered Banquo" stand before us; all that passed through the mind of Macbeth passes, without the loss of a tittle, through our's.

All that could actually take place, and all that is only possible to be conceived, what was said and what was done, the workings of passion, the spells of magic, are brought before us with the same absolute truth and vividness. Shakspeare excelled in the openings of his plays: that of Macbetch is the most striking of any. The wildness of the scenery, the sudden shifting of the situations and characters, the bustle, the expectations excited, are equally extraordinary. From the first entrance of the Witches and the description of them when they meet Macbeth, "What are these So wither'd and so wild in their attire, That look not like the inhabitants of the earth And yet are on't?" the mind is prepared for all that follows.

This tragedy is alike distinguished for the lofty imagination it displays, and for the tumultuous vehemence of the action; and the one is made the moving principle of the other. The overwhelming pressure of preternatural agency urges on the tide of human passion with redoubled force. Macbeth himself appears driven along by the violence of his fate like a vessel drifting before a storm: he reels to and fro like a drunken man; he staggers under the weight of his own purposes and the suggestions of others; he stands at bay with his situation; and from the superstitious awe and breathless suspense into which the communications of the Weird Sisters throw him, is hurried on with daring impatience to verify their predictions, and with impious and bloody hand to tear aside the veil which hides the uncertainty of the future. He is not equal to the struggle with fate and conscience.

He now "bends up each corporal instrument to the terrible feat;" at other times his heart misgives him, and he is cowed and abashed by his success. "The deed, no less than the attempt, confounds him." His mind is assailed by the stings of remorse, and full of "preternatural solicitings." His speeches and soliloquies are dark riddles on human life, baffling solution, and entangling him in their labyrinths. In thought he is absent and perplexed, sudden and desperate in act, from a distrust of his own resolution.

His energy springs from the anxiety and agitation of his mind. His blindly rushing forward on the objects of his ambition and revenge, or his recoiling from them, equally betrays the harassed state of his feelings. This part of his character is admirably set off by being brought in connection with that of Lady Macbeth, whose obdurate strength of will and masculine firmness give her the ascendancy over her husband's faultering virtue. She at once seizes on the opportunity that offers for the accomplishment of all their wished for greatness, and never flinches from her object till all is over. The magnitude of her resolution almost covers the magnitude of her guilt. She is a great bad woman, whom we hate, but whom we fear more than we hate.

She does not excite our loathing and abhorrence like Regan and Gonerill. She is only wicked to gain a great end; and is perhaps more distinguished by her commanding presence of mind and inexorable self will, which do not suffer her to be diverted from a bad purpose, when once formed, by weak and womanly regrets, than by the hardness of her heart or want of natural affections. The impression which her lofty determination of character makes on the mind of Macbeth is well described where he exclaims,

—"Bring forth men children only; For thy undaunted mettle should compose, Nothing but males!"

Nor do the pains she is at to "screw his courage to the sticking–place," the reproach to him, not to be "lost so poorly in himself," the assurance that "a little water clears them of this deed," shew anything but her greater consistency in depravity. Her strong nerved ambition furnishes ribs of steel to "the sides of his intent;" and she is herself wound up to the execution of her baneful project with the same unshrinking fortitude in crime, that in other circumstances she would probably have shewn patience in suffering. The deliberate sacrifice of all other considerations to the gaining "for their future days and nights sole sovereign sway and masterdom," by the murder of Duncan, is gorgeously expressed in her invocation on hearing of "his fatal entrance under her battlements:"

"Come all you spirits That tend on mortal thoughts, unsex me here: And fill me, from the crown to the toe, top–full of direst cruelty; make thick my blood, Stop up the access and passage to remorse, That no compunctious visitings of nature Shake my fell purpose, nor keep peace between The effect and it. Come to my woman's breasts, And take my milk for gall, you murthering ministers, Wherever in your sightless substances ,You wait on nature's mischief. Come, thick night! And pall thee in the dunnest smoke of hell, That my keen knife see not the wound it makes, Nor heav'n peep through the blanket of the dark, To cry, hold, hold!"

When she first hears that "Duncan comes there to sleep" she is so overcome by the news, which is beyond her utmost expectations, that she answers the messenger, "Thou'rt mad to say it:" and on receiving her husband's account of the predictions of the Witches, conscious of his instability of purpose, and that her presence is necessary to goad him on to the consummation of his promised greatness, she exclaims– "Hie thee hither, That I may pour my spirits in thine ear, And chastise with the valour of my tongue All that impedes thee from the golden round, Which fate and metaphysical aid doth seem To have thee crowned withal."

This swelling exultation and keen spirit of triumph, this uncontroulable eagerness of anticipation, which seems to dilate her form and take possession of all her faculties, this solid, substantial flesh and blood display of passion, exhibit a striking contrast to the cold, abstracted, gratuitous, servile malignity of the Witches, who are equally instrumental in urging Macbeth to his fate for the mere love of mischief, and from a disinterested delight in deformity and cruelty. They are hags of mischief, obscene panders to iniquity, malicious from their impotence of enjoyment, enamoured of destruction, because they are themselves unreal, abortive, half existences who become sublime from their exemption from all human sympathies and contempt for all human affairs, as Lady Macbeth does by the force of passion! Her fault seems to have been an excess of that strong principle of self interest and family aggrandisement, not amenable to the common feelings of compassion and justice, which is so marked a feature in barbarous nations and times. A passing reflection of this kind, on the resemblance of the sleeping king to her father, alone prevents her from slaying Duncan with her own hand.

In speaking of the character of Lady Macbeth, we ought not to pass over Mrs. Siddons's manner of acting that part. We can conceive of nothing grander. It was something above nature. It seemed almost as if a being of a superior order had dropped from a higher sphere to awe the world with the majesty of her appearance. Power was seated on her brow, passion emanated from her breast as from a shrine; she was tragedy personified. In coming on in the sleepingm scene, her eyes were open, but their sense was shut. She was like a person bewildered and unconscious of what she did. Her lips moved involuntarily all her gestures were involuntary and mechanical. She glided on and off the stage like an apparition. To have seen her in that character was an event in every one's life, not to be forgotten.

The dramatic beauty of the character of Duncan, which excites the respect and pity even of his murderers, has been often pointed out. It forms a picture of itself. An instance of the author's power of giving a striking effect to a common reflection, by the manner of introducing it, occurs in a speech of Duncan, complaining of his having been deceived in his opinion of the Thane of Cawdor, at the very moment that he is expressing the most unbounded confidence in the loyalty and services of Macbeth.

"There is no art To find the mind's construction in the face: He was a gentleman, on whom I built An absolute trust. O worthiest cousin, (addressing himself to Macbeth.) The sin of my Ingratitude e'en now Was great upon me," *etc.*

Another passage to shew that Shakspeare lost sight of nothing that could in any way give relief or heightening to his subject, is the conversation which takes place between Banquo and Fleance immediately before the murder scene of Duncan.

Banquo: How goes the night, boy?

Fleance: The moon is down: I have not heard the clock.

Banquo: And she goes down at twelve.

Fleance: I take't, 'tis later, Sir.

Banquo: Hold, take my sword. There's husbandry in heav'n, Their candles are all out.

A heavy summons lies like lead upon me, And yet I would not sleep: Merciful Powers, Restrain in me the cursed thoughts that nature Gives way to in repose."

In like manner, a fine idea is given of the gloomy coming on of evening, just as Banquo is going to be assassinated.

"Light thickens and the crow Makes wing to the rooky wood." "Now spurs the lated traveller apace To gain the timely inn." Macbeth (generally speaking) is done upon a stronger and more systematic principle of contrast than any other of Shakspeare's plays. It moves upon the verge of an abyss, and is a constant struggle between life and death. The action is desperate and the reaction is dreadful. It is a huddling together of fierce extremes, a war of opposite natures which of them shall destroy the other.

There is nothing but what has a violent end or violent beginnings. The lights and shades are laid on with a determined hand; the transitions from triumph to despair, from the height of terror to the repose of death, are sudden and startling; every passion brings in its fellow contrary, and the thoughts pitch and jostle against each other as in the dark. The whole play is an unruly chaos of strange and forbidden things, where the ground rocks under our feet. Shakspeare's genius here took its full swing and trod upon the farthest bounds of nature and passion.

This circumstance will account for the abruptness and violent antitheses of the style, the throes and labour which run through the expression and from defects will turn them into beauties. "So fair and foul a day I have not seen," *etc.* "Such welcome and unwelcome news together." Men's lives are like the flowers in their caps, dying or ere they sicken. "Look like the innocent flower, but be the serpent under it." The scene before the castle gate follows the appearance of the Witches on the heath, and is followed by a midnight murder. Duncan is cut off betimes by treason leagued with witchcraft, and Macduff is ripped untimely from his mother's womb to avenge his death.

Macbeth, after the death of Banquo, wishes for his presence in extravagant terms, "To him and all we thirst," and when his ghost appears, cries out, "Avaunt and quit my sight," and being gone, he is "himself again." Macbeth resolves to get rid of Macduff, that "he may sleep in spite of thunder;" and cheers his wife on the doubtful intelligence of Banquo's taking off with the encouragement. "Then be thou jocund: ere the bat has flown his cloistered flight; ere to black Hecate's summons the shard–born beetle has rung night's yawning peal, there shall be done a deed of dreadful note." In Lady Macbethes speech "Had he not resembled my father as he slept, I had done 't," there is murder and filial piety together; and in urging him to fulfil his vengeance against the defenceless king, her thoughts spare the blood neither of infants nor old age.

The description of the Witches is full of the same contradictory principle; they "rejoice when good kings bleed," they are neither of the earth nor the air, but both; they "should be women, but their beards forbid it;" they take all the pains possible to lead Macbeth on to the height of his ambition, only to betray him "in deeper consequence," and after showing him all the pomp of their art, discover their' malignant delight in his disappointed hopes, by that bitter taunt, "Why stands Macbeth thus amazedly?" We might multiply such instances every where.

The leading features in the character of Macbeth are striking enough, and they form what may be thought at first only a bold, rude, Gothic outline. By comparing it with other characters of the same author we shall perceive the absolute truth and identity which is observed in the midst of the giddy whirl and rapid career of events. Macbeth in Shakspeare no more loses his identity of character in the fluctuations of fortune or the storm of passion, than Macbeth in himself would have lost the identity of his person.

Thus he is as distinct a being from Richard III as it is possible to imagine, though these two characters in common hands, and indeed in the hands of any other poet, would have been a repetition of the same general idea, more or less exaggerated. For both are tyrants, usurpers, murderers, both aspiring and ambitious, both courageous, cruel, treacherous. But Richard is cruel from nature and constitution. Macbeth becomes so from accidental circumstances. Richard is from his birth deformed in body and mind, and naturally incapable of good. Macbeth is full of "the milk of human kindness," is frank, sociable, generous. He is tempted to the commission of guilt by golden opportunities, by the instigations of his wife, and by prophetic warnings.

Fate and metaphysical aid conspire against his virtue and his loyalty. Richard on the contrary needs no prompter, but wades through a series of crimes to the height of his ambition from the ungovernable violence of his temper and a reckless love of mischief.

He is never gay but in the prospect or in the success of his villainies: Macbeth is full of horror at the thoughts of the murder of Duncan, which he is with difficulty prevailed on to commit, and of remorse after its perpetration. Richard has no mixture of common humanity in his composition, no regard to kindred or posterity, he owns no fellowship with others, he is "himself alone." Macbeth is not destitute of feelings of sympathy, is accessible to pity, is even made in some measure the dupe of his uxoriousness, ranks the loss of friends, of the cordial love of his followers, and of his good name, among the causes which have made him weary of life, and regrets that he has ever seized the crown by unjust means, since he cannot transmit it to his posterity—

"For Banquo's issue have I fil'd my mind—For them the gracious Duncan have I murther'd, To make them kings, the seed of Banquo kings." In the agitation of his mind, he envies those whom he has sent to peace. "Duncan is in his grave; after life's fitful fever he sleeps well." It is true, he becomes more callous as he plunges deeper in guilt, "direness is thus rendered familiar to his slaughterous thoughts," and he in the end anticipates his wife in the boldness and bloodiness of his enterprises, while she for want of the same stimulus of action, "is troubled with thick coming fancies that rob her of her rest," goes mad and dies.

Macbeth endeavours to escape from reflection on his crimes by repelling their consequences, and banishes remorse for the past by the meditation of future mischief. This is not the principle of Richard's cruelty, which displays the wanton malice of a fiend as much as the frailty of human passion. Macbeth is goaded on to acts of violence and retaliation by necessity; to Richard, blood is a pastime.

There are other decisive differences inherent in the two characters. Richard may be regarded as a man of the world, a plotting, hardened knave, wholly regardless of everything but his own ends, and the means to secure them. Not so Macbeth. The superstitions of the age, the rude state of society, the local scenery and customs, all give a wildness and imaginary grandeur to his character. From the strangeness of the events that surround him, he is full of amazement and fear; and stands in doubt between the world of reality and the world of fancy. He sees sights not shewn to mortal eye, and hears unearthly music. All is tumult and disorder within and without his mind; his purposes recoil upon himself, are broken and disjointed; he is the double thrall of his passions and his evil destiny. Richard is not a character either of imagination or pathos, but of pure selfwill. There is no conflict of opposite feelings in his breast. The apparitions which he sees only haunt him in his sleep; nor does he live like Macbeth in a waking dream.

Macbeth has considerable energy and manliness of character; but then he is "subject to all the skyey influences." He is sure of nothing but the present moment. Richard in the busy turbulence of his projects never loses his self possession, and makes use of every circumstance that happens as an instrument of his long reaching designs. In his last extremity we can only regard him as a wild beast taken in the toils: while we never entirely lose our concern for Macbeth; and he calls back all our sympathy by that fine close of thoughtful melancholy, "My way of life is fallen into the sear, The yellow leaf; and that which should accompany old age, As honour, troops of friends, I must not look to have; But in their stead, curses not loud but deep, Mouth–honour, breath, which the poor heart Would fain deny, and dare not."

We can conceive a common actor to play Richard tolerably well; we can conceive no one to play Macbeth properly, or to look like a man that had encountered the Weird Sisters. All the actors that we have ever seen, appear as if they had encountered them on the boards of Coventgarden or Drury lane, but not on the heath at Fores, and as if they did not believe what they had seen. The Witches of Macbeth indeed are ridiculous on the modern stage, and we doubt if the Furies of Aeschylus would be more respected. The progress of manners and knowledge has an influence on the stage, and will in time perhaps destroy both tragedy and comedy.

Filch's picking pockets in the Beggar's Opera is not so good a jest as it used to be: by the force of the police and of philosophy, Lillo's murders and the ghosts in Shakspeare will become obsolete. At last, there will be nothing left, good nor bad, to be desired or dreaded, on the theatre or in real life. A question has been started with respect to the originality of Shakspeare's witches, which has been well answered by Mr. Lamb in his notes to the "Specimens of Early Dramatic Poetry."

Though some resemblance may be traced between the charms in Macbeth, and the incantations in this play, (The Witch of Middleton) which is supposed to have preceded it, this coincidence will not detract much from the originality of Shakspeare. His Witches are distinguished from the Witches of Middleton by essential differences. These are creatures to whom man or woman plotting some dire mischief might resort for occasional consultation. Those originate deeds of blood, and begin bad impulses to men. From the moment that their eyes first meet with Macbethes, he is spell bound.

That meeting sways his destiny. He can never break the fascination. These Witches can hurt the body; those have power over the soul. Hecate in Middleton has a son, a low buffoon: the hags of Shakspeare have neither child of their own, nor seem to be descended from any parent. They are foul anomalies, of whom we know not whence they are sprung, nor whether they have beginning or ending. As they are without human passions, so they seem to be without human relations. They come with thunder and lightning, and vanish to airy music. This is all we know of them. Except Hecate, they have no names, which heightens their mysteriousness. The names, and some of the properties which Middleton has given to his hags, excite smiles. The Weird Sisters are serious things.

Their presence cannot co-exist with mirth. But, in a lesser degree, the Witches of Middleton are fine creations. Their power too is, in some measure, over the mind. They raise jars, jealousies, strifes, like a thick scurf o'er life.

IAGO

The character of Iago is one of the supererogations of Shakspeare's genius. Some persons, more nice than wise, have thought this whole character unnatural, because his villainy is without a sufficient motive. Shakspeare, who was as good a philosopher as he was a poet, thought otherwise. He knew that the love of power, which is another name for the love of mischief, is natural to man. He would know this as well or better than if it had been demonstrated to him by a logical diagram, merely from seeing children paddle in the dirt or kill flies for sport.

Iago in fact belongs to a class of character, common to Shakspeare and at the same time peculiar to him; whose heads are as acute and active as their hearts are hard and callous. Iago is to be sure an extreme instance of the kind; that is to say, of diseased intellectual activity, with the most perfect indifference to moral good or evil, or rather with a decided preference of the latter, because it falls more readily in with his favourite propensity, gives greater zest to his thoughts and scope to his actions. He is quite or nearly as indifferent to his own fate as to that of others; he runs all risks for a trifling and doubtful advantage; and is himself the dupe and victim of his ruling passion an insatiable craving after action of the most difficult and dangerous kind. "Our ancient" is a philosopher, who fancies that a lie that kills has more point in it than an alliteration or an antithesis; who thinks a fatal experiment on the peace of a family a better thing than watching the palpitations in the heart of a flea in a microscope; who plots the ruin of his friends as an exercise for his ingenuity, and stabs men in the dark to prevent ennui. His gaiety, such as it is, arises from the success of his treachery; his ease from the torture he has inflicted on others. He is an amateur of tragedy in real life; and instead of employing his invention on imaginary characters, or long forgotten incidents, he takes the bolder and more desperate course of getting up his plot at home, casts the principal parts among his nearest friends and connections, and rehearses it in downright earnest, with steady nerves and unabated resolution. We will just give an illustration or two.

One of his most characteristic speeches is that immediately after the marriage of Othello.

Roderigo: What a full fortune does the thick lips owe, If he can carry her thus!

Iago: Call up her father:

Rouse him (Othello) make after him, poison his delight, Proclaim him in the streets, incense her kinsmen, And tho' he in a fertile climate dwell, Plague him with flies: tho' that his joy be joy, Yet throw such changes of vexation on it, As it may lose some colour.

In the next passage, his imagination runs riot in the mischief he is plotting, and breaks out into the wildness, and impetuosity of real enthusiasm.

Roderigo: Here is her father's house: I'll call aloud.

Iago: Do, with like timourous accent and dire yell, As when, by night and negligence, the fire Is spied in populous cities."

One of his most favourite topics, on which he is rich indeed, and in descanting on which his spleen serves him for a Muse, is the disproportionate match between Desdemona and the Moor. This is a clue to the character of the lady which he is by no means ready to part with. It is brought forward in the first scene, and he recurs to it, when in answer to his insinuations against Desdemona, Roderigo says,

I cannot believe that in her—she's full of most blest conditions.

Iago: Bless'd fig's end. The wine she drinks is made of grapes. If she had been blest, she would never have married the Moor.

And again with still more spirit and fatal effect afterwards, when he turns this very suggestion arising in Othello's own breast to her prejudice.

Othello: And yet how nature erring from itself –

Iago: Ay, there's the point; as to be bold with you, Not to affect many proposed matches Of her own clime, complexion, and degree," *etc.*

This is probing to the quick. Iago here turns the character of poor Desdemona, as it were, inside out. It is certain that nothing but the genius of Shakspeare could have preserved the entire interest and delicacy of the part, and have even drawn an additional elegance and dignity from the peculiar circumstances in which she is placed.

The habitual licentiousness of Iago's conversation is not to be traced to the pleasure he takes in gross or lascivious images, but to his desire of finding out the worst side of everything, and of proving himself an over–match for appearances. He has none of "the milk of human kindness" in his composition. His imagination rejects everything that has not a strong infusion of the most unpalatable ingredients; his mind digests only poisons.

Virtue or goodness or whatever has the least "relish of salvation in it," is, to his depraved appetite, sickly and insipid: and he even resents the good opinion entertained of his own integrity, as if it were an affront cast on the masculine sense and spirit of his character. Thus at the meeting between Othello and Desdemona, he exclaims "Oh, you are well tuned now: but I'll set down the pegs that make this music, as honest as I am" his character of bonhommie not sitting at all easy upon him. In the scenes, where he tries to work Othello to his purpose, he is proportionably guarded, insidious, dark, and deliberate. We believe nothing ever came up to the profound dissimulation and dextrous artifice of the well known dialogue in the third act, where he first enters upon the execution of his design.

Iago: My noble lord.

Othello: What dost thou say, Iago?

Iago: Did Michael Cassio, When you woo'd my lady, know of your love?

Othello: He did from first to last. Why dost thou ask?

Iago: But for a satisfaction of my thought, No further harm.

Othello: Why of thy thought, Iago?

Iago: I did not think he had been acquainted with it.

Othello: O yes, and went between us very oft—

Iago: Indeed!

Othello: Indeed? Ay, indeed. Discern'st thou aught of that? Is he not honest?

Iago: Honest, my lord?

Othello: Honest? Ay, honest.

Iago: My lord, for aught I know.

Othello: What do'st thou think?

Iago: Think, my lord!

Othello: Think, my lord! Alas, thou echo'st me, As if there was some monster in thy thought Too hideous to be shewn.

The stops and breaks, the deep workings of treachery under the mask of love and honesty, the anxious watchfulness, the cool earnestness, and if we may so say, the passion of hypocrisy, marked in every line, receive their last finishing in that inconceivable burst of pretended indignation at Othello's doubts of his sincerity. "O grace! O Heaven forgive me! Are you a man?

Have you a soul or sense? God be wi' you; take mine office. O wretched fool, That lov'st to make thine honesty a vice! Oh monstrous world! Take note, take note, O world! To be direct and honest, is not safe. I thank you for this profit, and from hence I'll love no friend, since love breeds such offence."

If Iago is detestable enough when he has business on his hands and all his engines at work, he is still worse when he has nothing to do, and we only see into the hollowness of his heart. His indifference when Othello falls into a swoon, is perfectly diabolical.

Iago: How is it, General? Have you not hurt your head?
Othello: Do'st thou mock me?
Iago: I mock you not, by Heaven, *etc.*

The part indeed would hardly be tolerated, even as a foil to the virtue and generosity of the other characters in the play, but for its indefatigable industry and inexhaustible resources, which divert the attention of the spectator (as well as his own) from the end he has in view to the means by which it must be accomplished. Edmund the Bastard in Lear is something of the same character, placed in less prominent circumstances. Zanga is a vulgar caricature of it.

HAMLET

This is that Hamlet the Dane, whom we read of in our youth, and whom we may be said almost to remember in our after years; he who made that famous soliloquy on life, who gave the advice to the players, who thought "this goodly frame, the earth, a steril promontory, and this brave o'er hanging firmament, the air, this majestical roof fretted with golden fire, a foul and pestilent congregation of vapours;" whom "man delighted not, nor woman neither;" he who talked with the grave diggers, and moralised on Yorick's skull; the school fellow of Rosencrans and Guildenstern at Wittenberg; the friend of Horatio; the lover of Ophelia; he that was mad and sent to England; the slow avenger of his father's death; who lived at the court of Horwendillus five hundred years before we were born, but all whose thoughts we seem to know as well as we do our own, because we have read them in Shakspeare.

Hamlet is a name; his speeches and sayings but the idle coinage of the poet's brain. What then, are they not real? They are as real as our own thoughts. Their reality is in the reader's mind. It is we who are Hamlet. This play has a prophetic truth, which is above that of history. Whoever has become thoughtful and melancholy through his own mishaps or those of others;

whoever has borne about with him the clouded brow of reflection, and thought himself "too much i' the sun;" whoever has seen the golden lamp of day dimmed by envious mists rising in his own breast, and could find in the world before him only a dull blank with nothing left remarkable in it; whoever has known "the pangs of despised love, the insolence of office, or the spurns which patient merit of the unworthy takes;" he who has felt his mind sink within him, and sadness cling to his heart like a malady, who has had his hopes blighted and his youth staggered by the apparitions of strange things; who cannot be well at ease, while he sees evil hovering near him like a spectre; whose powers of action have been eaten up by thought, he to whom the universe seems infinite, and himself nothing; whose bitterness of soul makes him careless of consequences, and who goes to a play as his best resource to shove off, to a second remove, the evils of life by a mock representation of them this is the true Hamlet.

We have been so used to this tragedy that we hardly know how to criticise it any more than we should know how to describe our own faces. But we must make such observations as we can. It is the one of Shakspeare's plays that we think of the oftenest, because it abounds most in striking reflections on human life, and because the distresses of Hamlet are transferred, by the turn of his mind, to the general account of humanity. Whatever happens to him we apply to ourselves, because he applies it so himself as a means of general reasoning. He is a great moraliser; and what makes him worth attending to is, that he moralises on his own feelings and experience. He is not a common place pedant.

If Lear is distinguished by the greatest depth of passion, Hamlet is the most remarkable for the ingenuity, originality, and unstudied developement of character. Shakspeare had more magnanimity than any other poet, and he has shewn more of it in this play than in any other. There is no attempt to force an interest: everything is left for time and circumstances to unfold. The attention is excited without effort, the incidents succeed each other as matters of course, the characters think and speak and act just as they might do, if left entirely to themselves.

There is no set purpose, no straining at a point. The observations are suggested by the passing scene the gusts of passion come and go like sounds of music borne on the wind. The whole play is an exact transcript of what might be supposed to have taken place at the court of Denmark, at the remote period of time fixed upon, before the modern refinements in morals and manners were heard of. It would have been interesting enough to have been admitted as a by stander in such a scene, at such a time, to have heard and witnessed something of what was going on. But here we are more than spectators. We have not only "the outward pageants and the signs of grief;" but "we have that within which passes shew." We read the thoughts of the heart, we catch the passions living as they rise. Other dramatic writers give us very fine versions and paraphrases of nature; but Shakspeare, together with his own comments, gives us the original text, that we may judge for ourselves. This is a very great advantage.

The character of Hamlet stands quite by itself. It is not a character marked by strength of will or even of passion, but by refinement of thought and sentiment. Hamlet is as little of the hero as a man can well be: but he is a young and princely novice, full of high enthusiasm and quick sensibility the sport of circumstances, questioning with fortune and refining on his own feelings, and forced from the natural bias of his disposition by the strangeness of his situation. He seems incapable of deliberate action, and is only hurried into extremities on the spur of the occasion, when he has no time to reflect, as in the scene where he kills Polonius, and again, where he alters the letters which Rosencrans and Guildenstern are taking with them to England, purporting his death.

At other times, when he is most bound to act, he remains puzzled, undecided, and sceptical, dallies with his purposes, till the occasion is lost, and finds out some pretence to relapse into indolence and thoughtfulness again. For this reason he refuses to kill the King when he is at his prayers, and by a refinement in malice, which is in truth only an excuse for his own want of resolution, defers his revenge to a more fatal opportunity, when he shall be engaged in some act "that has no relish of salvation in it."

"He kneels and prays, And now I'll do't, and so he goes to heaven, And so am I reveng'd: that would be scann'd. He kill'd my father, and for that, I, his sole son, send him to heaven. Why this is reward, not revenge. Up sword and know thou a more horrid time, When he is drunk, asleep, or in a rage."

He is the prince of philosophical speculators; and because he cannot have his revenge perfect, according to the most refined idea his wish can form, he declines it altogether. So he scruples to trust the suggestions of the ghost, contrives the scene of the play to have surer proof of his uncle's guilt, and then rests satisfied with this confirmation of his suspicions, and the success of his experiment, instead of acting upon it. Yet he is sensible of his own weakness, taxes himself with it, and tries to reason himself out of it.

"How all occasions do inform against me, And spur my dull revenge! What is a man, If his chief good and market of his time Be but to sleep and feed? A beast; no more. Sure he that made us with such large discourse, Looking before and after, gave us not That capability and god–like reason To rust in us unus'd. Now whether it be Bestial oblivion, or some craven scruple Of thinking too precisely on the event, A thought which quarter'd, hath but one part wisdom, And ever three parts coward; I do not know Why yet I live to say, this thing's to do; Sith I have cause, and will, and strength, and means To do it.

Examples gross as earth exhort me: Witness this army of such mass and charge, Led by a delicate and tender prince, Whose spirit with divine ambition puff'd, Makes mouths at the invisible event, Exposing what is mortal and unsure To all that fortune, death, and danger dare, Even for an egg–shell. 'Tis not to be great Never to stir without great argument; But greatly to find quarrel in a straw, When honour's at the stake. How stand I then, That have a father kill'd, a mother stain'd, Excitements of my reason and my blood, And let all sleep, while to my shame I see The imminent death of twenty thousand men, That for a fantasy and trick of fame, Go to their graves like beds, fight for a plot Whereon the numbers cannot try the cause, which is not tomb enough and continent to hide the slain? O, from this time forth,My thoughts be bloody or be nothing worth."

Still he does nothing; and this very speculation on his own infirmity only affords him another occasion for indulging it. It is not from any want of attachment to his father or of abhorrence of his murder that Hamlet is thus dilatory, but it is more to his taste to indulge his imagination in reflecting upon the enormity of the crime and refining on his schemes of vengeance, than to put them into immediate practice. His ruling passion is to think, not to act: and any vague pretext that flatters this propensity instantly diverts him from his previous purposes.

The moral perfection of this character has been called in question, we think, by those who did not understand it. It is more interesting than according to rules; amiable, though not faultless. The ethical delineations of "that noble and liberal casuist" (as Shakspeare has been well called) do not exhibit the drab, coloured quakerism of morality. His plays are not copied either from The Whole Duty of Man, or from The Academy of Compliments!

We confess we are a little shocked at the want of refinement in those who are shocked at the want of refinement in Hamlet. The neglect of punctilious exactness in his behaviour either partakes of the "licence of the time," or else belongs to the very excess of intellectual refinement in the character, which makes the common rules of life, as well as his own purposes, sit loose upon him.

He may be said to be amenable only to the tribunal of his own thoughts, and is too much taken up with the airy world of contemplation to lay as much stress as he ought on the practical consequences of things. His habitual principles of action are unhinged and out of joint with the time. His conduct to Ophelia is quite natural in his circumstances. It is that of assumed severity only.

It is the effect of disappointed hope, of bitter regrets, of affection suspended, not obliterated, by the distractions of the scene around him! Amidst the natural and preternatural horrors of his situation, he might be excused in delicacy from carrying on a regular courtship. When "his father's spirit was in arms," it was not a time for the son to make love in. He could neither marry Ophelia, nor wound her mind by explaining the cause of his alienation, which he durst hardly trust himself to think of. It would have taken him years to have come to a direct explanation on the point. In the harassed state of his mind, he could not have done much otherwise than he did. His conduct does not contradict what he says when he sees her funeral,

"I loved Ophelia: forty thousand brothers Could not with all their quantity of love Make up my sum."

Nothing can be more affecting or beautiful than the Queen's apostrophe to Ophelia on throwing the flowers into the grave. "Sweets to the sweet, farewell. I hop'd thou should'st have been my Hamlet's wife: I thought thy bride–bed to have deck'd, sweet maid, And not have strew'd thy grave." Shakspeare was thoroughly a master of the mixed motives of human character, and he here shews us the Queen, who was so criminal in some respects, not without sensibility and affection in other relations of life. Ophelia is a character almost too exquisitely touching to be dwelt upon. Oh rose of May, oh flower too soon faded! Her love, her madness, her death, are described with the truest touches of tenderness and pathos.

It is a character which nobody but Shakspeare could have drawn in the way that he has done, and to the conception of which there is not even the smallest approach, except in some of the old romantic ballads. Her brother, Laertes, is a character we do not like so well: he is too hot and choleric, and somewhat rhodomontade. Polonius is a perfect character in its kind; nor is there any foundation for the objections which have been made to the consistency of this part. It is said that he acts very foolishly and talks very sensibly.

There is no inconsistency in that. Again, that he talks wisely at one time and foolishly at another; that his advice to Laertes is very excellent, and his advice to the King and Queen on the subject of Hamlet's madness very ridiculous. But he gives the one as a father, and is sincere in it; he gives the other as a mere courtier, a busy–body, and is accordingly officious, garrulous, and impertinent. In short, Shakspeare has been accused of inconsistency in this and other characters, only because he has kept up the distinction which there is in nature, between the understandings and the moral habits of men, between the absurdity of their ideas and the absurdity of their motives. Polonius is not a fool, but he makes himself so. His folly, whether in his actions or speeches, comes under the head of impropriety of intention.

We do not like to see our author's plays acted, and least of all, Hamlet. There is no play that suffers so much in being transferred to the stage. Hamlet himself seems hardly capable of being acted. Mr. Kemble unavoidably fails in this character from a want of case and variety.

The character of Hamlet is made up of undulating lines; it has the yielding flexibility of "a wave o' the sea." Mr. Kemble plays it like a man in armour, with a determined inveteracy of purpose, in one undeviating straight line, which is as remote from the natural grace and refined susceptibility of the character, as the sharp angles and abrupt starts which Mr. Kean introduces into the part. Mr. Kean's Hamlet is as much too splenetic and rash as Mr. Kemble's is too deliberate and formal. His manner is too strong and pointed. He throws a severity, approaching to virulence, into the common observations and answers.

There is nothing of this in Hamlet. He is, as it were, wrapped up in his reflections, and only thinks aloud. There should therefore be no attempt to impress what he says upon others by a studied exaggeration of emphasis or manner; no talking at his hearers. There should be as much of the gentleman and scholar as possible infused into the part, and as little of the actor. A pensive air of sadness should sit reluctantly upon his brow, but no appearance of fixed and sullen gloom. He is full of weakness and melancholy, but there is no harshness in his nature. He is the most amiable of misanthropes.

ROMEO AND JULIET

Romeo and Juliet is the only tragedy which Shakspeare has written entirely on a love-story. It is supposed to have been his first play, and it deserves to stand in that proud rank. There is the buoyant spirit of youth in every line, in the rapturous intoxication of hope, and in the bitterness of despair. It has been said of Romeo and Juliet by a great critic, that "whatever is most intoxicating in the odour of a southern spring, languishing in the song of the nightingale, or voluptuous in the first opening of the rose, is to be found in this poem." The description is true; and yet it does not answer to our idea of the play. For if it has the sweetness of the rose, it has its freshness too; if it has the languor of the nightingale's song, it has also its giddy transport; if it has the softness of a southern spring, it is as glowing and as bright.

There is nothing of a sickly and sentimental cast. Romeo and Juliet are in love, but they are not love sick. Everything speaks the very soul of pleasure, the high and healthy pulse of the passions: the heart beats, the blood circulates and mantles throughout. Their courtship is not an insipid interchange of sentiments lip deep, learnt at second hand from poems and plays, made up of beauties of the most shadowy kind, of "fancies wan that hang the pensive head," of evanescent smiles, and sighs that breathe not, of delicacy that shrinks from the touch, and feebleness that scarce supports itself, an elaborate vacuity of thought, and an artificial dearth of sense, spirit, truth, and nature! It is the reverse of all this. It is Shakspeare all over, and Shakspeare when he was young.

MIDSUMMER NIGHT'S DREAM

Puck, or Robin Good fellow, is the leader of the fairy band. He is the Ariel of the Midsummer Night's Dream; and yet as unlike as can be to the Ariel in the Tempest. No other poet could have made two such different characters out of the same fanciful materials and situations. Ariel is a minister of retribution, who is touched with the sense of pity at the woes he inflicts. Puck is a mad cap sprite, full of wantonness and mischief, who laughs at those whom he misleads "Lord, what fools these mortals be!" Ariel cleaves the air, and executes his mission with the zeal of a winged messenger; Puck is borne along on his fairy errand like the light and glittering gossamer before the breeze. He is, indeed, a most Epicurean little gentleman, dealing in quaint devices, and faring in dainty delights.

Prospero and his world of spirits are a set of moralists: but with Oberon and his fairies we are launched at once into the empire of the butterflies. How beautifully is this race of beings contrasted with the men and women actors in the scene, by a single epithet which Titania gives to the latter, "the human mortals"!

It is astonishing that Shakspeare should be considered, not only by foreigners, but by many of our own critics, as a gloomy and heavy writer, who painted nothing but "gorgons and hydras, and chimeras dire." His subtlety exceeds that of all other dramatic writers, insomuch that a celebrated person of the present day said that he regarded him rather as a metaphysician than a poet. His delicacy and sportive gaiety are infinite.

In the Midsummer Night's Dream alone, we should imagine, there is more sweetness and beauty of description than in the whole range of French poetry put together. What we mean is this, that we will produce out of that single play ten passages, to which we do not think any ten passages in the works of the French poets can be opposed, displaying equal fancy and imagery.

Shall we mention the remonstrance of Helena to Hermia, or Titania's description of her fairy train, or her disputes with Oberon about the Indian boy, or Puck's account of himself and his employments, or the Fairy Queen's exhortation to the elves to pay due attendance upon her favourite, Bottom; or Hippolita's description of a chace, or Theseus's answer? The two last are as heroical and spirited as the others are full of luscious tenderness. The reading of this play is like wandering in a grove by moonlight: the descriptions breathe a sweetness like odours thrown from beds of flowers.

The Midsummer Night's Dream, when acted, is converted from a delightful fiction into a dull pantomime. All that is finest in the play is lost in the representation. The spectacle was grand; but the spirit was evaporated, the genius was fled. Poetry and the stage do not agree well together. The attempt to reconcile them in this instance fails not only of effect, but of decorum. The ideal can have no place upon the stage, which is a picture without perspective: everything there is in the fore–ground. That which was merely an airy shape, a dream, a passing thought, immediately becomes an unmanageable reality.

Where all is left to the imagination (as is the case in reading) every circumstance, near or remote, has an equal chance of being kept in mind, and tells accordingly to the mixed impression of all that has been suggested. But the imagination cannot sufficiently qualify the actual impressions of the senses. Any offence given to the eye is not to be got rid of by explanation.

Thus Bottom's head in the play is a fantastic illusion, produced by magic spells: on the stage it is an ass's head, and nothing more; certainly a very strange costume for a gentleman to appear in. Fancy cannot be embodied any more than a simile can be painted; and it is as idle to attempt it as to personate Wall or Moonshine. Fairies are not incredible, but fairies six feet high are so. Monsters are not shocking, if they are seen at a proper distance. When ghosts appear at mid-day, when apparitions stalk along Cheapside, then may the Midsummer Night's Dream be represented without injury at Coventgarden or at Drury–lane. The boards of a theatre and the regions of fancy are not the same thing.

FALSTAFF

If Shakspeare's fondness for the ludicrous sometimes led to faults in his tragedies (which was not often the case) he has made us amends by the character of Falstaff. This is perhaps the most substantial comic character that ever was invented. Sir John carries a most portly presence in the mind's eye; and in him, not to speak it profanely, "we behold the fulness of the spirit of wit and humour bodily." We are as well acquainted with his person as his mind, and his jokes come upon us with double force and relish from the quantity of flesh through which they make their way, as he shakes his fat sides with laughter, or "lards the lean earth as he walks along."

Other comic characters seem, if we approach and handle them, to resolve themselves into air, "into thin air;" but this is embodied and palpable to the grossest apprehension: it lies "three fingers deep upon the ribs," it plays about the lungs and the diaphragm with all the force of animal enjoyment. His body is like a good estate to his mind, from which he receives rents and revenues of profit and pleasure in kind, according to its extent, and the richness of the soil. Wit is often a meagre substitute for pleasurable sensation; an effusion of spleen and petty spite at the comforts of others, from feeling none in itself.

Falstaff's wit is an emanation of a fine constitution; an exuberance of good–humour and good–nature; an overflowing of his love of laughter and good–fellowship; a giving vent to his heart's ease, and over contentment with himself and others. He would not be in character, if he were not so fat as he is; for there is the greatest keeping in the boundless luxury of his imagination and the pampered self–indulgence of his physical appetites. He manures and nourishes his mind with jests, as he does his body with sack and sugar. He carves out his jokes, as he would a capon or a haunch of venison, where there is cut and come again; and pours out upon them the oil of gladness. His tongue drops fatness, and in the chambers of his brain "it snows of meat and drink." He keeps up perpetual holiday and open house, and we live with him. in a round of invitations to a rump and dozen. Yet we are not to suppose that he was a mere sensualist.

All this is as much in imagination as in reality. His sensuality does not engross and stupify his other faculties, but "ascends me into the brain, clears away all the dull, crude vapours that environ it, and makes it full of nimble, fiery, and delectable shapes." His imagination keeps up the ball after his senses have done with it. He seems to have even a greater enjoyment of the freedom from restraint, of good cheer, of his ease, of his vanity, in the ideal exaggerated description which he gives of them, than in fact. He never fails to enrich his discourse with allusions to eating and drinking, but we never see him at table.

He carries his own larder about with him, and he is himself "a tun of man." His pulling out the bottle in the field of battle is a joke to shew his contempt for glory accompanied with danger, his systematic adherence to his Epicurean philosophy in the most trying circumstances. Again, such is his deliberate exaggeration of his own vices, that it does not seem quite certain whether the account of his hostess's bill, found in his pocket, with such an out of the way charge for capons and sack with only one halfpenny–worth of bread, was not put there by himself as a trick to humour the jest upon his favourite propensities, and as a conscious caricature of himself.

He is represented as a liar, a braggart, a coward, a glutton, *etc.* and yet we are not offended but delighted with him; for he is all these as much to amuse others as to gratify himself. He openly assumes all these characters to shew the humourous part of them. The unrestrained indulgence of his own ease, appetites, and convenience, has neither malice nor hypocrisy in it. In a word, he is an actor in himself almost as much as upon the stage, and we no more object to the character of Falstaff in a moral point of view than we should think of bringing an excellent comedian, who should represent him to the life, before one of the police offices.

We only consider the number of pleasant lights in which he puts certain foibles (the more pleasant as they are opposed to the received rules and necessary restraints of society) and do not trouble ourselves about the consequences resulting from them, for no mischievous consequences do result. Sir John is old as well as fat, which gives a melancholy retrospective tinge to the character; and by the disparity between his inclinations and his capacity for enjoyment, makes it still more ludicrous and fantastical. The secret of Falstaff's wit is for the most part a masterly presence of mind, an absolute self possession, which nothing can disturb. His repartees are involuntary suggestions of his self love; instinctive evasions of everything that threatens to interrupt the career of his triumphant jollity and self complacency.

His very size floats him out of all his difficulties in a sea of rich conceits; and he turns round on the pivot of his convenience, with every occasion and at a moment's warning. His natural repugnance to every unpleasant thought or circumstance, of itself makes light of objections, and provokes the most extravagant and licentious answers in his own justification. His indifference to truth puts no check upon his invention, and the more improbable and unexpected his contrivances are, the more happily does he seem to be delivered of them, the anticipation of their effect acting as a stimulus to the gaiety of his fancy. The success of one adventurous sally gives him spirits to undertake another: he deals always in round numbers, and his exaggerations and excuses are "open, palpable, monstrous as the father that begets them." His dissolute carelessness of what he says discovers itself in the first dialogue with the Prince.

Falstaff: By the lord, thou say'st true, lad; and is not mine hostess of the tavern a most sweet wench?

P. Henry: As the honey of Hibla, my old lad of the castle; and is not a buff–jerkin a most sweet robe of durance?

Falstaff: How now, how now, mad wag, what in thy quips and thy quiddities? what a plague have I to do with a buff jerkin?

P. Henry: Why, what a pox have I to do with mine hostess of the tavern?"

In the same scene he afterwards affects melancholy, from pure satisfaction of heart, and professes reform, because it is the farthest thing in the world from his thoughts. He has no qualms of conscience, and therefore would as soon talk of them as of anything else when the humour takes him.

Falstaff: But Hal, I pr'ythee trouble me no more with vanity. I would to God thou and I knew where a commodity of good names were to be bought: an old lord of council rated me the other day in the street about you, sir; but I mark'd him not, and yet he talked very wisely, and in the street too.

P. Henry: Thou didst well, for wisdom cries out in the street, and no man regards it.

Falstaff: O, thou hast damnable iteration, and art indeed able to corrupt a saint. Thou hast done much harm unto me, Hal; God forgive thee for it. Before I knew thee, Hal, I knew nothing, and now I am, if a man should speak truly, little better than one of the wicked. I must give over this life, and I will give it over, by the Lord; an I do not, I am a villain. I'll be damned for never a king's son in Christendom.

P. Henry: Where shall we take a purse tomorrow, Jack?

Falstaff: Where thou wilt, lad, I'll make one; an I do not, call me villain, and baffle me.

P. Henry: I see good amendment of life in thee, from praying to purse taking.

Falstaff: Why, Hal, 'tis my vocation, Hal. 'Tis no sin for a man to labour in his vocation.

Of the other prominent passages, his account of his pretended resistance to the robbers, "who grew from four men in buckram into eleven" as the imagination of his own valour increased with his relating it, his getting off when the truth is discovered by pretending he knew the Prince, the scene in which in the person of the old king he lectures the prince and gives himself a good character, the soliloquy on honour, and description of his new–raised recruits, his meeting with the chief justice, his abuse of the Prince and Poins, who overhear him, to Doll Tearsheet, his reconciliation with Mrs. Quickly who has arrested him for an old debt, and whom he persuades to pawn her plate to lend him ten pounds more, and the scenes with Shallow and Silence, are all inimitable. Of all of them, the scene in which Falstaff plays the part, first, of the King, and then of Prince Henry, is the one that has been the most often quoted. We must quote it once more in illustration of our remarks.

Falstaff: Harry, I do not only marvel where thou spendest thy time, but also how thou art accompanied: for though the camomile, the more it is trodden on, the faster it grows, yet youth, the more it is wasted, the sooner it wears. That thou art my son, I have partly thy mother's word, partly my own opinion; but chiefly, a villainous trick of thine eye, and a foolish hanging of thy nether lip, that doth warrant me. If then thou be son to me, here lies the point; Why, being son to me, art thou so pointed at? Shall the blessed sun of heaven prove a micher, and eat blackberries? A question not to be ask'd. Shall the son of England prove a thief, and take purses? a question to be ask'd. There is a thing, Harry, which thou hast often heard of, and it is known to many in our land by the name of pitch: this pitch, as ancient writers do report, doth defile; so doth the company thou keepest: for, Harry, now I do not speak to thee in drink, but in tears; not in pleasure, but in passion; not in words only, but in woes also: and yet there is a virtuous man, whom I have often noted in thy company, but I know not his name.

P. Henry: What manner of man, an it like your majesty?

Falstaff: A goodly portly man, i'faith, and a corpulent; of a cheerful look, a pleasing eye, and a most noble carriage; and as I think, his age some fifty, or, by'r–lady, inclining to threescore; and now I do remember me, his name is Falstaff: if that man should be lewdly given, he deceiveth me; for, Harry, I see virtue in his looks. If then the fruit may be known by the tree, as the tree by the fruit, then peremptorily I speak it, there is virtue in that Falstaff: him keep with, the rest banish. And tell me now, thou naughty varlet, tell me, where hast thou been this month?

P. Henry: Dost thou speak like a king? Do thou stand for me, and I'll play my father.

Falstaff: Depose me? if thou dost it half so gravely, so majestically, both in word and matter, hang me up by the heels for a rabbit–sucker, or a poulterer's hare.

P. Henry: Well, here I am set.

Falstaff: And here I stand: judge, my masters.

P. Henry: Now, Harry, whence come you?

Falstaff: My noble lord, from Eastcheap.

P. Henry: The complaints I hear of thee are grievous.

Falstaff: S'blood, my lord, they are false: nay, I'll tickle ye for a young prince, i'faith.

P. Henry: Swearest thou, ungracious boy? henceforth ne'er look on me. Thou art violently carried away from grace: there is a devil haunts thee, in the likeness of a fat old man; a tun of man is thy companion. Why dost thou converse with that trunk of humours, that bolting–hutch of beastliness, that swoln parcel of dropsies, that huge bombard of sack, that stuft cloak–bag of guts, that roasted Manning tree ox with the pudding in his belly, that reverend vice, that grey iniquity, that father ruffian, that vanity in years? wherein is he good, but to taste sack and drink it? wherein neat and cleanly, but to carve a capon and eat it? wherein cunning, but in craft? wherein crafty, but in villainy? wherein villainous, but in all things? wherein worthy, but in nothing?

Falstaff: I would, your grace would take me with you; whom means your grace?

P. Henry: That villainous, abominable mis–leader of youth, Falstaff, that old white–bearded Satan.

Falstaff: My lord, the man I know.

P. Henry: I know thou dost.

Falstaff: But to say, I know more harm in him than in myself, were to say more than I know. That he is old (the more the pity) his white hairs do witness it: but that he is (saving your reverence) a whore–master, that I utterly deny. If sack and sugar be a fault, God help the wicked! if to be old and merry be a sin, then many an old host that I know is damned: if to be fat be to be hated, then Pharoah's lean kine are to be loved. No, my good lord; banish Peto, banish Bardolph, banish Poins: but for sweet Jack Falstaff, kind Jack Falstaff, true Jack Falstaff, valiant Jack Falstaff, and therefore more valiant, being as he is, old Jack Falstaff, banish not him thy Harry's company; banish plump Jack, and banish all the world.

P. Henry: I do, I will.

Knocking; and Hostess and Bardolph go out.

Re–enter Bardolph, running.

Bardolph: O, my lord, my lord; the sheriff, with a most monstrous watch, is at the door.

Falstaff: Out, you rogue! play out the play: I have much to say in the behalf of that Falstaff.

One of the most characteristic descriptions of Sir John is that which Mrs. Quickly gives of him when he asks her "What is the gross sum that I owe thee?"

Hostess: Marry, if thou wert an honest man, thyself, and the money too. Thou didst swear to me upon a parcel gilt goblet, sitting in my Dolphin chamber, at the round table, by a sea–coal fire on Wednesday in Whitsun week, when the Prince broke thy head for likening his father to a singing man of Windsor; thou didst swear to me then, as I was washing thy wound, to marry me, and make me my lady thy wife. Canst thou deny it? Did not goodwife Keech, the butcher's wife, come in then, and call me gossip Quickly? coming in to borrow a mess of vinegar; telling us, she had a good dish of prawns; whereby thou didst desire to eat some; whereby I told thee they were ill for a green wound? And didst thou not, when she was gone down stairs, desire me to be no more so familiarity with such poor people; saying, that ere long they should call me madam? And didst thou not kiss me, and bid me fetch thee thirty shillings? I put thee now to thy book oath; deny it, if thou canst."

One of the topics of exulting superiority over others most common in Sir John's mouth is his corpulence and the exterior marks of good living which he carries about him, thus "turning his vices into commodity." He accounts for the friendship between the Prince and Poins, from "their legs being both of a bigness;" and compares Justice Shallow to "a man made after supper of a cheeseparing." There cannot be a more striking gradation of character than that beween Falstaff and Shallow, and Shallow and Silence.

It seems difficult at first to fall lower than the squire; but this fool, great as he is, finds an admirer and humble foil in his cousin Silence. Vain of his acquaintance with Sir John, who makes a butt of him, he exclaims, "Would, cousin Silence, that thou had'st seen that which this knight and I have seen!" "Aye, Master Shallow, we have heard the chimes at midnight," says Sir John. To Falstaff's observation, "I did not think Master Silence had been a man of this mettle," Silence answers, "Who, I? I have been merry twice and once ere now." What an idea is here conveyed of a prodigality of living? What good husbandry and economical self–denial in his pleasures? What a stock of lively recollections? It is curious that Shakspeare has ridiculed in Justice Shallow, who was "in some authority under the king," that disposition to unmeaning tautology which is the regal infirmity of later times, and which, it may be supposed, he acquired from talking to his cousin Silence, and receiving no answers.

Falstaff: You have here a goodly dwelling, and a rich.

Shallow: Barren, barren, barren; beggars all, beggars all, Sir John: marry, good air. Spread Davy, spread Davy. Well said, Davy.

Falstaff: This Davy serves you for good uses.

Shallow: A good varlet, a good varlet, a very good varlet. By the mass, I have drunk too much sack at supper. A good varlet. Now sit down, now sit down. Come, cousin."

The true spirit of humanity, the thorough knowledge of the stuff we are made of, the practical wisdom with the seeming fooleries in the whole of the garden scene at Shallow's country seat, and just before in the exquisite dialogue between him and Silence on the death of old Double, have no parallel anywhere else. In one point of view, they are laughable in the extreme; in another they are equally affecting, if it is affecting to shew what a little thing is human life, what a poor forked creature man is!

TWELFTH NIGHT; OR, WHAT YOU WILL

This is justly considered as one of the most delightful of Shakspeare's comedies. It is full of sweetness and pleasantry. It is perhaps too good–natured for comedy. It has little satire, and no spleen. It aims at the ludicrous rather than the ridiculous. It makes us laugh at the follies of mankind, not despise them, and still less bear any ill will towards them. Shakspeare's comic genius resembles the bee rather in its power of extracting sweets from weeds or poisons, than in leaving a sting behind it. He gives the most amusing exaggeration of the prevailing foibles of his characters, but in a way that they themselves, instead of being offended at, would almost join in to humour; he rather contrives opportunities for them to shew themselves off in the happiest lights, than renders them contemptible in the perverse construction of the wit or malice of others.

There is a certain stage of society in which people become conscious of their peculiarities and absurdities, affect to disguise what they are, and set up pretensions to what they are not. This gives rise to a corresponding style of comedy, the object of which is to detect the disguises of self love, and to make reprisals on these preposterous assumptions of vanity, by marking the contrast between the real and the affected character as severely as possible, and denying to those, who would impose on us for what they are not, even the merit which they have. This is the comedy of artificial life, of wit and satire, such as we see it in Congreve, Wycherley, Vanburgh, *etc.*

To this succeeds a state of society from which the same sort of affectation and pretence are banished by a greater knowledge of the world or by their successful exposure on the stage; and which by neutralising the materials of comic character, both natural and artificial, leaves no comedy at all but the sentimental. Such is our modern comedy. There is a period in the progress of manners anterior to both these, in which the foibles and follies of individuals are of nature's planting, not the growth of art or study; in which they are therefore unconscious of them themselves, or care not who knows them, if they can but have their whim out; and in which, as there is no attempt at imposition, the spectators rather receive pleasure from humouring the inclinations of the persons they laugh at, than wish to give them pain by exposing their absurdity.

This may be called the comedy of nature, and it is the comedy which we generally find in Shakspeare. Whether the analysis here given be just or not, the spirit of his comedies is evidently quite distinct from that of the authors above mentioned, as it is in its essence the same with that of Cervantes, and also very frequently of Moliee, though he was more systematic in his extravagance than Shakspeare. Shakspeare's comedy is of a pastoral and poetical cast. Folly is indigenous to the soil, and shoots out with native, happy, unchecked luxuriance. Absurdity has every encouragement afforded it; and nonsense has room to flourish in. Nothing is stunted by the churlish, icy hand of indifference or severity. The poet runs riot in a conceit, and idolises a quibble. His whole object is to turn tile meanest or rudest objects to a pleasurable account. The relish which he has of a pun, or of the quaint humour of a low character, does not interfere with the delight with which he describes a beautiful image, or the most refined love. The Clown's forced jests do not spoil the sweetness of the character of Viola; the same house is big enough to hold Malvolio, the Countess, Maria, Sir Toby, and Sir Andrew Ague cheek.

For instance, nothing can fall much lower than this last character in intellect or morals: yet how are his weaknesses nursed and dandled by Sir Toby into something "high fantastical," when on Sir Andrew's commendation of himself for dancing and fencing, Sir Toby answers "Wherefore are these things hid? Wherefore have these gifts a curtain before them? Are they like to take dust like mistress Moll's picture? Why dost thou not go to church in a galliard, and come home in a coranto? My very walk should be a jig! I would not so much as make water but in a cinque pace. What dost thou mean? Is this a world to hide virtues in?

I did think by the excellent constitution of thy leg, it was framed under the star of a galliard!" How Sir Toby, Sir Andrew, and the Clown afterwårds chirp over their cups, how they "rouse the night owl in a catch, able to draw three souls out of one weaver!" What can be better than Sir Toby's unanswerable answer to Malvolio, "Dost thou think because thou art virtuous, there shall be no more cakes and ale?"In a word, the best turn is given to everything, instead of the worst. There is a constant infusion of the romantic and enthusiastic, in proportion as the characters are natural and sincere: whereas, in the more artificial style of comedy, every thing gives way to ridicule and indifference, there being nothing left but affectation on one side, and incredulity on the other.

Much as we like Shakspeare's comedies, we cannot agree with Dr. Johnson that they are better than his tragedies; nor do we like them half so well. If his inclination to comedy sometimes led him to trifle with the seriousness of tragedy, the poetical and impassioned passages are the best parts of his comedies. The great and secret charm of Twelfth Nitht is the character of Viola. Much as we like catches and cakes and ale, there is something that we like better. We have a friendship for Sir Toby; we patronise Sir Andrew; we have an understanding with the Clown, a sneaking kindness for Maria and her rogueries; we feel a regard for Malvolio, and sympathise with his gravity, his smiles, his cross garters, his yellow stockings, and imprisonment in the stocks. But there is something that excites in us a stronger feeling than all this it is Viola's confession of her love.

Duke: What's her history?

Viola: A blank, my lord, she never told her love: She let concealment, like a worm i' the bud, Feed on her damask cheek: she pin'd in thought, And with a green and yellow melancholy, She sat like Patience on a monument, Smiling at grief. Was not this love indeed? We men may say more, swear more, but indeed, Our shews are more than will; for still we prove Much in our vows, but little in our love.

Duke: But died thy sister of her love, my boy?

Viola: I am all the daughters of my father's house, And all the brothers too; and yet I know not.

Shakspeare alone could describe the effect of his own poetry. "Oh, it came o'er the ear like the sweet south That breathes upon a bank of violets, Stealing and giving odour."

What we so much admire here is not the image of Patience on a monument, which has been generally quoted, but the lines before and after it. "They give a very echo to the seat where love is throned." How long ago it is since we first learnt to repeat them; and still, still they vibrate on the heart, like the sounds which the passing wind draws from the trembling strings of a harp left on some desert shore! There are other passages of not less impassioned sweetness. Such is Olivia's address to Sebastian, whom she supposes to have already deceived her in a promise of marriage. "Blame not this haste of mine: if you mean well, Now go with me and with this holy manInto the chantry by: there before him, And underneath that consecrated roof, Plight me the full assurance of your faith, That my most jealous and too doubtful soulMay live at peace."

5

Milton

Shakespeare discovers in his writings little religious enthusiasm, and an indifference to personal reputation; he had none of the bigotry of his age, and his political prejudices were not very strong. In these respects, as well as in every other, he formed a direct contrast to Milton. Milton's works are a perpetual invocation to the Muses; a hymn to Fame. He had his thoughts constantly fixed on the contemplation of the Hebrew theocracy, and of a perfect commonwealth; and he seized the pen with a hand just warm from the touch of the ark of faith. His religious zeal infused its character into his imagination; so that he devotes himself with the same sense of duty to the cultivation of his genius, as he did to the exercise of virtue, or the good of his country. The spirit of the poet, the patriot, and the prophet, vied with each other in his breast. His mind appears to have held equal communion with the inspired writers, and with the bards and sages of ancient Greece and Rome;

"Blind Thamyris, and blind Mæonides, And Tiresias, and Phineus, prophets old."

He had a high standard, with which he was always comparing himself, nothing short of which could satisfy his jealous ambition. He thought of nobler forms and nobler things than those he found about him. He lived apart, in the solitude of his own thoughts, carefully excluding from his mind whatever might distract its purposes, or alloy its purity, or damp its zeal. "With darkness and with dangers compassed round," he had the mighty models of antiquity always present to his thoughts, and determined to raise a monument of equal height and glory, "piling up every stone of lustre from the brook," for the delight and wonder of posterity.

He had girded himself tip, and as it were, sanctified his genius to this service front his youth. "For after," he says, "I had from my first years, by the ceaseless diligence and care of my father, been exercised to the tongues, and some sciences as my age could suffer, by sundry masters and teachers, it was found that whether aught was imposed upon me by them, or betaken to of my own choice, the style by certain vital signs it had, was likely to live; but much latelier, in the private academies of Italy, perceiving that some trifles which I had in memory, composed at under twenty or thereabout, met with acceptance above what was looked for; I began thus far to assent both to them and divers of my friends here at home, and not less to an inward prompting which now grew daily upon me, that by labour and intense study (which I take to be my portion in this life), joined with the strong propensity of nature, I might perhaps leave something so written to after–times as they should not willingly let it die.

The accomplishment of these intentions which have lived within me ever since I could conceive myself anything worth to my country, lies not but in a power above man's to promise; but that none hath by more studious ways endeavoured, and with more unwearied spirit that none shall, that I dare almost aver of myself, as far as life and free leisure will extend. Neither do I think it shame to covenant with any knowing reader, that for some few years yet, I may go on trust with him toward the payment of what I am now indebted, as being a work not to be raised from the heat of youth or the vapours of wine; like that which flows at waste from the pen of some vulgar amourist, or the trencher fury of a rhyming parasite, nor to be obtained by the invocation of Dame Memory and her Siren daughters, but by devout prayer to that eternal spirit, who can enrich with all utterance and knowledge, and sends out his Seraphim with the hallowed fire of his altar, to touch and purify the lips of whom he pleases: to this must be added industrious and select reading, steady observation, and insight into all seemly and generous arts and affairs.

Although it nothing content me to have disclosed thus much beforehand; but that I trust hereby to make it manifest with what small willingness I endure to interrupt the pursuit of no less hopes than these, and leave a calm and pleasing solitariness, fed with cheerful and confident thoughts, to embark in a troubled sea of noises and hoarse disputes, from beholding the bright countenance of truth in the quiet and still air of delightful studies.

So that of Spenser: "The noble heart that harbours virtuous thought, And is with child of glorious great intent, Can never rest until it forth hath brought The eternal brood of glory excellent."

Milton, therefore, did not write from casual impulse, but after a severe examination of his own strength, and with a resolution to leave nothing undone which it was in his power to do. He always labours, and almost always succeeds. He strives hard to say the finest things in the world, and he does say them. He adorns and dignifies his subject to the utmost: he surrounds it with every possible association of beauty or grandeur, whether moral, intellectual, or physical. He refines on his descriptions of beauty; loading sweets on sweets, till the sense aches at them; and raises his images of terror to a gigantic elevation, that "makes Ossa like a wart." In Milton there is always an appearance of effort: in Shakspeare, scarcely any.

Milton has borrowed more than any other writer, and exhausted every source of imitation, sacred or profane; yet he is perfectly distinct from every other writer. He is a writer of centos, and yet in originality scarcely inferior to Homer. The power of his mind is stamped on every line. The fervour of his imagination melts down and renders malleable, as in a furnace, the most contradictory materials. In reading his works, we feel ourselves under the influence of a mighty intellect, that the nearer it approaches to others, becomes more distinct from them. The quantity of art in him shews the strength of his genius: the weight of his intellectual obligations would have oppressed any other writer. Milton's learning has all the effect of intuition. He describes objects, of which he could only have read in books, with the vividness of actual observation. His imagination has the force of nature. He makes words tell as pictures.

"Him followed Rimmon, whose delightful seat Was fair Damascus, on the fertile banks Of Abbana and Pharphar, lucid streams." The word lucid here gives to the idea all the sparkling effect of the most perfect landscape.

And again: "As when a vulture on Imaus bred, Whose snowy ridge the roving Tartar bounds, Dislodging from a region scarce of prey, To gorge the flesh of lambs and yeanling kids On hills where flocks are fed, flies towards the springs Of Ganges or Hydaspes, Indian streams; But in his way lights on the barren plains Of Sericana, where Chineses drive With sails and wind their cany waggons light."

If Milton had taken a journey for the express purpose, he could not have described this scenery and mode of life better. Such passages are like demonstrations of natural history. Instances might be multiplied without end. We might be tempted to suppose that the vividness with which he describes visible objects, was owing to their having acquired an unusual degree of strength in his mind, after the privation of his sight; but we find the same palpableness and truth in the descriptions which occur in his early poems. In Lycidas, he speaks of "the great vision of the guarded mount," with that preternatural weight of impression with which it would present itself suddenly to "the pilot of some small night–foundered skiff;" and the lines in the Penseroso, describing "the wandering moon,

"Riding near her highest noon, Like one that had been led astray Through the heaven's wide pathless way," are as if he had gazed himself blind in looking at her. There is also the same depth of impression in his descriptions of the objects of all the different senses, whether colours, or sounds, or smells the same absorption of his mind in whatever engaged his attention at the time. It has been indeed objected to Milton, by a common perversity of criticism, that his ideas were musical rather than picturesque, as if because they were in the highest degree musical, they must be (to keep the sage critical balance even, and to allow no one man to possess two qualities at the same time) proportionably deficient in other respects. But Milton's poetry is not cast in any such narrow, common–place mould; it is not so barren of resources. His worship of the Muse was not so simple or confined. A sound arises "like a steam of rich distilled perfumes;" we hear the pealing organ, but the incense on the altars is also there, and the statues of the gods are ranged. If Milton had taken a journey for the express purpose, he could not have described this scenery and mode of life better. Such passages are like demonstrations of natural history. Instances might be multiplied without end.

We might be tempted to suppose that the vividness with which he describes visible objects, was owing to their having acquired an unusual degree of strength in his mind, after the privation of his sight; but we find the same palpableness and truth in the descriptions which occur in his early poems. In Lycidas, he speaks of "the great vision of the guarded mount," with that preternatural weight of impression with which it would present itself suddenly to "the pilot of some small night–foundered skiff;" and the lines in the Penseroso, describing "the wandering moon, "Riding near her highest noon, Like one that had been led astray Through the heaven's wide pathless way," are as if he had gazed himself blind in looking at her. There is also the same depth of impression in his descriptions of the objects of all the different senses, whether colours, or sounds, or smells the same absorption of his mind in whatever engaged his attention at the time. It has been indeed objected to Milton, by a common perversity of criticism, that his ideas were musical rather than picturesque, as if because they were in the highest degree musical, they must be (to keep the sage critical balance even, and to allow no one man to possess two qualities at the same time) proportionably deficient in other respects. But Milton's poetry is not cast in any such narrow, common place mould; it is not so barren of resources. His worship of the Muse was not so simple or confined.

A sound arises " like a steam of rich distilled perfumes;" we hear the pealing organ, but the incense on the altars is also there, and the statues of the gods are ranged around! The car indeed predominates over the eye, because it is more immediately affected, and because the language of music blends more immediately with, and forms a more natural accompaniment to, the variable and indefinite associations of ideas conveyed by words. But where the associations of the imagination are not the principal thing, the individual object is given by Milton with equal force and beauty. The strongest and best proof of this, as a characteristic power of his mind, is, that the persons of Adam and Eve, of Satan, *etc.* are always accompanied, in our imagination, with the grandeur of the naked figure; they convey to us the ideas of sculpture. As an instance, take the following:

"He soon Saw within ken a glorious Angel stand, The same whom John saw also in the sun: His back was turned, but not his brightness hid; Of beaming sunny rays a golden tiar Circled his head, nor less his locks behind Illustrious on his shoulders fledge with wings Lay waving round; on some great charge employ'd He seem'd, or fix'd in cogitation deep. Glad was the spirit impure, as now in hope To find who might direct his wand'ring flight To Paradise, the happy seat of man, His jourriey's end, mid our beginning woe. But first he casts to change his proper shape, Which else might work him danger or delay And now a stripling cherub he appears, Not of the prime, yet such as in his face Youth smiled celestial, and to every limb Suitable grace diffus'd, so well lie feign'd: Under a coronet his flowing hair In curls on either cheek play'd; wings he wore Of many a colour'd plume sprinkled with gold, His habit fit for speed succinct, and held Before his decent steps a silver wand." The figures introduced here have all the elegance and Precision of a Greek statue; glossy and impurpled, tinged with golden light, and musical as the strings of Memnon's harp!

Again, nothing can be more magnificent than the portrait of Beelzebub: "With Atlantean shoulders fit to bear The weight of mightiest monarchies:"

Or the comparison of Satan, as he "lay floating many a rood," to "that sea beast," "Leviathan, which God of all his works Created hugest that swim the ocean stream!"

What a force of imagination is there in this last expression! What an idea it conveys of the size of that hugest of created beings, as if it shrunk up the ocean to a stream, and took up the sea in its nostrils as a very little thing! Force of style is one of Milton's greatest excellences. Hence, perhaps, he stimulates us more in the reading, and less afterwards. The way to defend Milton against all inlpugners, is to take down the book and read it.

Milton's blank verse is the only blank verse in the language (except Shakspeare's) that deserves the name of verse. Dr. Johnson, who had modelled his ideas of versification on the regular sing–song of Pope, condemns the Paradise Lost as harsh and unequal. I shall not pretend to say that this is not sometimes the case; for where a degree of excellence beyond the mechanical rules of art is attempted, the poet must sometimes fail. But I imagine that there are more perfect examples in Milton of musical expression, or of an adaptation of the sound and movement of the verse to the meaning of the passage, than in all our other writers, whether of rhyme or blank verse, put together, (with the exception already mentioned).

Spenser is the most harmonious of our stanza writers, as Dryden is the most sounding and varied of our rhymists. But in neither is there anything like the same ear for music, the same power of approximating the varieties of poetical to those of musical rhythm, as there is in our great epic poet. The sound of his lines is moulded into the expression of the sentiment, almost of the very image. They rise or fall, pause or hurry rapidly on, with exquisite art, but without the least trick or affectation, as the occasion seems to require.

The following are some of the finest instances: "His hand was known In Heaven by many a tower'd structure high; Nor was his name unheard or unador'd In ancient Greece; and in the Ansonian land Men called him Mulciber; and how he fell From Heaven, they fabled, thrown by angry Jove Sheer o'er the crystal battlements; from morn To noon he fell, from noon to dewy eve, A summer's day; and with the setting sun Dropt from the zenith like a falling star On Lemnos, the Aegean isle: thus they relate, Erring."

"But chief the spacious hall Thick swarm'd, both on the ground and in the air, Brush'd with the hiss of rustling wings. As bees In spring time, when the sun with Taurus rides, Pour forth their populous youth about the hive In clusters; they among fresh dews and flow'rs Fly to and fro; or on the smoothed plank, The suburb of their straw built citadel, New rubb'd with balm, expatiate, and confer Their state affairs. So thick the airy crowd Swarm'd and were straiten'd; till the signal giv'n, Behold a wonder! They but now who seem'd In bigness to surpass earthes giant sons, Now less than smallest dwarfs, in narrow room Throng numberless, like that Pygmean race

Beyond the Indian mount, or fairy elves, Whose midnight revels by a forest side Or fountain, some belated peasant sees,Or dreams he sees, while over–head the moon Sits arbitress, and nearer to the earth Wheels her pale course: they on their mirth and dance Intent, with jocund music charm his ear; At once with joy and fear his heart rebounds."

I can give only another instance, though I have some difficulty in leaving off. "Round he surveys (and well might, where he stood So high above the circling canopy Of night's extended shade) from the eastern point Of Libra to the fleecy star that bears Andromeda far off Atlantic seas Beyond the horizon: then from pole to pole He views in breadth, and without longer pause Down right into the world's first region throws His flight precipitant, and winds with ease Through the pure marble air his oblique way Amongst innumerable stars that shone Stars distant, but nigh hand seem'd other worlds; Or other worlds they seem'd or happy isles," *etc.*

The verse, in this exquisitely modulated passage, floats up and down as if it had itself wings. Milton has himself given us the theory of his versification—"Such as the meeting soul may pierce In notes with many a winding bout Of linked sweetness long drawn out."

Dr. Johnson and Pope would have converted his vaulting Pegasus into a rocking–horse. Read any other blank verse but Milton's, Thomson's, Young's, Cowper's, Wordsworthes and it will be found, from the want of the same insight into "the hidden soul of harmony," to be mere lumbering prose.

To proceed to a consideration of the merits of Paradise Lost, in the most essential point of view, I mean as to the poetry of character and passion. I shall say nothing of the fable, or of other technical objections or excellences; but I shall try to explain at once the foundation of the interest belonging to the poem. I am ready to give up the dialogues in Heaven, where, as Pope justly observes, "God the Father turns a school divine;" nor do I consider the battle of the angels as the climax of sublimity, or the most successful effort of Milton's pen. In a word, the interest of the poem arises from the daring ambition and fierce passions of Satan, and from the account of the paradisaical happiness, and the loss of it by our first parents.

Threefourths of the work are taken up with these characters, and nearly all that relates to them is unmixed sublimity and beauty. The two first books alone are like too massy pillars of solid gold.

Satan is the most heroic subject that ever was chosen for a poem; and the execution is as perfect as the design is lofty. He was the first of created beings, who, for endeavouring to be equal with the highest, and to divide the empire of heaven with the Almighty, was hurled down to hell. His aim was no less than the throne of the universe; his means, myriads of angelic armies bright, the third part of the heavens, whom he hired after him with his countenance, and who durst defy the Omnipotent in arms. His ambition was the greatest, and his punishment was the greatest; but not so his despair, for his fortitude was as great as his sufferings. His strength of mind was matchless as his strength of body; the vastness of his designs did not surpass the firm, inflexible determination with which he submitted to his irreversible doom, and final loss of all good. His power of action and of suffering was equal. He was the greatest power that was ever overthrown, with the strongest will left to resist or to endure. He was baffled, not confounded. He stood like a tower; or

"As when Heaven's fire Hath scathed the forest oaks or mountain pines!" He is still surrounded with hosts of rebel angels, armed warriors, who own him as their sovereign leader, and with whose fate he sympathises as he views them round, far as the eye can reach; though he keeps aloof from them in his own mind, and holds supreme counsel only with his own breast. An outcast from Heaven, Hell trembles beneath his feet, Sin and Death are at his heels, and mankind are his easy prey.

"All is not lost; the unconquerable will, And study of revenge, immortal hate, And courage never to submit or yield, And what else is not to be overcome," are still his. The sense of his punishment seems lost in the magnitude of it; the fierceness of tormenting flames, is qualified and made innoxious by the greater fierceness of his pride; the loss of infinite happiness to himself is compensated in thought, by the power of inflicting infinite misery on others. Yet Satan is not the principle of malignity, or of the abstract love of evil but of the abstract love of power, of pride, of self–will personified, to which last principle all other good and evil, and even his own, are subordinate. From this principle he never once flinches.

His love of power and contempt for suffering are never once relaxed from the highest pitch of intensity. His thoughts burn like a hell within him; but the power of thought holds dominion in his mind over every other consideration. The consciousness of a determined purpose, of "that intellectual being, those thoughts that wander through eternity," though accompanied with endless pain, he prefers to nonentity, to "being swallowed up and lost in the wide womb of uncreated night." He expresses the sum and substance of all ambition in one line: "Fallen cherub, to be weak is miserable, doing or suffering!" After such a conflict as his, and such a defeat, to retreat in order, to rally, to make terms, to exist at all, is something; but he does more than this he founds a new empire in hell, and from it conquers this new world, whither he bends his undaunted flight, forcing his way through nether and surrounding fires.

The poet has not in all this given us a mere shadowy outline; the strength is equal to the magnitude of the conception. The Achilles of Homer is not more distinct; the Titans were not more vast; Prometheus chained to his rock was not a more terrific example of suffering and of crime. Wherever the figure of Satan is introduced, whether he walks or flies, "rising aloft incumbent on the dusky air," it is illustrated with the most striking and appropriate images: so that we see it always before us, gigantic, irregular, portentous, uneasy, and disturbed but dazzling in its faded splendour, the clouded ruins of a god. The deformity of Satan is only in the depravity of his will; he has no bodily deformity to excite our loathing or disgust.

The horns and tail are not there, poor emblems of the unbending, unconquered spirit, of the writhing agonies within. Milton was too magnanimous and open an antagonist to support his argument by the bye tricks of a hump and cloven foot; to bring into the fair field of controversy the good old catholic prejudices of which Tasso and Dante have availed themselves, and which the mystic German critics would restore. He relied on the justice of his cause, and did not scruple to give the devil his due. Some persons may think that he has carried his liberality too far, and injured the cause he professed to espouse by making him the chief person in his poem. Considering the nature of his subject, he would be equally in danger of running into this fault, from his faith in religion, and his love of rebellion; and perhaps each of these motives had its full share in determining the choice of his subject. Not only the figure of Satan, but his speeches in council, his soliloquies, his address to Eve, his share in the war in heaven, or in the fall of man, show the same decided superiority of character. To give only one instance, almost the first speech he makes:

"Is this the region, this the soil, the clime, Said then the lost archangel, this the seat That we must change for Heaven; this mournful gloom For that celestial light? Be it so, since he Who now is sov'rain can dispose and bid What shall be right: farthest from him is best, Whom reason hath equal'd, force hath made supreme Above his equals. Farewell happy fields, Where joy for ever dwells: Hail horrors, hail Infernal world, and thou profoundest Hell, Receive thy new possessor; one who brings A mind not to be chang'd by place or time. The mind is its own place, and in itself Can make a Heav'n of Hell, a Hell of Heav'n. What matter where, if I be still the same, And what I should be, all but less than he Whom thunder hath made greater? Here at least We shall be free; the Almighty hath not built Here for his envy, will not drive us hence: Here we may reign secure, and in my choice, To reign is worth ambition, though in Hell: Better to reign in Hell, than serve in Heaven."

The whole of the speeches and debates in Pandemonium are well worthy of the place and the occasion with Gods for speakers, and angels and archangels for hearers. There is a decided manly tone in the arguments and sentiments, an eloquent dogmatism, as if each person spoke from thorough conviction; an excellence which Milton probably borrowed from his spirit of partisanship, or else his spirit of partisanship from the natural firmness and vigour of his mind. In this respect Milton resembles Dante, (the only modern writer with whom he has any thing in common) and it is remarkable that Dante, as well as Milton, was a political partisan.

That approximation to the severity of impassioned prose which has been made an objection to Milton's poetry, and which is chiefly to be met with in these bitter invectives, is one of its great excellences. The author might here turn his philippics against Salmasius to good account. The rout in Heaven is like the fall of some mighty structure, nodding to its base, "with hideous ruin and combustion down." But, perhaps, of all the passages in Paradise Lost, the description of the employments of the angels during the absence of Satan, some of whom "retreated in a silent valley, sing with notes angelical to many a harp their own heroic deeds and hapless fall by doom of battle" is the most perfect example of mingled pathos and sublimity.

What proves the truth of this noble picture in every part, and that the frequent complaint of want of interest in it is the fault of the reader, not of the poet, is that when any interest of a practical kind takes a shape that can be at all turned into this, (and there is little doubt that Milton had some such in his eye in writing it,) each party converts it to its own purposes, feels the absolute identity of these abstracted and high speculations; and that, in fact, a noted political writer of the present day has exhausted nearly the whole account of Satan in the Paradise Lost, by applying it to a character whom he considered as after the devil, (though I do not know whether he would make even that exception) the greatest enemy of the human race. This may serve to show that Milton's Satan is not a very insipid personage.

Of Adam and Eve it has been said, that the ordinary reader can feel little interest in them, because they have none of the passions, pursuits, or even relations of human life, except that of man and wife, the least interesting of all others, if not to the parties concerned, at least to the by standers. The preference has on this account been given to Homer, who, it is said, has left very vivid and infinitely diversified pictures of all the passions and affections, public and private, incident to human nature, the relations of son, of brother, parent, friend, citizen, and many others.

Longinus preferred the Iliad to the Odyssey, on account of the greater number of battles it contains; but I can neither agree to his criticism, nor assent to the present objection. It is true, there is little action in this part of Milton's poem; but there is much repose, and more enjoyment. There are none of the everyday occurrences, contentions, disputes, wars, fightings, feuds, jealousies, trades, professions, liveries, and common handicrafts of life; "no kind of traffic; letters are not known; no use of service, of riches, poverty, contract, succession, bourn, bound of land, tilth, vineyard none; no occupation, no treason, felony, sword, pike, knife, gun, nor need of any engine." So much the better; thank Heaven, all these were yet to come. But still the die was cast, and in them our doom was sealed. In them:

"The generations were prepared; the pangs, The internal pangs, were ready, the dread strife Of poor humanity's afflicted will, Struggling in vain with ruthless destiny."

In their first false step we trace all our future woe, with loss of Eden. But there was a short and precious interval between, like the first blush of morning before the day is overcast with tempest, the dawn of the world, the birth of nature from "the unapparent deep," with its first dews and freshness on its cheek, breathing odours. Theirs was the first delicious taste of life, and on them depended all that was to come of it. In them hung trembling all our hopes and fears. They were as get alone in the world, in the eye of nature, wondering at their new being, full of enjoyment and enraptured with one another, with the voice of their Maker walking in the garden, and ministering angels attendant on their steps, winged messengers from heaven like rosy clouds descending in their sight. Nature played around them her virgin fancies wild; and spread for them a repast where no crude surfeit reigned. Was there nothing in this scene, which God and nature alone witnessed, to interest a modern critic? What need was there of action, where the heart was full of bliss and innocence without it! They had nothing to do but feel their own happiness, and "know to know no more." "They toiled not, neither did they spin; yet Solomon in all his glory was not arrayed like one of these."

All things seem to acquire fresh sweetness, and to be clothed with fresh beauty in their sight. They tasted as it were for themselves and us, of all that there ever was pure in human bliss. "In them the burthen of the mystery, the heavy and the weary weight of all this unintelligible world, is lightened." They stood awhile perfect, but they afterwards fell, and were driven out of Paradise, tasting the first fruits of bitterness as they had done of bliss. But their pangs were such as a pure spirit might feel at the sight their tears "such as angels weep."

The pathos is of that mild contemplative kind which arises from regret for the loss of unspeakable happiness, and resignation to inevitable fate. There is none of the fierceness of intemperate passion, none of the agony of mind and turbulence of action, which is the result of the habitual struggles of the will with circumstances, irritated by repeated disappointment, and constantly setting its desires most eagerly on that which there is an impossibility of attaining. This would have destroyed the beauty of the whole picture. They had received their unlooked for happiness as a free gift from their Creator's hands, and they submitted to its loss, not without sorrow, but without impious and stubborn repining.

"In either hand the hast'ning angel caught Our ling'ring parents, and to the eastern gate Led them direct, and down the cliff as fast To the subjected plain; then disappear'd. They looking back, all the eastern side beheld Of Paradise, so late their happy seat, Wav'd over by that flaming brand, the gate With dreadful faces throng'd, and fiery arms: Some natural tears they dropt, but wip'd them soon; The world was all before them, where to choose, Their place of rest, and Providence their guide."

6

Pope

The question, whether Pope was a poet, has hardly yet been settled, and is hardly worth settling; for if he was not a great poet, he must have been a great prose writer, that is, he was a great writer of some sort. He was a man of exquisite faculties, and of the most refined taste; and as he chose verse (the most obvious distinction of poetry) as the vehicle to express his ideas, he has generally passed for a poet, and a good one.

If, indeed, by a great poet, we mean one who gives the utmost grandeur to our conceptions of nature, or the utmost force to the passions of the heart, Pope was not in this sense a great poet; for the bent, the characteristic power of his mind, lay the clean contrary way; namely, in representing things as they appear to the indifferent observer, stripped of prejudice and passion, as in his Critical Essays; or in representing them in the most contemptible and insignificant point of view, as in his Satires; or in clothing the little with mock dignity, as in his poems of Fancy; or in adorning the trivial incidents and familiar relations of life with the utmost elegance of expression, and all the flattering illusions of friendship or self love, as in his Epistles. He was not then distinguished as a poet of lofty enthusiasm, of strong imagination, with a passionate sense of the beauties of nature, or a deep insight into the workings of the heart; but he was a wit, and a critic, a man of sense, of observation, and the world, with a keen relish for the elegances of art, or of nature when embellished by art, a quick tact for propriety of thought and manners as established by the forms and customs of society, a refined sympathy with the sentiments and habitudes of human life, as he felt them within the little circle of his family and friends.

He was, in a word, the poet, not of nature, but of art; and the distinction between the two, as well as I can make it out, is this, The poet of nature is one who, from the elements of beauty, of power, and of passion in his own breast, sympathises with whatever is beautiful, and grand, and impassioned in nature, in its simple majesty, in its immediate appeal to the senses, to the thoughts and hearts of all men; so that the poet of nature, by the truth, and depth, and harmony of his mind, may be said to hold communion with the very soul of nature; to be identified with and to foreknow and to record the feelings of all men at all times and places, as they are liable to the same impressions; and to exert the same power over the minds of his readers, that nature does.

He sees things in their eternal beauty, for he sees them as they are; he feels them in their universal interest, for he feels them as they affect the first principles of his and our common nature. Such was Homer, such was Shakspeare, whose works will last as long as nature, because they are a copy of the indestructible forms and everlasting impulses of nature, welling out from the bosom as from a perennial spring, or stamped upon the senses by the hand of their maker. The power of the imagination in them, is the representative power of all nature. It has its centre in the human soul, and makes the circuit of the universe. Pope was not assuredly a poet of this class, or in the first rank of it. He saw nature only dressed by art; he judged of beauty by fashion; he sought for truth in the opinions of the world; he judged of the feelings of others by his own. The capacious soul of Shakspeare had an intuitive and mighty sympathy with whatever could enter into the heart of man in all possible circumstances: Pope had an exact knowledge of all that he himself loved or hated, wished or wanted. Milton has winged his daring flight from heaven to earth, through Chaos and old Night.

Pope's Muse never wandered with safety, but from his library to his grotto, or from his grotto into his library back again. His mind dwelt with greater pleasure on his own garden, than on the garden of Eden; he could describe the faultless whole length mirror that reflected his own person, better than the smooth surface of the lake that reflects the face of heaven a piece of cut glass or a pair of paste buckles with more brilliance and effect, than a thousand dew drops glittering in the sun. He would be more delighted with a patent lamp, than with "the pale reflex of Cynthia's brow," that fills the skies with its soft silent lustre, that trembles through the cottage window, and cheers the watchful mariner on the lonely wave.

In short, he was the poet of personality and of polished life. That which was nearest to him, was the greatest; the fashion of the day bore sway in his mind over the immutable laws of nature. He preferred the artificial to the natural in external objects, because he had a stronger fellow feeling with the self love of the maker or proprietor of a gewgaw, than admiration of that which was interesting to all mankind. He preferred the artificial to the natural in passion, because the involuntary and uncalculating impulses of the one hurried him away with a force and vehemence with which he could not grapple; while he could trifle with the conventional and superficial modifications of mere sentiment at will, laugh at or admire, put them on or off like a masquerade dress, make much or little of them, indulge them for a longer or a shorter time, as lie pleased; and because while they amused his fancy and exercised his ingenuity, they never once disturbed his vanity, his levity, or indifference. His mind was the antithesis of strength and grandeur; its power was the power of indifference. He had none of the enthusiasm of poetry: he was in poetry what the sceptic is in religion.'

It cannot be denied, that his chief excellence lay more in diminishing, than in aggrandising objects; in checking, not in encouraging our enthusiasm; in sneering at the extravagances of fancy or passion, instead of giving a loose to them; in describing a row of pins and needles, rather than the embattled spears of Greeks and Trojans; in penning a lampoon or a compliment, and in praising Martha Blount.

Shakspeare says, "In Fortune's ray and brightness The herd hath more annoyance by the brize Than by the tyger: but when the splitting wind Makes flexible the knees of knotted oaks, And flies fled under shade, why then The thing of courage, As roused with rage, with rage doth sympathise; And with an accent tuned in the self same key, Replies to chiding Fortune." There is none of this rough work in Pope. His Muse was on a peace establishment, and grew somewhat effeminate by long ease and indulgence. He lived in the smiles of fortune, and basked in the favour of the great. In his smooth and polished verse we meet with no prodigies of nature, but with miracles of wit; the thunders of his pen are whispered flatteries; its forked lightnings pointed sarcasms; for "the gnarled oak," he gives us "the soft myrtle: "for rocks, and seas, and mountains, artificial grassplats, gravel walks, and tinkling rills; for earthquakes and tempests, the breaking of a flower pot, or the fall of a china jar; for the tug and war of the elements, or the deadly strife of the passions, we have: "Calm contemplation and poetic ease."

Yet within this retired and narrow circle how much, and that how exquisite, was contained! What discrimination, what wit, what delicacy, what fancy, what lurking spleen, what elegance of thought, what pampered refinement of sentiment! It is like looking at the world through a microscope, where everything assumes a new character and a new consequence, where things are seen in their minutest circumstances and slightest shades of difference; where the little becomes gigantic, the deformed beautiful, and the beautiful deformed. The wrong end of the magnifier is, to be sure, held to every thing, but still the exhibition is highly curious, and we know not whether to be most pleased or surprised. Such, at least, is the best account I am able to give of this extraordinary man, without doing injustice to him or others. It is time to refer to particular instances in his works. The Rape of the Lock is the best or most ingenious of these. It is the most exquisite specimen of fillagree work ever invented. It is admirable in proportion as it is made of nothing. "More subtle web Arachne cannot spin, Nor the fine nets, which oft we woven see of scorched dew, do not in the air more lightly flee."

It is made of gauze and silver spangles. The most glittering appearance is given to every thing, to paste, pomatum, billet–doux, and patches. Airs, languid airs, breathe around; the atmosphere is perfumed with affectation. A toilette is described with the solemnity of an altar raised to the goddess of vanity, and the history of a silver bodkin is given with all the pomp of heraldry. No pains are spared, no profusion of ornament, no splendour of poetic diction, to set off the meanest things. The balance between the concealed irony and the assumed gravity, is as nicely trimmed as the balance of power in Europe. The little is made great, and the great little. You hardly know whether to laugh or weep. It is the triumph of insignificance, the apotheosis of foppery and folly. It is the perfection of the mock heroic! I will give only the two following passages in illustration' of these remarks. Can anything be more elegant and graceful than the description of Belinda, in the beginning of the second canto?

"Not with more glories, in the ethereal plain, The sun first rises o'er the purpled main, Than, issuing forth, the rival of his beams Launch'd on the bosom of the silver Thames. Fair nymphs, and well drest youths around her shone, But ev'ry eye was fix'd on her alone. On her white breast a sparkling cross she wore, Which Jews might kiss, and infidels adore. Her lively looks a sprightly mind disclose, Quick as her eyes, and as unfix'd as those: Favours to none, to all she smiles extends; Oft she rejects, but never once offends. Bright as the sun, her eyes the gazers strike; And like the sun, they shine on all alike. Yet graceful ease, and sweetness void of pride, Might hide her faults, if belles had faults to hide: If to her share some female errors fall, Look on her face, and you'll forget 'em all. This nymph, to the destruction of mankind, Nourish'd two locks, which graceful hung behind In equal curls, and well conspir'd to deck With shining ringlets the smooth iv'ry neck."

The following is the introduction to the account of Belinda's assault upon the baron bold, who had dissevered one of these locks "from her fair head for ever and for ever."

"Now meet thy fate, incens'd Belinda cry'd, And drew a deadly bodkin from her side. (The same his ancient personage to deck, Her great, great grandsire wore about his neck, In three seat–rings; which after, melted down, Form'd a vast buckle for his widow's gown: Her infant grandame's whistle next it grew, The bells she jingled, and the whistle blew: Then in a bodkin grac'd her mother's hairs, Which long she wore, and now Belinda wears.)"

I do not know how far Pope was indebted for the original idea, or the delightful execution of this poem, to the Lutrin of Boileau. The Rape of the Lock is a double refined essence of wit and fancy, as the Essay on Criticism is of wit and sense. The quantity of thought and observation in this work, for so young a' man as Pope was when he wrote it, is wonderful: unless we adopt the supposition, that most men of genius spend the rest of their lives in teaching others what they themselves have learned under twenty. The conciseness and felicity of the expression is equally remarkable. Thus in reasoning on the variety of men's opinions, he says—

"Tis with our judgments, as our watches; none Go just alike, yet each believes his own." Nothing can be more original and happy than the general remarks and illustrations in the Essay: the critical rules laid down are too much those of a school, and of a confined one. There is one passage in the Essay on Criticism in which the author speaks with that eloquent enthusiasm of the fame of ancient writers, which those will always feel who have themselves any hope or chance of immortality. I have quoted the passage elsewhere, but I will repeat it here. "Still green with bays each ancient altar stands, Above the reach of sacrilegious hands; Secure from flames, from envy's fiercer rage, Destructive war, and all involving age. Hail, bards triumphant, born in happier days, Immortal heirs of universal praise! Whose honours with increase of ages grow, As streams roll down, enlarging as they flow."

These lines come with double force and beauty on the reader as they were dictated by the writer's despair of ever attaining that lasting glory which he celebrates with such disinterested enthusiasm in others, from the lateness of the age in which he lived, and from his writing in a tongue, not understood by other nations, and that grows obsolete and unintelligible to ourselves at the end of every second century. But he needed not have thus antedated his own poetical doom the loss and entire oblivion of that which can never die. If he had known, he might have boasted that his "little bark" wafted down the stream of time,

"With theirs should sail, Pursue the triumph and partake the gale", if those who know how to set a due value on the blessing, were not the last to decide confidently on their own pretensions to it. There is a cant in the present day about genius, as every thing in poetry: there was a cant in the time of Pope about sense, as performing all sorts of wonders. It was a kind of watchword, the shibboleth of a critical party of the day. As a proof of the exclusive attention which it occupied in their minds, it is remarkable that in the Essay on Criticism (not a very long poem) there are no less than half a score successive couplets rhyming to the word sense. This appears almost incredible without giving the instances, and no less so when they are given.

"But of the two, less dangerous is the offence,To tire our patience than mislead our sense." lines 3, 4. "In search of wit these lose their common sense,And then turn critics in their own defence." l. 28, 29. "Pride, where wit fails, steps in to our defence,And fills up all the mighty void of sense." l. 209, 10. "Some by old words to fame have made pretence,Ancients in phrase, mere moderns in their sense." l. 324, 5. "Tis not enough no harshness gives offence;The sound must seem an echo to the sense." l. 364, 5. "At every trifle scorn to take offence;That always shews great pride, or little sense." l. 386, 7. "Be silent always, when you doubt your sense,And speak, though sure, with seeming diffidence." l. 366, 7.

"Be niggards of advice on no pretence,For the worst avarice is that of sense." l. 578, 9. "Strain out the last dull dropping of their sense, And rhyme with all the rage of impotence." l. 608, 9. "Horace still charms with graceful negligence,And without method talks us into sense." l. 653, 4.

I have mentioned this the more for the sake of those critics who are bigotted idolisers of our author, chiefly on the score of his correctness. These persons seem to be of opinion that "there is but one perfect writer, even Pope." This is, however, a mistake: his excellence is by no means faultlessness. If he had no great faults, he is full of little errors. His grammatical construction is often lame and imperfect. In the Abelard and Eloise, he says—

"There died the best of passions, Love and Fame."

This is not a legitimate ellipsis. Fame is not a passion, though love is: but his ear was evidently confused by the meeting of the sounds "love and fame," as if they of themselves immediately implied "love, and love of fame." Pope's rhymes are constantly defective, being rhymes to the eye instead of the ear; and this to a greater degree, not only than in later, but than in preceding writers. The praise of his versification must be confined to its uniform smoothness and harmony. In the translation of the Iliad, which has been considered as his masterpiece in style and execution, he continually changes the tenses in the same sentence for the purpose of the rhyme, which shews either a want of technical resources, or great inattention to punctilious exactness. But to have done with this.

The Epistle of Eloise to Abelard is the only exception I can think of, to the general spirit of the foregoing remarks; and I should be disingenuous not to acknowledge that it is an exception. The foundation is in the letters themselves of Abelard and Eloise, which are quite as impressive, but still in a different way. It is fine as a poem: it is finer as a piece of high wrought eloquence. No woman could be supposed to write a finer love letter in verse. Besides the richness of the historical materials, the high gusto of the original sentiments which Pope had to work upon, there were perhaps circumstances in his own situation which made him enter into the subject with even more than a poet's feeling. The tears shed are drops gushing from the heart: the words are burning sighs breathed from the soul of love. Perhaps the poem to which it bears the greatest similarity in our language, is Dryden's Tancred and Sigismunda, taken from Boccaccio. Pope's Eloise will bear this comparison; and after such a test, with Boccaccio for the original author, and Dryden for the translator, it need shrink from no other. There is something exceedingly tender and beautiful in the sound of the concluding lines:

"If ever chance two wandering lovers brings To Paraclete's white walls and silver springs," *etc.* The Essay on Man is not Pope's best work. It is a theory which Bolingbroke is supposed to have given him, and which he expanded into verse. But "he spins the thread of his verbosity finer than the staple of his argument." All that he says, "the very words, and to the selfsame tune," would prove just as well that whatever is, is wrong, as that whatever is, is right. The Dunciad has splendid passages, but in general it is dull, heavy, and mechanical. The sarcasm already quoted on Settle, the Lord Mayor's poet, (for at that time there was a city as well as a court poet). "Now night descending, the proud scene is o'er, But lives in Settle's numbers one day more" is the finest inversion of immortality conceivable. It is even better than his serious apostrophe to the great heirs of glory, the triumphant bards of antiquity!

The finest burst of severe moral invective in all Pope, is the prophetical conclusion of the epilogue to-the-Satires:

"Virtue may chuse the high or low degree, Tis just alike to virtue, and to me; Dwell in a monk, or light upon a king, She's still the same belov'd, contented thing. Vice is undone if she forgets her birth, And stoops from angels to the dregs of earth. But 'tis the Fall degrades her to a whore: Let Greatness own her, and she's mean no more. Her birth, her beauty, crowds and courts confess, Chaste matrons praise her, and grave bishops bless; In golden chains the willing world she draws, And hers the gospel is, and hers the laws; Mounts the tribunal, lifts her scarlet head, And sees pale Virtue carted in her stead. Lo! at the wheels of her triumphal car, Old England's Genius, rough with many a scar, Dragged in the dust! his arms hang idly round, His flag inverted trails along the ground! Our youth, all livery'd o'er with foreign gold, Before her dance; behind her, crawl the old! See thronging millions to the Pagod run, And offer country, parent, wife, or son!

Hear her black trumpet through the land proclaim, That not to be corrupted is the shame. In soldier, churchman, patriot, man in pow'r, 'Tis av'rice all, ambition is no more! See all our nobles begging to be slaves! See all our fools aspiring to be knaves! The wit of cheats, the courage of a whore, Are what ten thousand envy and adore: All, all look up with reverential awe, At crimes that 'scape or triumph o'er the law; While truth, worth, wisdom, daily they decry: Nothing is sacred now but villainy. Yet may this verse (if such a verse remain) Show there was one who held it in disdain."

His Satires are not in general so good as his Epistles. His enmity is effeminate and petulant from a sense of weakness, as his friendship was tender from a sense of gratitude. I do not like, for instance, his character of Chartres, or his characters of women. His delicacy often borders upon sickliness; his fastidiousness makes others fastidious. But his compliments are divine; they are equal in value to a house or an estate. Take the following. In addressing Lord Mansfield, he speaks of the grave as a scene, "Where Murray, long enough his country's pride, Shall be no more than Tully, or than Hyde."

To Bolingbroke he says—

Why rail they then if but one wreath of mine, Oh all–accomplished St. John, deck thy shrine?

Again, he has bequeathed this praise to Lord Cornbury, "Despise low thoughts, low gains: Disdain whatever Cornbury disdains; Be virtuous and be happy for your pains."

One would think (though there is no knowing) that a descendant of this nobleman, if there be such a person living, could hardly be guilty of a mean or paltry action.

The finest piece of personal satire in Pope (perhaps in the world) is his character of Addison; and this, it may be observed, is of a mixed kind, made up of his respect for the man, and a cutting sense of his failings. The other finest one is that of Buckingham, and the best part of that is the pleasurable.

"Alas! how changed from him, That life of pleasure, and that soul of whim: Gallant and gay, in Cliveden's proud alcove, The bower of wanton Shrewsbury and love!"

Among his happiest and most inimitable effusions are the Epistles to Arbuthnot, and to Jervas the painter; amiable patterns of the delightful unconcerned life, blending ease with dignity, which poets and painters then led. Thus he says to Arbuthnot—

"Why did I write? What sin to me unknown Dipp'd me in ink, my parents' or my own? As yet a child, nor yet a fool to fame, I lisped in numbers, for the numbers came. I left no calling for this idle trade, No duty broke, no father disobey'd The Muse but served to ease some friend, not wife; To help me through this long disease, my life; To second, Arbuthnot! thy art and care, And teach the being you preserv'd to bear. But why then publish? Granville the polite, And knowing Walsh, would tell me I could write; Well natur'd Garth, inflam'd with early praise, And Congreve lov'd, and Swift endur'd my lays; The courtly Talbot, Somers, Sheffield read; E'en mitred Rochester would nod the head; And St. John's self (great Dryden's friend before) With open arms receiv'd one poet more.

Happy my studies, when by these approv'd! Happier their author, when by these belov'd! From these the world will judge of men and books, Not from the Burnets, Oldmixons, and Cooks." I cannot help giving also the conclusion of the Epistle to Jervas. "Oh, lasting as those colours may they shine, Free as thy stroke, yet faultless as thy line; New graces yearly like thy works display, Soft without weakness, without glaring gay; Led by some rule, that guides, but not constrains; And finish'd more through happiness than pains. The kindred arts shall in their praise conspire, One dip the pencil, and one string the lyre. Yet should the Graces all thy figures place, And breathe an air divine on ev'ry face; Yet should the Muses bid my numbers roll Strong as their charms, and gentle as their soul; With Zeuxis' Helen thy Bridgewater vie, And these be sung till Granville's Myra die: Alas! how little from the grave we claim! Thou but preserv'st a face, and I a name."

And shall we cut ourselves off from beauties like these with a theory? Shall we shut up our books, and seal up our senses, to please the dull spite and inordinate vanity of those "who have eyes, but they see not ears, but they hear not-and understandings, but they understand not," and go about asking our blind guides, whether Pope was a poet or not? It will never do. Such persons, when you point out to them a fine passage in Pope, turn it off to something of the same sort in some other writer. Thus they say that the line, "I lisp'd in numbers, for the numbers came," is pretty, but taken from that of Ovid Et quum conabar scribcre, versus crat. They are safe in this mode of criticism: there is no danger of any one's tracing their writings to the classics.

Pope's letters and prose writings neither take away from, nor add to his poetical reputation. There is, occasionally, a littleness of manner, and an unnecessary degree of caution. He appears anxious to say a good thing in every word, as well as every sentence. They, however, give a very favourable idea of his moral character in all respects; and his letters to Atterbury, in his disgrace and exile, do equal honour to both. If I had to choose, there are one or two persons, and but one or two, that I should like to have been better than Pope!

The English Novelists

There is an exclamation in one of Gray's Letters, "Be mine to read eternal new romances of Marivaux and Crebillon!", If I did not utter a similar aspiration at the conclusion of the last new novel which I read (I would not give offence by being more particular as to the name) it was not from any want of affection for the class of writing to which it belongs: for, without going so far as the celebrated French philosopher, who thought that more was to be learnt from good novels and romances than from the gravest treatises on history and morality, yet there are few works to which I am oftener tempted to turn for profit or delight, than to the standard productions in this species of composition. We find there a close imitation of men and manners; we see the very web and texture of society as it really exists, and as we meet with it when we come into the world. If poetry has "something more divine in it," this savours more of humanity. We are brought acquainted with the motives and characters of mankind, imbibe our notions of virtue and vice from practical examples, and are taught a knowledge of the world through the airy medium of romance. As a record of past manners and opinions, too, such writings afford the best and fullest information. For example, I should be at a loss where to find in any authentic documents of the same period so satisfactory an account of the general state of society, and of moral, political, and religious feeling in the reign of George II, as we meet with in the Adventures of Joseph Andrews and his friend Mr. Abraham Adams.

This work, indeed, I take to be a perfect piece of statistics in its kind. In looking into any regular history of that period, into a learned and eloquent charge to a grand jury or the clergy of a diocese, or into a tract on controversial divinity, we should hear only of the ascendancy of the Protestant succession, the horrors of Popery, the triumph of civil and religious liberty, the wisdom and moderation of the sovereign, the happiness of the subject, and the flourishing state of manufactures and commerce.

But if we really wish to know what all these fine sounding names come to, we cannot do better than turn to the works of those, who having no other object than to imitate nature, could only hope for success from the fidelity of their pictures; and were bound (in self-defence) to reduce the boasts of vague theorists and the exaggerations of angry disputants to the mortifying standard of reality. Extremes are said to meet: and the works of imagination, as they are called, sometimes come the nearest to truth and nature. Fielding in speaking on this subject, and vindicating the use and dignity of the style of writing in which he excelled against the loftier pretensions of professed historians, says that in their productions nothing is true but the names and dates, whereas in his everything is true but the names and dates. If so, he has the advantage on his side.

I will here confess, however, that I am a little prejudiced on the point in question; and that the effect of many fine speculations has been lost upon me, from an early familiarity with the most striking passages in the work to which I have just alluded. Thus nothing can be more captivating than the description somewhere given by Mr. Burke of the indissoluble connection between learning and nobility; and of the respect universally paid by wealth to piety and morals. But the effect of this ideal representation has always been spoiled by my recollection of Parson Adams sitting over his cup of ale in Sir Thomas Booby's kitchen. Echard "On the Contempt of the Clergy" is, in like manner, a very good book, and "worthy of all acceptation:" but, somehow, an unlucky impression of the reality of Parson Trulliber involuntarily checks the emotions of respect, to which it might otherwise give rise: while, on the other hand, the lecture which Lady Booby reads to Lawyer Scout on the immediate expulsion of Joseph and Fanny from the parish casts no very favourable light on the flattering accounts of our practical jurisprudence which are to be found in Blackstone or De Lolme.

The most moral writers, after all, are those who do not pretend to inculcate any moral. The professed moralist almost unavoidably degenerates into the' partisan of a system; and the philosopher is too apt to warp the evidence to his own purpose. But the painter of manners gives the facts of human nature, and leaves us to draw the inference: if we are not able to do this, or do it ill, at least it is our own fault.

The first rate writers in this class, of course, are few; but those few we may reckon among the greatest ornaments and best benefactors of our kind. There is a certain set of them who, as it were, take their rank by the side of reality, and are appealed to as evidence on all questions concerning human nature. The principal of these are Cervantes and Le Sage, who may be considered as having been naturalised among ourselves; and, of native English growth, Fielding, Smollett, Richardson, and Sterne. As this is a department of criticism which deserves more attention than has been usually bestowed upon it, I shall here venture to recur (not from choice, but necessity) to what I have said upon it in a well-known periodical publication; and endeavour to contribute my mite towards settling the standard of excellence, both as to degree and kind, in these several writers. . . .

There is very little to warrant the common idea that Fielding was an imitator of Cervantes, except his own declaration of such an intention in the title page of Joseph Andrews, the romantic turn of the character of Parson Adams (the only romantic character in his works), and the proverbial humour of Partridge, which is kept up only for a few pages. Fielding's novels are, in general, thoroughly his own; and they are thoroughly English. What they are most remarkable for, is neither sentiment, nor imagination, nor wit, nor even humour, though there is an immense deal of this last quality; but profound knowledge of human nature, at least of English nature; and masterly pictures of the characters of men as he saw them existing. This quality distinguishes all his works, and is shown almost equally in all of them.

As a painter of real life, he was equal to Hogarth; as a mere observer of human nature, he was little inferior to Shakspeare, though without any of the genius and poetical qualities of his mind. His humour is less rich and laughable than Smollett's; his wit as often misses as hits; he has none of the fine pathos of

Richardson or Sterne; but he has brought together a greater variety of characters in common life, marked with more distinct peculiarities, and without an atom of caricature, than any other novel writer whatever. The extreme subtlety of observation on the springs of human conduct in ordinary characters, is only equalled by the ingenuity of contrivance in bringing those springs into play, in such a manner as to lay open their smallest irregularity. The detection is always complete, and made with the certainty and skill of a philosophical experiment, and the obviousness and familiarity of a casual observation. The truth of the imitation is indeed so great, that it has been argued that Fielding must have had his materials ready made to his hands, and was merely a transcriber of local manners and individual habits. For this conjecture, however, there seems to be no foundation. His representations, it is true, are local and individual; but they are not the less profound and conclusive. The feeling of the general principles of human nature, operating in particular circumstances, is always intense, and uppermost in his mind; and he makes use of incident and situation only to bring out character.

It is scarcely necessary to give any illustrations. Tom Jones is full of them. There is the account, for example, of the gratitude of the elder Blifil to his brother, for assisting him to obtain the fortune of Miss Bridget Alworthy by marriage; and of the gratitude of the poor in his neighbourhood to Alworthy himself, who had done so much good in the country that he had made every one in it his enemy. There is the account of the Latin dialogues between Partridge and his maid, of the assault made on him during one of these by Mrs. Partridge, and the severe bruises he patiently received on that occasion, after which the parish of Little Baddington rung with the story, that the school-master had killed his wife.

There is the exquisite keeping in the character of Blifil, and the want of it in that of Jones. There is the gradation in the lovers of Molly Seagrim; the philosopher Square succeeding to Tom Jones, who again finds that he himself had succeeded to the accomplished Will. Barnes, who had the first possession of her person, and had still possession of her heart, Jones being only the instrument of her vanity, as Square was of her interest. Then there is the discreet honesty of Black George, the learning of Thwackum and Square, and the profundity of Squire Western, who considered it as a physical impossibility that his daughter should fall in love with Tom Jones. We have also that gentleman's disputes with his sister, and the inimitable appeal of that lady to her niece. "I was never so handsome as you, Sophy: yet I had something of you formerly. I was called the cruel Parthenissa. Kingdoms and states, as Tully Cicero says, undergo alteration, and so must the human form!" The adventure of the same lady with the highwayman, who robbed her of her jewels while he complimented her beauty, ought not to be passed over, nor that of Sophia and her muff, nor the reserved coquetry of her cousin Fitzpatrick, nor the description of Lady Bellaston, nor the modest overtures of the pretty widow Hunt, nor the indiscreet babblings of Mrs. Honour.

The moral of this book has been objected to, without much reason; but a more serious objection has been made to the want of refinement and elegance in two principal characters. We never feel this objection, indeed, while we are reading the book; but at other times we have something like a lurking suspicion that Jones was but an awkward fellow, and Sophia a pretty simpleton. I do not know how to account for this effect, unless it is that Fielding's constantly assuring us of the beauty of his hero, and the good sense of his heroine, at last produces a distrust of both. The story of Tom Jones is allowed to be unrivalled: and it is this circumstance, together with the vast variety of characters, that has given the History of a Foundling so decided a preference over Fielding's other novels.

The characters themselves, both in Amelia and Joseph Andrews, are quite equal to any of those in Tom Jones. The account of Miss Matthews and Ensign Hibbert, in the former of these; the way in which that lady recon ciles herself to the death of her father; the inflexible Colonel Bath; the insipid Mrs. James, the complaisant Colonel Trent, the demure, sly, intriguing, equivocal Mrs. Bennet, the lord who is her seducer, and who attempts afterwards to seduce Amelia by the same mechanical process of a concert ticket, a book, and the disguise of a great coat; his little, fat, short-nosed, red-faced, good humoured accomplice, the keeper of the lodging-house, who, having no pretensions to gallantry herself, has a disinterested delight in forwarding the intrigues and pleasures of others (to say nothing of honest Atkinson, the story of the miniaturepicture of Amelia, and the hashed mutton, which are in a different style,) are masterpieces of description. The whole scene at the lodging house, the masquerade, *etc.*, in Amelia, are equal in interest to the parallel scenes in Tom Jones, and even more refined in the knowledge of character. For instance, Mrs. Bennet is superior to Mrs. Fitzpatrick in her own way.

The uncertainty, in which the event of her interview with her former seducer is left, is admirable. Fielding was a master of what may be called the double entendre of character, and surprises you no less by what he leaves in the dark, (hardly known to the persons themselves) than by the unexpected discoveries he makes of the real traits and circumstances in a character with which, till then, you find you were unacquainted. There is nothing at all heroic, however, in the usual style of his delineations. He does not draw lofty characters or strong passions; all his persons are of the ordinary stature as to intellect; and possess little elevation of fancy, or energy of purpose. Perhaps, after all, Parson Adams is his finest character. It is equally true to nature, and more ideal than any of the others. Its unsuspecting simplicity makes it not only more amiable, but doubly amusing, by gratifying the sense of superior sagacity in the reader. Our laughing at him does not once lessen our respect for him. His declaring that he would willingly walk ten miles to fetch his sermon on vanity, merely to convince Wilson of his thorough contempt of this vice, and his consoling himself for the loss of his Aeschylus, by suddenly recollecting that he could not read it if he had it, because it is dark, are among the finest touches of naïvete.

The night adventures at Lady Booby's with Beau Didapper, and the amiable Slipslop, are the most ludicrous; and that with the huntsman, who draws off the hounds from the poor Parson, because they would be spoiled by following vermin, the most profound. Fielding did not often repeat himself; but Dr. Harrison, in Amelia, may be considered as a variation of the character of Adams: so also is Goldsmithes Vicar of Wakefield; and the latter part of that work, which sets out so delightfully, an almost entire plagiarism from Wilson's account of himself, and Adams's domestic history.

Smollett's first novel, Roderick Random, which is also his best, appeared about the same time as Fielding's Tom Jones; and yet it has a much more modern air with it: but this may be accounted for from the circumstance that Smollett was quite a young man at the time, whereas Fielding's manner must have been formed long before. The style of Roderick Random is more easy and flowing than that of Tom Jones; the incidents follow one another more rapidly (though, it must be confessed, they never come in such a throng, or are brought out with the same dramatic effect); the humour is broader, and as effectual; and there is very nearly, if not quite, an equal interest excited by the story. What, then, is it that gives the superiority to Fielding?

It is the superior insight into the springs of human character, and the constant developement of that character through every change of circumstance. Smollett's humour often arises from the situation of the persons, or the peculiarity of their external appearance; as, from Roderick Random's carrotty locks, which hung down over his shoulders like a pound of candles, or Strap's ignorance of London, and the blunders that follow from it. There is a tone of vulgarity about all his productions.

He exhibits the ridiculous accidents and reverses to which human life is liable, not "the stuff" of which it is composed. He seldom probes to the quick, or penetrates beyond the surface; and, therefore, he leaves no stings in the minds of his readers, and in this respect is far less interesting than Fielding. His novels always enliven, and never tire us: we take them up with pleasure, and lay them down without any strong feeling of regret. We look on and laugh, as spectators of a highly amusing scene, without closing in with the combatants, or being made parties in the event. We read Roderick Random as an entertaining story; for the particular accidents and modes of life which it describes have ceased to exist: but we regard Tom Jones as a real history; because the author never stops short of those essential principles which lie at the bottom of all our actions, and in which we feel an immediate interest intus et in cute. Smollett excels most as the lively caricaturist: Fielding as the exact painter and profound metaphysician. I am far from maintaining that this account applies uniformly to the productions of these two writers; but I think that, as far as they essentially differ, what I have stated is the general distinction between them. Roderick Random is the purest of Smollett's novels: I mean in point of style and description. Most of the incidents and characters are supposed to have been taken from the events of his own life; and are, therefore, truer to nature.

There is a rude conception of generosity in some of his characters, of which Fielding seems to have been incapable, his amiable persons being merely good natured. It is owing to this that Strap is superior to Partridge; as there is a heartiness and warmth of feeling in some of the scenes between Lieutenant Bowling and his nephew, which is beyond Fielding's power of impassioned writing. The whole of the scene on ship board is a most admirable and striking picture, and, I imagine, very little if at all exaggerated, though the interest it excites is of a very unpleasant kind, because the irritation and resistance to petty oppression can be of no avail.

The picture of the little profligate French friar, who was Roderick's travelling companion, and of whom he always kept to the windward, is one of Smollett's most masterly sketches. Peregrine Pickle is no great favourite of mine, and Launcelot Greaves was not worthy of the genius of the author.

Humphry Clinker and Count Fathom are both equally admirable in their way. Perhaps the former is the most pleasant gossiping novel that ever was written; that which gives the most pleasure with the least effort to the reader. It is quite as amusing as going the journey could have been; and we have just as good an idea of what happened on the road, as if we had been of the party. Humphry Clinker himself is exquisite; and his sweetheart, Winifred Jenkins, not much behind him.

Matthew Bramble, though not altogether original, is excellently supported, and seems to have been the prototype of Sir Anthony Absolute in the Rivals. But Lismahago is the flower of the flock. His tenaciousness in argument is not so delightful as the relaxation of his logical severity, when he finds his fortune mellowing in the wintry smiles of Mrs. Tabitha Bramble. This is the bestpreserved and most severe of all

Smollett's characters. The resemblance to Don Quixote is only just enough to make it interesting to the critical reader, without giving offence to any body else. The indecency and filth in this novel are what must be allowed to all Smollett's writings.

The subject and characters in Count Fathom are, in general, exceedingly disgusting: the story is also spun cut to a degree of tediousness in the serious and sentimental parts; but there is more power of writing occasionally shewn in it than in any of his works. I need only refer to the fine and bitter irony of the Count's address to the country of his ancestors on his landing in England; to the robber scene in the forest, which has never been surpa. .ed; to the Parisian swindler who personates a raw English country squire (Western is tame in the comparison); and to the story of the seduction in the west of England. It would be difficult to point out, in any author, passages written with more force and mastery than these.

It is not a very difficult undertaking to class Fielding or Smollett; the one as an observer of the characters of human life, the other as a describer of its various eccentricities. But it is by no means so easy to dispose of Richardson, who was neither an observer of the one, nor a describer of the other; but who seemed to spin his materials entirely out of his own brain, as if there had been nothing existing in the world beyond the little room in which he sat writing.

They have the romantic air of a pure fiction, with the literal minuteness of a common diary. The author had the strongest matter of fact imagination that ever existed, and wrote the oddest mixture of poetry and prose. He does not appear to have taken advantage of anything in actual nature, from one end of his works to the other; and yet, throughout all his works, voluminous as they are (and this, to be sure, is one reason why they are so) he sets about describing every object and transaction, as if the whole had been given in on evidence by all eye witness. This kind of high finishing from imagination is an anomaly in the history of human genius; and, certainly, nothing so fine was ever produced by the same accumulation of minute parts. There is not the least distraction, the least forgetfulness of the end: every circumstance is made to tell. I cannot agree that this exactness of detail produces heaviness;

on the contrary, it gives an appearance of truth, and a positive interest to the story; and we listen with the same attention as we should to the particulars of a confidential communication. I at one time used to think some parts of Sir Charles Grandison rather trifling and tedious, especially the long description of Miss Harriet Byron's wedding clothes, till I was told of two young ladies who had severally copied out the whole of that very description for their own private gratification. After that, I could not blame the author.

The effect of reading this work is like an increase of kindred. You find yourself all of a sudden introduced into the midst of a large family, with aunts and cousins to the third and fourth generation, and grandmothers both by the father's and mother's side; and a very odd set of people they are, but people whose real existence and personal identity you can no more dispute than your own senses, for you see and hear all that they do or say. What is still more extraordinary, all this extreme elaborateness in working out the story, seems to have cost the author nothing; for it is said, that the published works are mere abridgments. I have heard (though this I suspect must be a pleasant exaggeration) that Sir Charles Grandison was originally written in eight and twenty volumes.

Pamela is the first of Richardson's productions, and the very child of his brain. Taking the general idea of the character of a modest and beautiful country girl, and of the ordinary situation in which she is placed, he makes out all the rest, even to the smallest circumstance, by the mere force of a reasoning imagination. It would seem as if a step lost, would be as fatal here as in a mathematical demonstration. The development of the character is the most simple, and comes the nearest to nature that it can do, without being the same thing.

The interest of the story increases with the dawn of understanding and reflection in the heroine: her sentiments gradually expand themselves, like opening flowers. She writes better every time, and acquires a confidence in herself, just as a girl would do, writing such letters in such circumstances; and yet it is certain that no girl would write such letters in such circumstances. What I mean is this: Richardson's nature is always the nature of sentiment and reflection, not of impulse or situation. He furnishes his characters, on every occasion, with the presence of mind of the author.

He makes them act, not as they would from the impulse of the moment, but as they might upon reflection, and upon a careful review of every motive and circumstance in their situation. They regularly sit down to write letters: and if the business of life consisted in letter writing, and was carried on by the post (like a Spanish game at chess), human nature would be what Richardson represents it. All actual objects and feelings are blunted and deadened by being presented through a medium which may be true to reason, but is false in nature. He confounds his own point of view with that of the immediate actors in the scene; and hence presents you with a conventional and factitious nature, instead of that which is real.

Dr. Johnson seems to have preferred this truth of reflection to the truth of nature, when he said that there was more knowledge of the human heart in a page of Richardson, than in all Fielding. Fielding, however, saw more of the practical results, and understood the principles as well; but he had not the same power of speculating upon their possible results, and combining them in certain ideal forms of passion and imagination, which was Richardson's real excellence.

It must be observed, however, that it is this mutual good understanding, and comparing of notes between the author and the persons he describes; his infinite circumspection, his exact process of ratiocination and calculation, which gives such an appearance of coldness and formality to most of his characters, which makes prudes of his women, and coxcombs of his men. Every thing is too conscious in his works. Every thing is distinctly brought home to the mind of the actors in the scene, which is a fault undoubtedly: but then it must be confessed, every thing is brought home in its full force to the mind of the reader also; and we feel the same interest in the story as if it were our own.

Can anything be more beautiful or more affecting than Pamela's reproaches to her "lumpish heart," when she is sent away from her master's at her own request; its lightness, when she is sent for back; the joy which the conviction of the sincerity of his love diffuses in her heart, like the coming on of spring;

the artifice of the stuff gown; the meeting with Lady Davers after her marriage; and the trial scene with her husband? Who ever remained insensible to the passion of Lady Clementina, except Sir Charles Grandison himself, who was the object of it? Clarissa is, however, his masterpiece, if we except Lovelace. If she is fine in herself, she is still finer in his account of her. With that foil, her purity is dazzling indeed: and she who could triumph by her virtue, and the force of her love, over the regality of Lovelace's mind, his wit, his person, his accomplishments, and his spirit, conquers all hearts.

I should suppose that never sympathy more deep or sincere was excited than by the heroine of Richardson son's romance, except by the calamities of real life. The links in this wonderful chain of interest are not more finely wrought, than their whole weight is overwhelming and irresistible. Who can forget the exquisite gradations of her long dying–scene, or the closing of the coffin lid, when Miss Howe comes to take her last leave of her friend; or the heart breaking reflection that Clarissa makes on what was to have been her wedding day? Well does a certain writer exclaim: "Books are a real world, both pure and good, Round which, with tendrils strong as flesh and blood, Our pastime and our happiness may grow!"

Richardson's wit was unlike that of any other writer his humour was so too. Both were the effect of intense activity of mind laboured, and yet completely effectual. I might refer to Lovelace's reception and description of Hickman, when he calls out Death in his ear, as the name of the person with whom Clarissa had fallen in love; and to the scene at the glove shop. What can be more magnificent than his enumeration of his companions: "Belton, so pert and so pimply Tourville, so fair and so foppish!" *etc.* In casuistry this author is quite at home; and, with a boldness greater even than his puritanical severity, has exhausted every topic on virtue and vice.

There is another peculiarity in Richardson, not perhaps so uncommon, which is, his systematically preferring his most insipid characters to his finest, though both were equally his own invention, and he must be supposed to have understood something of their qualities. Thus he preferred the little, selfish, affected, insignificant Miss Byron, to the divine Clementina;

and again, Sir Charles Grandison, to the nobler Lovelace. I have nothing to say in favour of Lovelace's morality; but Sir Charles is the prince of coxcombs, whose eye was never once taken from his own person, and his own virtues; and there is nothing which excites so little sympathy as this excessive egotism.

It remains to speak of Sterne; and I shall do it in few words. There is more of mannerism and affectation in him, and a more immediate reference to preceding authors; but his excellences, where he is excellent, are of the first order. His characters are intellectual and inventive, like Richardson's; but totally opposite in the execution. The one are made out by continuity, and patient repetition of touches: the others, by glancing transitions and graceful apposition.

His works consist only of morceaux of brilliant passages. I wonder that Goldsmith, who ought to have known better, should call him "a dull fellow." His wit is poignant, though artificial; and his characters (though the groundwork of some of them had been laid before) have yet invaluable original differences; and the spirit of the execution, the masterstrokes constantly thrown into them, are not to be surpassed. It is sufficient to name them; Yorick, Dr. Slop, Mr. Shandy, My Uncle Toby, Trim, Susanna, and the Widow Wadman. In these he has contrived to oppose, with equal felicity and originality, two characters, one of pure intellect, and the other of pure good nature, in My Father and My Uncle Toby. There appears to have been in Sterne a vein of dry, sarcastic humour, and of extreme tenderness of feeling; the latter sometimes carried to affectation, as in the tale of Maria, and the apostrophe to the recording angel: but at other times pure, and without blemish. The story of Le Fevre is perhaps the finest in the English language.

My Father's restlessness, both of body and mind, is inimitable. It is the model from which all those despicable performances against modern philosophy ought to have been copied, if their authors had known any thing of the subject they were writing about. My Uncle Toby is one of the finest compliments ever paid to human nature. He is the most unoffending of God's creatures; or, as the French express it, un tel petit bon homme! Of his bowling green, his sieges, and his amours, who would say or think any thing amiss!

8

Character of Mr. Burke, 1807

The following speech is perhaps the fairest specimen I could give of Mr. Burke's various talents as a speaker. The subject itself is not the most interesting, nor does it admit of that weight and closeness of reasoning which he displayed on other occasions. But there is no single speech which can convey a satisfactory idea of his powers of mind: to do him justice, it would be necessary to quote all his works; the only specimen of Burke is, all that he wrote. With respect to most other speakers, a specimen is generally enough, or more than enough.

When you are acquainted with their manner, and see what proficiency they have made in the mechanical exercise of their profession, with what facility they can borrow a simile, or round a period, how dexterously they can argue, and object, and rejoin, you are satisfied; there is no other difference in their speeches than what arises from the difference of the subjects.

But this was not the case with Burke. He brought his subjects along with him; he drew his materials from himself. The only limits which circumscribed his variety were the stores of his own mind. His stock of ideas did not consist of a few meagre facts, meagrely stated, of half a dozen common places tortured in a thousand different ways: but his mine of wealth was a profound understanding, inexhaustible as the human heart, and various as the sources of nature. He therefore enriched every subject to which he applied himself, and new subjects were only the occasions of calling forth fresh powers of mind which had not been before exerted.

It would therefore be in vain to look for the proof of his powers in any one of his speeches or writings: they all contain some additional proof of power. In speaking of Burke, then, I shall speak of the whole compass and circuit of his mind not of that small part or section of him which I have been able to give: to do otherwise would be like the story of the man who put the brick in his pocket, thinking to shew it as the model of a house. I have been able to manage pretty well with respect to all my other speakers, and curtailed them down without remorse. It was easy to reduce them within certain limits, to fix their spirit, and condense their variety; by having a certain quantity given, you might infer all the rest; it was only the same thing over again. But who can bind Proteus, or confine the roving flight of genius?

Burke's writings are better than his speeches, and indeed his speeches are writings. But he seemed to feel himself more at ease, to have a fuller possession of his faculties in addressing the public, than in addressing the House of Commons. Burke was raised into public life: and he seems to have been prouder of this new dignity than became so great a man. For this reason, most of his speeches have a sort of parliamentary preamble to them: there is an air of affected modesty, and ostentatious trifling in them: he seems fond of coqueting with the House of Commons, and is perpetually calling the Speaker out to dance a minuet with him, before he begins.

There is also something like an attempt to stimulate the superficial dulness of his hearers by exciting their surprise, by running into extravagance: and he sometimes demeans himself by condescending to what may be considered as bordering too much upon buf foonery, for the amusement of the company. Those lines of Milton were admirably applied to him by some one "The elephant to make them sport wreathed his proboscis lithe." The truth is, that he was out of his place in the House of Commons; he was eminently qualified to shine as a man of genius, as the instructor of mankind, as the brightest luminary of his age: but he had nothing in common with that motley crew of knights, citizens, and burgesses.

He could not be said to be "native and endued unto that element." He was above it; and never appeared like himself, but when, forgetful of the idle clamours of party, and of the little views of little men, he appealed to his country, and the enlightened judgment of mankind.

I am not going to make an idle panegyric on Burke (he has no need of it); but I cannot help looking upon him as the chief boast and ornament of the English House of Commons. What has been said of him is, I think, strictly true, that "he was the most eloquent man of his time: his wisdom was greater than his eloquence." The only public man that in my opinion can be put in any competition with him, is Lord Chatham: and he moved in a sphere so very remote, that it is almost impossible to compare them. But though it would perhaps be difficult to determine which of them excelled most in his particular way, there is nothing in the world more easy than to point out in what their peculiar excellences consisted.

They were in every respect the reverse of each other. Chatham's eloquence was popular: his wisdom was altogether plain and practical. Burke's eloquence was that of the poet; of the man of high and unbounded fancy: his wisdom was profound and contemplative. Chatham's eloquence was calculated to make men act; Burke's was calculated to make them think. Chatham could have roused the fury of a multitude, and wielded their physical energy as he pleased: Burke's eloquence carried conviction into the mind of the retired and lonely student, opened the recesses of the human breast, and lighted up the face of nature around him. Chatham supplied his hearers with motives to immediate action: Burke furnished them with reasons for action which might have little effect upon them at the time, but for which they would be the wiser and better all their lives after.

In research, in originality, in variety of knowledge, in richness of invention, in depth and comprehension of mind, Burke had as much the advantage of Lord Chatham as he was excelled by him in plain common sense, in strong feeling, in steadiness of purpose, in vehemence, in warmth, in enthusiasm, and energy of mind. Burke was the man of genius, of fine sense, and subtle reasoning; Chatham was a man of clear understanding, of strong sense, and violent passions. Burke's mind was satisfied with speculation: Chatham's was essentially active: it could not rest without an object. The power which governed Burke's mind was his Imagination; that which gave its impetus to Chathamn's was Will. The one was almost the creature of pure intellect, the other of physical temperament.

There are two very different ends which a man of genius may propose to himself either in writing or speaking, and which will accordingly give birth to very different styles. He can have but one of these two objects; either to enrich or strengthen the mind; either to furnish us with new ideas, to lead the mind into new trains of thought, to which it was before unused, and which it was incapable of striking out for itself; or else to collect and embody what we already knew, to rivet our old impressions more deeply; to make what was before plain still plainer, and to give to that which was familiar all the effect of novelty.

In the one case we receive an accession to the stock of our ideas; in the other, an additional degree of life and energy is infused into them: our thoughts continue to flow in the same channels, but their pulse is quickened and invigorated. I do not know how to distinguish these different styles better than by calling them severally the inventive and refined, or the impressive and vigorous styles. It is only the subjectmatter of eloquence, however, which is allowed to be remote or obscure. The things in themselves may be subtle and recondite, but they must be dragged out of their obscurity and brought struggling to the light; they must be rendered plain and palpable, (as far as it is in the wit of man to do so) or they are no longer eloquence.

That which by its natural impenetrability, and in spite of every effort, remains dark and difficult, which is impervious to every ray, on which the imagination can shed no lustre, which can be clothed with no beauty, is not a subject for the orator or poet. At the same time it cannot be expected that abstract truths or profound observations should ever be placed in the same strong and dazzling points of view as natural objects and mere matters of fact. It is enough if they receive a reflex and borrowed lustre, like that which cheers the first dawn of morning, where the effect of surprise and novelty gilds every object, and the joy of beholding another world gradually emerging out of the gloom of night, "a new creation rescued from his reign," fills the mind with a sober rapture.

Philosophical eloquence is in writing what chiaro scuro is in painting; he would be a fool who should object that the colours in the shaded part of a picture were not so bright as those on the opposite side; the eye of the connoisseur receives an equal delight from both, balancing the want of brilliancy and effect with the greater delicacy of the tints, and difficulty of the execution. In judging of Burke, therefore, we are to consider first the style of eloquence which he adopted, and secondly the effects which he produced with it. If he did not produce the same effects on vulgar minds, as some others have done, it was not for want of power, but from the turn and direction of his mind.

It was because his subjects, his ideas, his arguments, were less vulgar. The question is not whether he brought certain truths equally home to us, but how much nearer he brought them than they were before. In my opinion, he united the two extremes of refinement and strength in a higher degree than any other writer whatever.

The subtlety of his mind was undoubtedly that which rendered Burke a less popular writer and speaker than he otherwise would have been. It weakened the impression of his observations upon others, but I cannot admit that it weakened the observations themselves; that it took anything from their real weight and solidity. Coarse minds think all that is subtle, futile: that because it is not gross and obvious and palpable to the senses, it is therefore light and frivolous, and of no importance in the real affairs of life; thus making their own confined understandings the measure of truth, and supposing that whatever they do not distinctly perceive, is nothing.

Seneca, who was not one of the vulgar; also says, that subtle truths are those which have the least substance in them, and consequently approach nearest to nonentity. But for my own part I cannot help thinking that the most important truths must be the most refined and subtle; for that very reason, that they must comprehend a great number of particulars, and instead of referring to any distinct or positive fact, must point out the combined effects of an extensive chain of causes, operating gradually, remotely, and collectively, and therefore imperceptibly.

General principles are not the less true or important because from their nature they elude immediate observation; they are like the air, which is not the less necessary because we neither see nor feel it, or like that secret influence which binds the world together, and holds the planets in their orbits. The very same persons who are the most forward to laugh at all systematic reasoning as idle and impertinent, you will the next moment hear exclaiming bitterly against the baleful effects of new fangled systems of philosophy, or gravely descanting on the immense importance of instilling sound principles of morality into the mind. It would not be a bold conjecture, but an obvious truism to say, that all the great changes which have been brought about in the moral world, either for the better or worse, have been introduced not by the bare statement of facts, which are things already known, and which must always operate nearly in the same manner, but by the development of certain opinions and abstract principles of reasoning on life and manners, on the origin of society and man's nature in general, which being obscure and uncertain, vary from time to time, and produce correspondent changes in the human mind. They are the wholesome dew and rain, or the mildew and pestilence that silently destroy. To this principle of generalisation all religious creeds, the institutions of wise lawgivers, and the systems of philosophers, owe their influence.

It has always been with me a test of the sense and candour of any one belonging to the opposite party, whether he allowed Burke to be a great man. Of all the persons of this description that I have ever known, I never met with above one or two who would make this concession; whether it was that party feelings ran too high to admit of any real candour, or whether it was owing to an essential vulgarity in their habits of thinking, they all seemed to be of opinion that he was a wild enthusiast, or a hollow sophist, who was to be answered by bits of facts, by smart logic, by shrewd questions, and idle songs.

They looked upon him as a man of disordered intellects, because he reasoned in a style to which they had not been used and which confounded their dim perceptions. If you said that though you differed with him in sentiment, yet you thought him an admirable reasoner, and a close observer of human nature, you were answered with a loud laugh, and some hackneyed quotation. "Alas! Leviathan was not so tamed!" They did not know whom they had to contend with. The corner stone, which the builders rejected, became the head corner, though to the Jews a stumbling block, and to the Greeks foolishness; for indeed I cannot discover that he was much better understood by those of his own party, if we may judge from the little affinity there is between his mode of reasoning and theirs. The simple clue to all his reasonings on politics is, I think, as follows. He did not agree with some writers, that that mode of government is necessarily the best which is the cheapest.

He saw in the construction of society other principles at work, and other capacities of fulfilling the desires, and perfecting the nature of man, besides those of securing the equal enjoyment of the means of animal life, and doing this at as little expense as possible. He thought that the wants and happiness of men were not to be provided for, as we provide for those of a herd of cattle, merely by attending to their physical necessities. He thought more nobly of his fellows. He knew that man had affections and passions and powers of imagination, as well as hunger and thirst and the sense of heat and cold.

He took his idea of political society from the pattern of private life, wishing, as he himself expresses it, to incorporate the domestic charities with the orders of the state, and to blend them together. He strove to establish an analogy between the compact that binds together the community at large, and that which binds together the several families that compose it. He knew that the rules that form the basis of private morality are not founded in reason, that is, in the abstract properties of those things which are the subjects of them, but in the nature of man, and his capacity of being affected by certain things from habit, from imagination, and sentiment, as well as from reason.

Thus, the reason why a man ought to be attached to his wife and children is not, surely, that they are better than others, (for in this case every one else ought to be of the same opinion) but because he must be chiefly interested in those things which are nearest to him, and with which he is best acquainted, since his understanding cannot reach equally to every thing; because he must be most attached to those objects which he has known the longest, and which by their situation have actually affected him the most, not those which in themselves are the most affecting, whether they have ever made any impression on him or no; that is, because he is by his nature the creature of habit and feeling, and because it is reasonable that he should act in conformity to his nature. Burke was so far right in saying that it is no objection to an institution that it is founded in prejudice, but the contrary, if that prejudice is natural and right; that is, if it arises from those circumstances which are properly subjects of feeling and association, not from any defect or perversion of the understanding in those things which fall strictly under its jurisdiction.

On this profound maxim he took his stand. Thus he contended, that the prejudice in favour of nobility was natural and proper, and fit to be encouraged by the positive institutions of society; not on account of the real or personal merit of the individuals, but because such an institution has a tendency to enlarge and raise the mind, to keep alive the memory of past greatness, to connect the different ages of the world together, to carry back the imagination over a long tract of time, and feed it with the contemplation of remote events: because it is natural to think highly of that which inspires us with high thoughts, which has been connected for many generations with splendour, and affluence, and dignity, and power, and privilege.

He also conceived, that by transferring the respect from the person to the thing, and thus rendering it steady and permanent, the mind would be habitually formed to sentiments of deference, attachment, and fealty, to whatever else demanded its respect: that it would be led to fix its view on what was elevated and lofty, and be weaned from that low and narrow jealousy which never willingly or heartily admits of any superiority in others, and is glad of every opportunity to bring down all excellence to a level with its own miserable standard. Nobility did not therefore exist to the prejudice of the other orders of the state, but by, and for them. The inequality of the different orders of society did not destroy the unity and harmony of the whole. The health and well being of the moral world was to be promoted by the same means as the beauty of the natural world; by contrast, by change, by light and shade, by variety of parts, by order and proportion.

To think of reducing all mankind to the same insipid level, seemed to him the same absurdity as to destroy the inequalities of surface in a country, for the benefit of agriculture and commerce. In short, he believed that the interests of men in society should be consulted, and their several stations and employments assigned, with a view to their nature, not as physical, but as moral beings, so as to nourish their hopes, to lift their imagination, to enliven their fancy, to rouse their activity, to strengthen their virtue, and to furnish the greatest number of objects of pursuit and means of enjoyment to beings constituted as man is, consistently with the order and stability of the whole.

The same reasoning might be extended farther. I do not say that his arguments are conclusive; but they are profound and true, as far as they go. There may be disadvantages and abuses necessarily interwoven with his scheme, or opposite advantages of infinitely greater value, to be derived from another order of things and state of society.

This however does not invalidate either the truth or importance of Burke's reasoning; since the advantages he points out as connected with the mixed form of government are really and necessarily inherent in it: since they are compatible in the same degree with no other; since the principle itself on which he rests his argument (whatever we may think of the application) is of the utmost weight and moment; and since on whichever side the truth lies, it is impossible to make a fair decision without having the opposite side of the question clearly and fully stated to us. This Burke has done in a masterly manner. He presents to you one view or face of society. Let him, who thinks he can, give the reverse side with equal force, beauty, and clearness. It is said, I know, that truth is one; but to this I cannot subscribe, for it appears to me that truth is many. There are as many truths as there are things and causes of action and contradictory principles at work in society. In making up the account of good and evil, indeed, the final result must be one way or the other; but the particulars on which that result depends are infinite and various.

It will be seen from what I have said, that I am very far from agreeing with those who think that Burke was a man without understanding, and a merely florid writer. There are two causes which have given rise to this calumny; namely, that narrowness of mind which leads men to suppose that the truth lies entirely on the side of their own opinions, and that whatever does not make for them is absurd and irrational; secondly, a trick we have of confounding reason with judgment, and supposing that it is merely the province of the understanding to pronounce sentence, and not to give in evidence, or argue the case; in short, that it is a passive, not an active faculty. Thus there are persons who never run into any extravagance, because they are so buttressed up with the opinions of others on all sides, that they cannot lean much to one side or the other; they are so little moved with any kind of reasoning, that they remain at an equal distance from every extreme, and are never very far from the truth, because the slowness of their faculties will not suffer them to make much progress in error. These are persons of great judgment. The scales of the mind are pretty sure to remain even, when there is nothing in them.

In this sense of the word, Burke must be allowed to have wanted judgment, by all those who think that he was wrong in his conclusions. The accusation of want of judgment, in fact, only means that you yourself are of a different opinion. But if in arriving at one error he discovered a hundred truths, I should consider myself a hundred times more indebted to him than if, stumbling on that which I consider as the right side of the question, he had committed a hundred absurdities in striving to establish his point. I speak of him now merely as an author, or as far as I and other readers are concerned with him; at the same time, I should not differ from any one who may be disposed to contend that the consequences of his writings as instruments of political power have been tremendous, fatal, such as no exertion of wit or knowledge or genius can ever counteract or atone for.

Burke also gave a hold to his antagonists by mixing up sentiment and imagery with his reasoning; so that being unused to such a sight in the region of politics, they were deceived, and could not discern the fruit from the flowers. Gravity is the cloke of wisdom; and those who have nothing else think it an insult to affect the one without the other, because it destroys the only foundation on which their pretensions are built.

The easiest part of reason is dulness; the generality of the world are therefore concerned in discouraging any example of unnecessary brilliancy that might tend to show that the two things do not always go together. Burke in some measure dissolved the spell. It was discovered, that his gold was not the less valuable for being wrought into elegant shapes, and richly embossed with curious figures; that the solidity of a building is not destroyed by adding to it beauty and ornament; and that the strength of a man's understanding is not always to be estimated in exact proportion to his want of imagination. His understanding was not the less real, because it was not the only faculty he possessed. He justified the description of the poet: "How charming is divine philosophy! Not harsh and crabbed as dull fools suppose, But musical as is Apollo's lute!"

Those who object to this union of grace and beauty with reason, are in fact weak sighted people, who cannot distinguish the noble and majestic form of Truth from that of her sister Folly, if they are dressed both alike! But there is always a difference even in the adventitious ornaments they wear, which is sufficient to distinguish them.

Burke was so far from being a gaudy or flowery writer, that he was one of the severest writers we have. His words are the most like things; his style is the most strictly suited to the subject. He unites every extreme and every variety of composition; the lowest and the meanest words and descriptions with the highest. He exults in the display of power, in shewing the extent, the force, and intensity of his ideas; he is led on by the mere impulse and vehemence of his fancy, not by the affectation of dazzling his readers by gaudy conceits or pompous images.

He was completely carried away by his subject. He had no other object but to produce the strongest impression on his reader, by giving the truest, the most characteristic, the fullest, and most forcible description of things, trusting to the power of his own mind to mould them into grace and beauty. He did not produce a splendid effect by setting fire to the light vapours that float in the regions of fancy, as the chemists make fine colours with phosphorus, but by the eagerness of his blows struck fire from the flint, and melted the hardest substances in the furnace of his imagination. The wheels of his imagination did not catch fire from the rottenness of the materials, but from the rapidity of their motion. One would suppose, to hear people talk of Burke, that his style was such as would have suited the "Lady's Magazine"; soft, smooth, showy, tender, insipid, full of fine words, without any meaning.

The essence of the gaudy or glittering style consists in producing a momentary effect by fine words and images brought together, without order or connexion. Burke most frequently produced an effect by the remoteness and novelty of his combinations, by the force of contrast, by the striking manner in which the most opposite and unpromising materials were harmoniously blended together; not by laying his hands on all the fine things he could think of, but by bringing together those things which he knew would blaze out into glorious light by their collision. The florid style is a mixture of affectation and common place. Burke's was an union of untameable vigour and originality.

Burke was not a verbose writer. If he sometimes multiplies words, it is not for want of ideas, but because there are no words that fully express his ideas, and he tries to do it as well as he can by different ones. He had nothing of the set or formal style, the measured cadence, and stately phraseology of Johnson, and most of our modern writers. This style, which is what we understand by the artificial, is all in one key. It selects a certain set of words to represent all ideas whatever, as the most dignified and elegant, and excludes all others as low and vulgar.

The words are not fitted to the things, but the things to the words. Every thing is seen through a false medium. It is putting a mask on the face of nature, which may indeed hide some specks and blemishes, but takes away all beauty, delicacy, and variety. It destroys all dignity or elevation, because nothing can be raised where all is on a level, and completely destroys all force, expression, truth, and character, by arbitrarily confounding the differences of things, and reducing every thing to the same insipid standard. To suppose that this stiff uniformity can add any thing to real grace or dignity, is like supposing that the human body in order to be perfectly graceful, should never deviate from its upright posture.

Another mischief of this method is, that it confounds all ranks in literature. Where there is no room for variety, no discrimination, no nicety to be shewn in matching the idea with its proper word, there can be no room for taste or elegance. A man must easily learn the art of writing, when every sentence is to be cast in the same mould: where he is only allowed the use of one word, he cannot choose wrong, nor will he be in much danger of making himself ridiculous by affectation or false glitter, when, whatever subject he treats of, he must treat of it in the same way. This indeed is to wear golden chains for the sake of ornament. Burke was altogether free from the pedantry which I have here endeavoured to expose. His style was as original, as expressive, as rich and varied, as it was possible; his combinations were as exquisite, as playful, as happy, as unexpected, as bold and daring, as his fancy. If any thing, he ran into the opposite extreme of too great an inequality, if truth and nature could ever be carried to an extreme.

Those who are best acquainted with the writings and speeches of Burke will not think the praise I have here bestowed on them exaggerated. Some proof will be found of this in the following extracts. But the full proof must be sought in his works at large, and particularly in the "Thoughts on the Discontents"; in his "Reflections on the French Revolution"; in his "Letter to the Duke of Bedford"; and in the "Regicide Peace."

The two last of these are perhaps the most remarkable of all his writings, from the contrast they afford to each other. The one is the most delightful exhibition of wild and brilliant fancy, that is to be found in English prose, but it is too much like a beautiful picture painted upon gauze; it wants something to support it: the other is without ornament, but it has all the solidity, the weight, the gravity of a judicial record. It seems to have been written with a certain constraint upon himself, and to shew those who said he could not reason, that his arguments might be stripped of their ornaments without losing any thing of their force. It is certainly, of all his works, that in which he has shewn most power of logical deduction, and the only one in which he has made any important use of facts.

In general he certainly paid little attention to them: they were the playthings of his mind. He saw them as he pleased, not as they were; with the eye of the philosopher or the poet, regarding them only in their general principle, or as they might serve to decorate his subject.

This is the natural consequence of much imagination: things that are probable are elevated into the rank of realities. To those who can reason on the essences of things, or who can invent according to nature, the experimental proof is of little value. This was the case with Burke. In the present instance, however, he seems to have forced his mind into the service of facts: and he succeeded completely.

His comparison between our connection with France or Algiers, and his account of the conduct of the war, are as clear, as convincing, as forcible examples of this kind of reasoning, as are any where to be met with. Indeed I do not think there is any thing in Fox (whose mind was purely historical) or in Chatham, (who attended to feelings more than facts) that will bear a comparison with them.

Burke has been compared to Cicero, I do not know for what reason. Their excellences are as different, and indeed as opposite, as they well can be. Burke had not the polished elegance, the glossy neatness, the artful regularity, the exquisite modulation of Cicero: he had a thousand times more richness and originality of mind, more strength and pomp of diction.

It has been well observed, that the ancients had no word that properly expresses what we mean by the word genius. They perhaps had not the thing. Their minds appear to have been too exact, too retentive, too minute and subtle, too sensible to the external differences of things, too passive under their impressions, to admit of those bold and rapid combinations, those lofty flights of fancy, which, glancing from heaven to earth, unite the most opposite extremes, and draw the happiest illustrations from things the most remote. Their ideas were kept too confined and distinct by the material form or vehicle in which they were conveyed, to unite cordially together, or be melted down in the imagination.

Their metaphors are taken from things of the same class, not from things of different classes; the general analogy, not the individual feeling, directs them in their choice. Hence, as Dr. Johnson observed, their similes are either repetitions of the same idea, or so obvious and general as not to lend any additional force to it; as when a huntress is compared to Diana, or a warrior rushing into battle to a lion rushing on his prey. Their forte was exquisite art and perfect imitation. Witness their statues and other things of the same kind. But they had not that high and enthusiastic fancy which some of our own writers have shewn. For the proof of this, let any one compare Milton and Shakspeare with Homer and Sophocles, or Burke with Cicero.

It may be asked whether Burke was a poet. He was so only in the general vividness of his fancy, and in richness of invention. There may be poetical passages in his works, but I certainly think that his writings in general are quite distinct from poetry; and that for the reason before given, namely, that the subject-matter of them is not poetical. The finest part of them are illustrations or personifications of dry abstract ideas; and the union between the idea and the illustration is not of that perfect and pleasing kind as to constitute poetry, or indeed to be admissible, but for the effect intended to be produced by it; that is, by every means in our power to give animation and attraction to subjects in themselves barren of ornament, but which at the same time are pregnant with the most important consequences, and in which the understanding and the passions are equally interested.

I have heard it remarked by a person, to whose opinion I would sooner submit than to a general council of critics, that the sound of Burke's prose is not musical; that it wants cadence; and that instead of being so lavish of his imagery as is generally supposed, he seemed to him to be rather parsimonious in the use of it, always expanding and making the most of his ideas. This may be true if we compare him with some of our poets, or perhaps with some of our early prose writers, but not if we compare him with any of our political writers or parliamentary speakers. There are some very fine things of Lord Bolingbroke's on the same subjects, but not equal to Burke's. As for Junius, he is at the head of his class; but that class is not the highest. He has been said to have more dignity than Burke. Yes if the stalk of a giant is less dignified than the strut of a petit maitre. I do not mean to speak disrespectfully of Junius, but grandeur is not the character of his composition; and if it is not to be found in Burke, it is to be found nowhere.

Wants cadence; and that instead of being so lavish of his imagery as is generally supposed, he seemed to him to be rather parsimonious in the use of it, always expanding and making the most of his ideas. This may be true if we compare him with some of our poets, or perhaps with some of our early prose writers, but not if we compare him with any of our political writers or parliamentary speakers. There are some very fine things of Lord Bolingbroke's on the same subjects, but not equal to Burke's. As for Junius, he is at the head of his class; but that class is not the highest. He has been said to have more dignity than Burke.

It is one of the innovations of the time. It partakes of, and is carried along with, the revolutionary movement of our age: the political changes of the day were the model on which he formed and conducted his poetical experiments. His Muse (it cannot be denied, and without this we cannot explain its character at all) is a levelling one. It proceeds on a principle of equality, and strives to reduce all things to the same standard. It is distinguished by a proud humility. It relies upon its own resources, and disdains external show and relief. It takes the commonest events and objects, as a test to prove that nature is always interesting from its inherent truth and beauty, without any of the ornaments of dress or pomp of circumstances to set it off.

Hence the unaccountable mixture of seeming simplicity and real abstruseness in the Lyrical Ballads. Fools have laughed at, wise men scarcely understand them. He takes a subject or a story merely as pegs or loops to hang thought and feeling on; the incidents are trifling, in proportion to his contempt for imposing appearances; the reflections are profound, according to the gravity and aspiring pretensions of his mind.

His popular, inartificial style gets rid (at a blow) of all the trappings of verse, of all the high places of poetry: "the cloud capt towers, the solemn temples, the gorgeous through the withered fern. No sad vicissitude of fate, no overwhelming catastrophe in nature deforms his page: but the dewdrop glitters on the bending flower, the tear collects in the glistening' eye. "Beneath the hills, along the flowery vales, The generations are prepared; the pangs, The internal pangs are ready; the dread strife Of poor humanity's afflicted will, Struggling in vain with ruthless destiny." As the lark ascends from its low bed on fluttering wing, and salutes the morning skies; so Mr. Wordsworthes unpretending Muse, in russet guise, scales the summits of reflection, while it makes the round earth its footstool, and its home!

Possibly a good deal of this may be regarded as the effect of disappointed views and an inverted ambition. Prevented by native pride and indolence from climbing the ascent of learning or greatness, taught by political opinions to say to the vain pomp and glory of the world, "I hate ye," seeing the path of classical and artificial poetry blocked up by the cumbrous ornaments of style and turgid commonplaces, so that nothing more could be achieved in that direction but by the most ridiculous bombast or the tamest servility; he has turned back partly from the bias of his mind, partly perhaps from a judicious policy has struck into the sequestered vale of humble life, sought out the Muse among sheep cotes and hamlets and the peasant's mountain haunts, has discarded all the tinsel pageantry of verse, and endeavoured (not in vain) to aggrandise the trivial and add the charm of novelty to the familiar.

No one has shown the same imagination in raising trifles into importance: no one has displayed the same pathos in treating of the simplest feelings of the heart. Reserved, yet haughty, having no unruly or violent passions, (or those passions having been early suppressed,) Mr. Wordsworth has passed his life in solitary musing, or in daily converse with the face of nature. He exemplifies in an eminent degree the power of association; for his poetry has no other source or character. He has dwelt among pastoral scenes, till each object has become connected with a thousand feelings, a link in the chain of thought, a fibre of his own heart.

Every one is by habit and familiarity strongly attached to the place of his birth, or to objects that recall the most pleasing and eventful circumstances of his life. But to the author of the Lyrical Ballads, nature is a kind of home; and he may be said to take a personal interest in the universe. There is no image so insignificant that it has not in some mood or other found the way into his heart: no sound that does not awaken the memory of other years: "To him the meanest flower that blows can give Thoughts that do often lie too deep for tears."

The daisy looks up to him with sparkling eye as an old acquaintance: the cuckoo haunts him with sounds of early youth not to be expressed: a linnet's nest startles him with boyish delight: an old withered thorn is weighed down with a heap of recollections: a grey cloak, seen on some wild moor, torn by the wind, or drenched in the rain, afterwards becomes an object of imagination to him: even the lichens on the rock have a life and being in his thoughts. He has described all these objects in a way and with an intensity of feeling that no one else had done before him, and has given a new view or aspect of nature.

He is in this sense the most original poet now living, and the one whose writings could the least be spared: for they have no substitute elsewhere. The vulgar do not read them, the learned, who see all things through books, do not understand them; the great despise, the fashionable may ridicule them: but the author has created himself an interest in the heart of the retired and lonely student of nature, which can never die. Persons of this class will still continue to feel what he has felt: he has expressed what they might in vain wish to express, except with glistening eye and faultering tongue! There is a lofty philosophic tone, a thoughtful humanity, infused into his pastoral vein. Remote from the passions and events of the great world, he has communicated interest and dignity to the primal movements of the heart of man, and ingrafted his own conscious reflections on the casual thoughts of hinds and shepherds. Nursed amidst the grandeur of mountain scenery, he has stooped to have a nearer view of the daisy under his feet, or plucked a branch of white thorn from the spray: but in describing it, his mind seems imbued with the majesty and solemnity of the objects around him the tall rock lifts its head in the erectness of his spirit; the cataract roars in the sound of his verse; and in its dim and mysterious meaning, the mists seem to gather in the hollows of Helvellyn, and the forked Skiddaw hovers in the distance. There is little mention of mountainous scenery in Mr. Wordsworthes poetry; but by internal evidence one might be almost sure that it is written in a mountainous country, from its bareness, its simplicity, its loftiness, and its depth!

His later philosophic productions have a somewhat different character. They are a departure from, a dereliction of his first principles. They are classical and courtly. They are polished in style, without being gaudy; dignified in subject, without affectation. They seem to have been composed not in a cottage at Grasmere, but among the halfinspired groves and stately recollections of Cole–Orton. We might allude in particular, for examples of what we mean, to the lines on a Picture by Claude Lorraine, and to the exquisite poem, entitled Laodamia. The last of these breathes the pure spirit of the finest fragments of antiquity, the sweetness, the gravity, the strength, the beauty and the languor of death: "Calm contemplation and majestic pains."

Its glossy brilliancy arises from the perfection of the finishing, like that of careful sculpture, not from gaudy colouring, the texture of the thoughts has the smoothness and solidity of marble. It is a poem that might be read aloud in Elysium, and the spirits of departed heroes and sages would gather round to listen to it! Mr. Wordsworthes philosophic poetry, with a less glowing aspect and less tumult in the veins than Lord Byron's on similar occasions, bends a calmer and keener eye on mortality; the impression, if less vivid, is more pleasing and permanent; and we confess it (perhaps it is a want of taste and proper feeling) that there are lines and poems of our author's, that we think of ten times for once that we recur to any of Lord Byron's.

Or if there are any of the latter's writings, that we can dwell upon in the same way, that is, as lasting and heart felt sentiments, it is when, laying aside his usual pomp and pretension, he descends with Mr. Wordsworth to the common ground of a disinterested humanity. It may be considered as characteristic of our poet's writings, that they either make no impression on the mind at all, seem mere nonsense verses, or that they leave a mark behind them that never wears out. They either

"Fall blunted from the indurated breast", without any perceptible result, or they absorb it like a passion. To one class of readers he appears sublime, to another (and, we fear the largest) ridiculous. He has probably realised Milton's wish, "and fit audience found, though few:" but we suspect he is not reconciled to the alternative. There are delightful passages in the Excursion, both of natural description and of inspired reflection (passages of the latter kind that in the sound of the thoughts and of the swelling language resemble heavenly symphonies, mournful requiems over the grave of human hopes); but we must add, in justice and in sincerity, that we think it impossible that this work should ever become popular, even in the same degree as the Lyrical Ballads. It affects a system without having any intelligible clue to one; and instead of unfolding a principle in various and striking lights, repeats the same conclusions till they become flat and insipid. Mr. Wordsworthes mind is obtuse, except as it is the organ and the receptacle of accumulated feelings: it is not analytic, but synthetic; it is reflecting, rather than theoretical. The Excursion, we believe, fell still born from the press. There was something abortive, and clumsy, and ill judged in the attempt. It was long and laboured.

The personages, for the most part, were low, the fare rustic: the plan raised expectations which were not fulfilled, and the effect was like being ushered into a stately hall and invited to sit down to a splendid banquet in the company of clowns, and with nothing but successive courses of apple dumplings served up. It was not even toujours perdrix!

Mr. Wordsworth, in his person, is above the middle size, with marked features, and an air somewhat stately and Quixotic. He reminds one of some of Holbein's heads, grave, saturnine, with a slight indication of sly humour, kept under by the manners of the age or by the pretensions of the person. He has a peculiar sweetness in his smile, and great depth and manliness and a rugged harmony, in the tones of his voice. His manner of reading his own poetry is particularly imposing; and in his favourite passages his eye beams with preternatural lustre, and the meaning labours slowly up from his swelling breast. No one who has seen him at these moments could go away with an impression that he was a "man of no mark or likelihood."

Perhaps the comment of his face and voice is necessary to convey a full idea of his poetry. His language may not be intelligible, but his manner is not to be mistaken. It is clear that he is either mad or inspired. In company, even in a tete-a-tete, Mr. Wordsworth is often silent, indolent, and reserved. If he is become verbose and oracular of late years, he was not so in his better days. He threw out a bold or an indifferent remark without either effort or pretension, and relapsed into musing again. He shone most (because he seemed most roused and animated) in reciting his own poetry, or in talking about it. He sometimes gave striking views of his feelings and trains of association in composing certain passages; or if one did not always understand his distinctions, still there was no want of interest there was a latent meaning worth inquiring into, like a vein of ore that one cannot exactly hit upon at the moment, but of which there are sure indications. His standard of poetry is high and severe, almost to exclusiveness. He admits of nothing below, scarcely of any thing above himself. It is fine to hear him talk of the way in which certain subjects should have been treated by eminent poets, according to his notions of the art.

Thus he finds fault with Dryden's description of Bacchus in the Alexander's Feast, as if he were a mere good looking youth, or boon companion: "Flushed with a purple grace, He shows his honest face" instead of representing the God returning from the conquest of India, crowned with vine-leaves, and drawn by panthers, and followed by troops of satyrs, of wild men and animals that he had tamed. You would think, in hearing him speak on this subject, that you saw Titian's picture of the meeting of Bacchus and Ariadne so classic were his conceptions, so glowing his style. Milton is his great idol, and he sometimes dares to compare himself with him. His Sonnets, indeed, have something of the same high raised tone and prophetic spirit. Chaucer is another prime favourite of his, and he has been at the pains to modernize some of the Canterbury Tales. Those persons who look upon Mr. Wordsworth as a merely puerile writer, must be rather at a loss to account for his strong predilection for such geniuses as Dante and Michael Angelo.

We do not think our author has any very cordial sympathy with Shakspeare. How should he? Shakspeare was the least of an egotist of anybody in the world. He does not much relish the variety and scope of dramatic composition. "He hates those interlocutions between Lucius and Caius." Yet Mr. Wordsworth himself wrote a tragedy when he was young; and we have heard the following energetic lines quoted from it, as put into the mouth of a person smit with remorse for some rash crime:

"Action is momentary, The motion of a muscle this way or that; Suffering is long, obscure, and infinite!"

Perhaps for want of light and shade, and the unshackled spirit of the drama, this performance was never brought forward. Our critic has a great dislike to Gray, and a fondness for Thomson and Collins. It is mortifying to hear him speak of Pope and Dryden, whom, because they have been supposed to have all the possible excellences of poetry, he will allow to have none. Nothing, however, can be fairer, or more amusing, than the way in which he some times exposes the unmeaning verbiage of modern poetry. Thus, in the beginning of Dr. Johnson Vanity of Human Wishes: "Let observation with extensive view Survey mankind from China to Peru" he says there is a total want of imagination accompanying the words, the same idea is repeated three times under the disguise of a different phraseology: it comes to this " let observation, with extensive observation, observe mankind;" or take away the first line, and the second, "Survey mankind from China to Peru,"

Literally conveys the whole. Mr. Wordsworth is, we must say, a perfect Drawcansir as to prose writers. He complains of the dry reasoners and matter of fact people for their want of passion; and he is jealous of the rhetorical declaimers and rhapsodists as trenching on the province of poetry. He condemns all French writers (as well of poetry as prose) in the lump. His list in this way is indeed small. He approves of Walton's Angler, Paley, and some other writers of an inoffensive modesty of pretension. He also likes books of voyages and travels, and Robinson Crusoe.

In art, he greatly esteems Bewick's woodcuts, and Waterloo's sylvan etchings. But he sometimes takes a higher tone, and gives his mind fair play. We have known him enlarge with a noble intelligence and enthusiasm on Nicolas Poussin's fine landscape compositions, pointing out the unity of design that pervades them, the superintending mind, the imaginative principle that brings all to bear on the same end; and declaring he would not give a rush for any landscape that did not express the time of day, the climate, the period of the world it was meant to illustrate, or had not this character of wholeness in it.

His eye also does justice to Rembrandt's fine and masterly effects. In the way in which that artist works something out of nothing, and transforms the stump of a tree, a common figure into an ideal object, by the gorgeous light and shade thrown upon it, he perceives an analogy to his own mode of investing the minute details of nature with an atmosphere of sentiment; and in pronouncing Rembrandt to be a man of genius, feels that he strengthens his own claim to the title.

It has been said of Mr. Wordsworth, that "he hates conchology, that he hates the Venus of Medicis." But these, we hope, are mere epigrams and jecx–d'esprit, as far from truth as they are free from malice; a sort of running satire or critical clenches: "Where one for sense and one for rhyme Is quite sufficient at one time."

We think, however, that if Mr. Wordsworth had been a more liberal and candid critic, he would have been a more sterling writer. If a greater number of sources of pleasure had been open to him, he would have communicated pleasure to the world more frequently. Had he been less fastidious in pronouncing sentence on the works of others, his own would have been received more favourably, and treated more leniently. The current of his feelings is deep, but narrow; the range of his understanding is lofty and aspiring rather than discursive.

The force, the originality, the absolute truth and identity with which he feels some things, makes him indifferent to so many others. The simplicity and enthusiasm of his feelings, with respect to nature, renders him bigotted and intolerant in his judgments of men and things. But it happens to him, as to others, that his strength lies in his weakness; and perhaps we have no right to complain. We might get rid of the cynic and the egotist, and find in his stead a common place man. We should "take the good the Gods provide us:" a fine and original vein of poetry is not one of their most contemptible gifts, and the rest is scarcely worth thinking of, except as it may be a mortification to those who expect perfection from human nature; or who have been idle enough at some period of their lives, to deify men of genius as possessing claims above it. But this is a chord that jars, and we shall not dwell upon it.

Lord Byron we have called, according to the old proverb, "the spoiled child of fortune:" Mr. Wordsworth might plead, in mitigation of some peculiarities, that he is "the spoiled child of disappointment." We are convinced, if he had been early a popular poet, he would have borne his honours meekly, and would have been a person of great bonhominie and frankness of disposition. But the sense of injustice and of undeserved ridicule sours the temper and narrows the views. To have produced works of genius, and to find them neglected or treated with scorn is one of the heaviest trials of human patience.

We exaggerate our own merits when they are denied by others, and are apt to grudge and cavil at every particle of praise bestowed on those to whom we feel a conscious superiority. In mere self defence we turn against the world, when it turns against us; brood over the undeserved slights we receive; and thus the genial current of the soul is stopped, or vents itself in effusions of petulance and self conceit. Mr. Wordsworth has thought too much of contemporary critics and criticism; and less than he ought of the award of posterity, and of the opinion, we do not say of private friends, but of those who were made so by their admiration of his genius. He did not court popularity by a conformity to established models, and he ought not to have been surprised that his originality was not understood as a matter of course. He has gnawed too much on the bridle; and has often thrown out crusts to the critics, in mere defiance or as a point of honour when he was challenged, which otherwise his own good sense would have withheld. We suspect that Mr. Wordsworthes feelings are a little morbid in this respect, or that he resents censure more than he is gratified by praise. Otherwise, the tide has turned much in his favour of late years he has a large body of determined partisans and is at present sufficiently in request with the public to save or relieve him from the last necessity to which a man of genius can be reduced that of becoming the God of his own idolatry!

9

Mr. Coleridge

The present is an age of talkers, and not of doers; and the reason is, that the world is growing old. We are so far advanced in the Arts and Sciences, that we live in retrospect, and doat on past achievements. The accumulation of knowledge has been so great, that we are lost in wonder at the height it has reached, instead of attempting to climb or add to it; while the variety of objects distracts and dazzles the looker on. What niche remains unoccupied? What path untried? What is the use of doing anything, unless we could do better than all those who have gone before us? What hope is there of this?

We are like those who have been to see some noble monument of art, who are content to admire without thinking of rivalling it; or like guests after a feast, who praise the hospitality of the donor "and thank the bounteous Pan", perhaps carrying away some trifling fragments; or like the spectators of a mighty battle, who still hear its sound afar off, and the clashing of armour and the neighing of the war horse and the shout of victory is in their ears, like the rushing of innumerable waters!

Mr. Coleridge has "a mind reflecting ages past:" his voice is like the echo of the congregated roar of the "dark rearward and abyss" of thought. He who has seen a mouldering tower by the side of a chrystal lake, hid by the mist, but glittering in the wave below, may conceive the dim, gleaming, uncertain intelligence of his eye: he who has marked the evening clouds uprolled (a world of vapours), has seen the picture of his mind, unearthly, unsubstantial, with gorgeous tints and ever varying forms: "That which was now a horse, even with a thought, The rack dislimns, and makes it indistinct As water is in water."

Our author's mind is (as he himself might express it) tangential. There is no subject on which he has not touched, none on which he has rested. With an understanding fertile, subtle, expansive, "quick, forgetive, apprehensive," beyond all living precedent, few traces of it will perhaps remain. He lends himself to all impressions alike; he gives up his mind and liberty of thought to none. He is a general lover of art and science, and wedded to no one in particular. He pursues knowledge as a mistress, with outstretched hands and winged speed; but as he is about to embrace her, his Daphne turns alas! not to a laurel! Hardly a speculation has been left on record from the earliest time, but it is loosely folded up in Mr. Coleridge's memory, like a rich, but somewhat tattered piece of tapestry: we might add (with more seeming than real extravagance), that scarce a thought can pass through the mind of man, but its sound has at some time or other passed over his head with rustling pinions.

On whatever question or author you speak, he is prepared to take up the theme with advantage from Peter Abelard down to Thomas Moore, from the subtlest metaphysics to the politics of the Courier. There is no man of genius, in whose praise he descants, but the critic seems to stand above the author, and "what in him is weak, to strengthen, what is low, to raise and support:" nor is there any work of genius that does not come out of his hands like an illuminated Missal, sparkling even in its defects. If Mr. Coleridge had not been the most impressive talker of his age, he would probably have been the finest writer; but he lays down his pen to make sure of an auditor, and mortgages the admiration of posterity for the stare of an idler. If he had not been a poet, he would have been a powerful logician; if he had not dipped his wing in the Unitarian controversy, he might have soared to the very summit of fancy. But in writing verse, he is' trying to subject the Muse to transcendental theories: in his abstract reasoning, he misses his way by strewing it with flowers.

All that he has done of moment, he had done twenty years ago; since then, he may be said to have lived on the sound of his own voice. Mr. Coleridge is too rich in intellectual wealth, to need to task himself to any drudgery: he has only to draw the sliders of his imagination, and a thousand subjects expand before him, startling him with their brilliancy, or losing themselves in endless obscurity: "And by the force of blear illusion' They draw him on to his confusion." What is the little he could add to the stock, compared with the countless stores that lie about him, that he should stoop to pick up a name, or to polish an idle fancy? He walks abroad in the majesty of an universal understanding, eyeing the "rich strond," or golden sky above him, and "goes sounding on his way," in eloquent accents, uncompelled and free!

Persons of the greatest capacity are often those, who for this reason do the least; for surveying themselves from the highest point of view, amidst the infinite variety of the universe, their own share in it seems trifling, and scarce worth a thought, and they prefer the contemplation of all that is, or has been, or can be, to the making a coil about doing what, when done, is no better than vanity. It is hard to concentrate all our attention and efforts on one pursuit, except from ignorance of others; and without this concentration of our faculties, no great progress can be made in any one thing. It is not merely that the mind is not capable of the effort; it does not think the effort worth making.

Action is one; but thought is manifold. He whose restless eye glances through the wide compass of nature and art, will not consent to have "his own nothings monstered:" but he must do this, before he can give his. whole soul to them. The mind, after "letting contemplation have its fill," or "Sailing with supreme dominion Through the azure deep of air," sinks down on the ground, breathless, exhausted, powerless, inactive; or if it must have some vent to its feelings, seeks the most easy and obvious; is soothed by friendly flattery, lulled by the murmur of immediate applause, thinks as it were aloud, and babbles in its dreams! A scholar (so to speak) is a more disinterested and abstracted character than a mere author. The first looks at the numberless volumes of a library, and says, "All these are mine:" the other points to a single volume (perhaps it may be an immortal one) and says, "My name is written on the back of it." This is a puny and groveling ambition, beneath the lofty amplitude of Mr. Coleridge's mind. No, he revolves in his wayward soul, or utters to the passing wind, or discourses to his own shadow, things mightier and more various! Let us draw the curtain, and unlock the shrine.

Learning rocked him in his cradle, and while yet a child, He lisped in numbers, for the numbers came.

At sixteen he wrote his Ode on Chatterton, and he still reverts to that period with delight, not so much as it relates to himself (for that string of his own early promise of fame rather jars than otherwise) but as exemplifying the youth of a poet. Mr. Coleridge talks of himself, without being an egotist, for in him the individual is always merged in the abstract and general. He distinguished himself at school and at the University by his knowledge of the classics, and gained several prizes for Greek epigrams. How many men are there (great scholars, celebrated names in literature) who having done the same thing in their youth, have no other idea all the rest of their lives but of this achievement, of a fellowship and dinner, and who, installed in academic honours, would look down on our author as a mere strolling bard!

At Christ's Hospital, where he was brought up, he was the idol of those among his schoolfellows, who mingled with their bookish studies the music of thought and of humanity; and he was usually attended round the cloisters by a group of these (inspiring and inspired) whose hearts, even then, burnt within them as he talked, and where the sounds yet linger to mock ELIA on his way, still turning pensive to the past! One of the finest and rarest parts of Mr. Coleridge's conversation, is when he expatiates on the Greek tragedians (not that he is not well acquainted, when he pleases, with the epic poets, or the philosophers, or orators, or historians of antiquity) on the subtle reasonings and melting pathos of Euripides, on the harmonious gracefulness of Sophocles, tuning his love laboured song, like sweetest warblings from a sacred grove; on the high wrought, trumpet tongued eloquence of Aeschylus, whose Prometheus, above all, is like an Ode to Fate, and a pleading with Providence, his thoughts being let loose as his body is chained on his solitary rock, and his afflicted will (the emblem of mortality); "Struggling in vain with ruthless destiny."

As the impassioned critic speaks and rises in his theme, you would think you heard the voice of the Man hated by the Gods, contending with the wild winds as they roar, and his eye glitters with the spirit of Antiquity! Next, he was engaged with Hartley's tribes of mind, "etherial braid, thought woven," and he busied himself for a year or two with vibrations and vibratiuncles, and the great law of association that binds all things in its mystic chain, and the doctrine of Necessity (the mild teacher of Charity) and the Millennium, anticipative of a life to come and he plunged deep into the controversy on Matter and Spirit, and, as an escape from Dr. Priestley's Materialism, where he felt himself imprisoned by the logician's spell, like Ariel in the cloven pine tree, he became suddenly enamoured of Bishop Berkeley's fairy world, and used in all companies to build the universe, like a brave poetical fiction, of fine words and he was deep read in Malebranche, and in Cudworthes Intellectual System (a huge pile of learning, unwieldy, enormous) and in Lord Brook's hieroglyphic theories, and in Bishop Butler's Sermons, and in the Duchess of Newcastle's fantastic folios, and in Clarke and South and Tillotson, and all the fine thinkers and masculine reasoners of that age and Leibnitz's Pre-established Harmony reared its arch above his head, like the rainbow in the cloud, covenanting with the hopes of man and then he fell plump, ten thousand fathoms down (but his wings saved him harmless) into the hortus siccus of Dissent, where he pared religion down to the standard of reason, and stripped faith of mystery, and preached Christ crucified and the Unity of the Godhead, and so dwelt for a while in the spirit of John Huss and Jerome offs Prague and Socinus and old John Zisca, and ran through Neal's History of the Puritans, and Calamy's Non-Conformists' Memorial, having like thoughts and passions with them but then Spinoza became his God, and he took up the vast chain of being in his hand, and the round world became the centre and the soul of all things in some shadowy sense, forlorn of meaning, and around him he beheld the living traces and the sky–pointing proportions of the mighty Pan but poetry redeemed him from this spectral philosophy, and he bathed his heart in beauty, and gazed at the golden light of heaven, and drank of the spirit of the universe, and wandered at eve by fairy stream or fountain,

"When he saw nought but beauty, When he heard the voice of that Almighty One In every breeze that blew, or wave that murmured" and wedded with truth in Plato's shade, and in the writings of Proclus and Plotinus saw the ideas of things in the eternal mind, and unfolded all mysteries with the Schoolmen and fathomed the depths of Duns Scotus and Thomas Aquinas, and entered the third heaven with Jacob Behmen, and walked hand in hand with Swedenborg through the pavilions of the New Jerusalem, and sung his faith in the promise and in the word in his Religious Musings and lowering himself from that dizzy height, poised himself on Milton's wings, and spread out his thoughts in charity with the glad prose of Jeremy Taylor, and wept over Bowles's Sonnets, and studied Cowper's blank verse, and betook him self to Thomson's Castle of Indolence, and sported with the wits of Charles the Second's days and of Queen Anne, and relished Swift's style and that of the John Bull.

Arbuthnot's we mean, not Mr. Croker's and dallied with the British Essayists and Novelists, and knew all qualities of more modern writers with a learned spirit, Johnson, and Goldsmith, and Junius, and Burke, and Godwin, and the Sorrows of Werter, and Jean Jacques Rousseau, and Voltaire, and Marivaux, and Crebillon, and thousands more now "laughed with Rabelais in his easy chair" or pointed to Hogarth, or afterwards dwelt on Claude's classic scenes, or spoke with rapture of Raphael, and compared the women at Rome to figures that had walked out of his pictures, or visited the Oratory of Pisa, and described the works of Giotto and Ghirlandaio and Massaccio, and gave the moral of the picture of the Triumph of Death, where the beggars and the wretched invoke his dreadful dart, but the rich and mighty of the earth quail and shrink before it; and in that land of siren sights and sounds, saw a dance of peasant girls, and was charmed with lutes and gondolas, or wandered into Germany and lost himself in the labyrinths of the Hartz Forest and of the Kantean philosophy, and amongst the cabalistic names of Fichtè and Schelling and Lessing, and God knows who this was long after, but all the former while he had nerved his heart and filled his eyes with tears, as he hailed the rising orb of liberty, since quenched in darkness and in blood, and had kindled his affections at the blaze of the French Revolution, and sang for joy when the towers of the Bastile and the proud places of the insolent and the oppressor fell, and would have floated his bark, freighted with fondest fancies, across the Atlantic wave with Southey and others to seek for peace and freedom—

"In Philarmonia's undivided dale!"

Alas! "Frailty, thy name is Genius!" What is become of all this mighty heap of hope, of thought, of learning, and humanity? It has ended in swallowing doses of oblivion and in writing paragraphs in the Courier. Such and so little is the mind of man!

It was not to be supposed that Mr. Coleridge could keep on at the rate he set off; he could not realize all he knew or thought, and less could not fix his desultory ambition; other stimulants supplied the place, and kept up the intoxicating dream, the fever and the madness of his early impressions. Liberty (the philosopher's and the poet's bride) had fallen a victim, meanwhile, to the murderous practice of the hag, Legitimacy. Proscribed by court hirelings, too romantic for the herd of vulgar politicians, our enthusiast stood at bay, and at last turned on the pivot of a subtle casuistry to the unclean side: but his discursive reason would not let him trammel himself into a poet laureate or stamp distributor, and he stopped, ere he had quite passed that well known "bourne from whence no traveller returns" and so has sunk into torpid, uneasy repose, tantalised by useless resources, haunted by vain imaginings, his lips idly moving, but his heart for ever still, or, as the shattered chords vibrate of themselves, making melancholy music to the ear of memory! Such is the fate of genius in an age, when in the unequal contest with sovereign wrong, every man is ground to powder who is not either a born slave, or who does not willingly and at once offer up the yearnings of humanity and the dictates of reason as a welcome sacrifice to besotted prejudice and loathsome power.

Of all Mr. Coleridge's productions, the Ancient Mariner is the only one that we could with confidence put into any person's hands, on whom we wished to impress a favourable idea of his extraordinary powers. Let whatever other objections be made to it, it is unquestionably a work of genius –of wild, irregular, overwhelming imagination, and has that rich, varied movement in the verse, which gives a distant idea of the lofty or changeful tones of Mr. Coleridge's voice. In the Christobcl, there is one splendid passage on divided friendship. The Translation of Schiller's Wallenstein is also a masterly production in its kind, faithful and spirited. Among his smaller pieces there are occasional bursts of pathos and fancy, equal to what we might expect from him; but these form the exception, and not the rule. Such, for instance, is his affecting Sonnet to the author of the Robbers.

"Schiller! that hour I would have wish'd to die,

If through the shudd'ring midnight I had sent From the dark dungeon of the tower time rent,

That fearful voice, a famish'd father's cry—

That in no after–moment aught less vast Might stamp me mortal! A triumphant shout Black horror scream'd, and all her goblin rout

From the more withering scene diminish'd pass'd. Ah! Bard tremendous in sublimity!

Could I behold thee in thy loftier mood, Wand'ring at eve, with finely frenzied eye, Beneath some vast old tempest–swinging wood! Awhile, with mute awe gasing, I would brood, Then weep aloud in a wild ecstasy."

His Tragedy, entitled Remorse, is full of beautiful and striking passages, but it does not place the author in the first rank of dramatic writers. But if Mr. Coleridge's works do not place him in that rank, they injure instead of conveying a just idea of the man, for he himself is certainly in the first class of general intellect.

If our author's poetry is inferior to his conversation, hi; prose is utterly abortive. Hardly a gleam is to be found in it of the brilliancy and richness of those stores of thought and language that he pours out incessantly, when they are lost like drops of water in the ground. The principal work, in which he has attempted to embody his general view of things, is the friend, of which, though it contains some noble passages and fine trains of thought, prolixity and obscurity are the most frequent characteristics.

10

Mr. Southey

Perhaps the most pleasing and striking of all Mr. Southey's poems are not his triumphant taunts hurled against oppression, are not his glowing effusions to Liberty, but those in which, with a mild melancholy, he seems conscious of his own infirmities of temper, and to feel a wish to correct by thought and time the precocity and sharpness of his disposition. May the quaint but affecting aspiration expressed in one of these be fulfilled, that as he mellows, into maturer age, all such asperities may wear off, and he himself become, "Like the high leaves upon the holly tree!

Mr. Southey's prosestyle can hardly be too much praised. It is plain, clear, pointed, familiar, perfectly modern in its texture, but with a grave and sparkling admixture of archaisms in its ornaments and occasional phraseology. He is the best and most natural prose writer of any poet of the day; we mean that he is far better than Lord Byron, Mr. Wordsworth, or Mr. Coleridge, for instance. The manner is perhaps superior to the matter, that is, in his Essays and Reviews. There is rather a want of originality and even of impetus: but there is no want of playful or biting satire, of ingenuity, of casuistry, of learning and of information. He is "full of wise saws and modern" (as well as ancient) "instances." Mr. Southey may not always convince his opponents; but he seldom fails to stagger, never to gall them.

In a word, we may describe his style by saying that it has not the body or thickness of port wine, but it is like clear sherry, with kernels of old authors thrown into it! He also excels as an historian and prosetranslator. His histories abound in information, and exhibit proofs of the most indefatigable patience and industry.

By no uncommon process of the mind, Mr. Southey seems willing to steady the extreme levity of his opinions and feelings by an appeal to facts. His translations of the Spanish and French romances are also executed con amore, and with the literary fidelity of a mere linguist. That of the Cid, in particular, is a masterpiece. Not a word coull be altered for the better in the old scriptural style which it adopts in conformity to the original. It is no less interesting in itself, or as a record of high and chivalrous feelings and manners, than it is worthy of perusal as a literary curiosity.

Mr. Southey's conversation has a little resemblance to a common place book; his habitual deportment to a piece of clock work. He is not remarkable either as a reasoner or an observer: but he is quick, unaffected, replete with anecdote, various and retentive in his reading, and exceedingly happy in his play upon words, as most scholars are who give their minds this sportive turn.

We have chiefly seen Mr. Southey in company where few people appear to advantage, we mean in that of Mr. Coleridge. He has not certainly the same range of speculation, nor the same flow of sounding words, but he makes up by the details of knowledge and by a scrupulous correctness of statement for what he wants in originality of thought, or impetuous declamation.

The tones of Mr. Coleridge's voice are eloquence: those of Mr. Southey are meagre, shrill, and dry. Mr. Coleridge's forte is conversation, and he is conscious of this: Mr. Southey evidently considers writing as his stronghold, and if gravelled in an argument, or at a loss for an explanation, refers to something he has written on the subject, or brings out his portfolio, doubled down in dog ears, in confirmation of some fact. He is scholastic and professional in his ideas. He sets more value on what he writes than on what he says: he is perhaps prouder of his library than of his own productions themselves a library! He is more simple in his manners than his friend Mr. Coleridge; but at the same time less cordial or conciliating. He is less vain, or has less hope of pleasing, and therefore lays himself less out to please.

There is an air of condescension in his civility. With a tall, loose figure, a peaked austerity of countenance, and no inclination to embonpoint, you would say he has something puritanical, something ascetic in his appearance. He answers to Mandeville's description of Addison, "a parson in a tye wig." He is not a boon companion, nor does he indulge in the pleasures of the table, nor in any other vice; nor are we aware that Mr. Southey is chargeable with any human frailty but want of charity! Having fewer errors to plead guilty to, he is less lenient to those of others. He was born an age too late. Had he lived a century or two ago, he would have been a happy as well as blameless character.

But the distraction of the time has unsettled him, and the multiplicity of his pretensions have jostled with each other. No man in our day (at least no man of genius) has led so uniformly and entirely the life of a scholar from boyhood to the present hour, devoting himself to learning with the enthusiasm of an early love, with the severity and constancy of a religious vow and well would it have been for him if he had confined himself to this, and not undertaken to pull down or to patch up the State!

However irregular in his opinions, Mr. Southey is constant, unremitting, mechanical in his studies, and the performance of his duties. There is nothing Pindaric'or Shandean here. In all the relations and charities of private life, he is correct, exemplary, generous, just. We never heard a single impropriety laid to his charge; and if he has many enemies, few men can boast more numerous or stauncher friends. The variety and piquancy of his writings form a striking contrast to the mode in which they are produced. He rises early, and writes or reads till breakfast time. He writes or reads after breakfast till dinner, after dinner till tea, and from tea till bed time, "And follows so the ever running year With profitable labour to his grave."

On Derwent's banks, beneath the foot of Skiddaw. Study serves him for business, exercise, recreation. He passes from verse to prose, from history to poetry, from reading to writing, by a stop watch. He writes a fair hand without blots, sitting upright in his chair, leaves off when he comes to the bottom of the page, and changes the subject for another, as opposite as the Antipodes. His mind is after all rather the recipient and transmitter of knowledge, than the originator of it. He has hardly grasp of thought enough to arrive at any great leading truth. His passions do not amount to more than irritability. With some gall in his pen, and coldness in his manner, he has a great deal of kindness in his heart. Rash in his opinions, he is steady in his attachments and is a man, in many particulars admirable, in all respectable, his political inconsistency alone excepted!

11

Sir Walter Scott

Sir Walter has found out (oh, rare discovery!) that facts are better than fiction; that there is no romance like the romance of real life; and that if we can but arrive at what men feel, do, and say in striking and singular situations, the result will be "more lively, audible, and full of vent," than the fine spun cobwebs of the brain. With reverence be it spoken, he is like the man who having to imitate the squeaking of a pig upon the stage, brought the animal under his coat with him.

Our author has conjured up the actual people he has to deal with, or as much as he could get of them, in "their habits as they lived." He has ransacked old chronicles, and poured the contents upon his page; he has squeezed out musty records; he has consulted wayfaring pilgrims, bed rid sybils; he has invoked the spirits of the air; he has conversed with the living and the dead, and let them tell their story their own way; and by borrowing of others, has enriched his own genius with everlasting variety, truth, and freedom. He has taken his materials from the original, authentic sources, in large concrete masses, and not tampered with or too much frittered them away. He is only the amanuensis of truth and history. It is impossible to say how fine his writings in consequence are, unless we could describe how fine nature is. All that portion of the history of his country that he has touched upon (wide as the scope is) the manners, the personages, the events, the scenery, lives over again sister, and old David Deans, the patriarch of St. Leonard's Crags, and Butler, and Dumbiedikes, eloquent in his silence, and Mr. Bartoline Saddle tree and his prudent helpmate, and Porteous swinging in the wind, and Madge Wildfire, full of finery and madness, and her ghastly mother.

Again, there is Meg Merrilies, standing on her rock, stretched on her bier with "her head to the east," and Dirk

Hatterick (equal to Shakspeare's Master Barnardine), and Glossin, the soul of an attorney, and Dandy Dinmont, with his terrier pack and his pony Dumple, and the fiery Colonel Mannering, and the modish old counsellor Pleydell, and Dominie Sampson, and Rob Roy (like the eagle in his eyry), and Baillie Nicol Jarvie, and the inimitable Major Galbraith, and Rashleigh Osbaldistone, and Die Vernon, the best of secret keepers; and in the Antiquary, the ingenious and abstruse Mr. Jonathan Oldbuck, and the old beadsman Edie Ochiltree, and that preternatural figure of old Edith Elspeith, a living shadow, in whom the lamp of life had been long extinguished, had it not been fed by remorse and "thick coming" recollections; and that striking picture of the effects of feudal tyranny and fiendish pride, the unhappy Earl of Glenallan; and the Black Dwarf, and his friend Habbie of the Heughfoot (the cheerful hunter), and his cousin Grace Armstrong, fresh and laughing like the morning; and the Children of the Mist, and the baying of the bloodhound that tracks their steps at a distance (the hollow echoes are in our ears now), and Amy and her hapless love, and the villain Varney, and the deep voice of George of Douglas and the immoveable Balafre, and Master Oliver the Barber in Quentin Durward and the quaint humour of the Fortunes of Nigel, and the comic spirit of Peveril of the Peak and the fine old English romance of Ivanhoe.

What a list of names! What a host of associations! What a thing is human life! What a power is that of genius! What a world of thought and feeling is thus rescued from oblivion! How many hours of heartfelt satisfaction has our author given to the gay and thoughtless! How many sad hearts has he soothed in pain and solitude! It is no wonder that the public repay with lengthened applause and gratitude the pleasure they receive. He writes as fast as they can read, and he does not write himself down. He is always in the public eye, and we do not tire of him. His worst is better than any other person's best. His backgrounds (and his later works are little else but backgrounds capitally made out) are more attractive than the principal figures and most complicated actions of other writers. His works (taken together) are almost like a new edition of human nature. This is indeed to be an author!

The political bearing of the Scotch Novels has been a considerable recommendation to them. They are a relief to the mind, rarefied as it has been with modern philosophy, and heated with ultra radicalism. At a time also, when we bid fair to revive the principles of the Stuarts, it is interesting to bring us acquainted with their persons and misfortunes. The candour of Sir Walter's historic pen levels our bristling prejudices on this score, and sees fair play between Roundheads and Cavaliers, between Protestant and Papist. He is a writer reconciling all the diversities of human nature to the reader. He does not enter into the distinctions of hostile sects or parties, but treats of the strength or the infirmity of the human mind, of the virtues or vices of the human breast, as they are to be found blended in the whole race of mankind.

Nothing can show more handsomely or be more gallantly executed. There was a talk at one time that our author was about to take Guy Faux for the subject of one of his novels, in order to put a more liberal and humane construction on the Gunpowder Plot than our "No Popery" prejudices have hitherto permitted. Sir Walter is a professed clarifier of the age from the vulgar and still lurking old English antipathy to Popery and Slavery. Through some odd process of servile logic, it should seem, that in restoring the claims of the Stuarts by the courtesy of romance, the House of Brunswick are more firmly seated in point of fact, and the Bourbons, by collateral reasoning, become legitimate! In any other point of view, we cannot possibly conceive how Sir Walter imagines "he has done something to revive the declining spirit of loyalty" by these novels.

His loyalty is founded on would be treason: he props the actual throne by the shadow of rebellion. Does he really think of making us enamoured of the "good old times" by the faithful and harrowing portraits, he has drawn of them? Would he carry us back to the early stages of barbarism, of clanship, of the feudal system as "a consummation devoutly to be wished?" Is he infatuated enough, or does he so dote and drivel over his own slothful and self willed prejudices, as to believe that he will make a single convert to the beauty of Legitimacy, that is, of lawless power and savage bigotry, when he himself is obliged to apologize for the horrors he describes, and even render his descriptions credible to the modern reader by referring to the authentic history of these delectable times?

He is indeed so besotted as to the moral of his own story, that he has even the blindness to go out of his way to have a fling at flints and dungs (the contemptible ingredients, as he would have us believe, of a modern rabble) at the very time when he is describing a mob of the twelfth century a mob (one should think) after the writer's own heart, without one was a talk at one time that our author was about to take Guy Faux for the subject of one of his novels, in order to put a more liberal and humane construction on the Gunpowder Plot than our "No Popery" prejudices have hitherto permitted. Sir Walter is a professed clarifier of the age from the vulgar and still lurking old English antipathy to Popery and Slavery. Through some odd process of servile logic, it should seem, that in restoring the claims of the Stuarts by the courtesy of romance, the House of Brunswick are more firmly seated in point of fact, and the Bourbons, by collateral reasoning, become legitimate! In any other point of view, we cannot possibly conceive how Sir Walter imagines "he has done something to revive the declining spirit of loyalty" by these novels.

His loyalty is founded on would be treason: he props the actual throne by the shadow of rebellion. Does he really think of making us enamoured of the "good old times" by the faithful and harrowing portraits, he has drawn of them? Would he carry us back to the early stages of barbarism, of clanship, of the feudal system as "a consummation devoutly to be wished?" Is he infatuated enough, or does he so dote and drivel over his own slothful and self willed prejudices, as to believe that he will make a single convert to the beauty of Legitimacy, that is, of lawless power and savage bigotry, when he himself is obliged to apologize for the horrors he describes, and even render his descriptions credible to the modern reader by referring to the authentic history of these delectable times?

He is indeed so besotted as to the moral of his own story, that he has even the blindness to go out of his way to have a fling at flints and dungs (the contemptible ingredients, as he would have us believe, of a modern rabble) at the very time when he is describing a mob of the twelfth century a mob (one should think) after the writer's own heart, without one men are no longer strung up like acorns on trees without judge or jury, or hunted like wild beasts through thickets and glens, who have abated the cruelty of priests, the pride of nobles, the divinity of kings in former times; to whom we owe it, that we no longer wear round our necks the collar of Gurth the swineherd, and of Wamba the jester; that the castles of great lords are no longer the dens of banditti, whence they issue with fire and sword to lay waste the land; that we no longer expire in loathsome dungeons without knowing the cause, or have our right hands struck off for raising them in self defence against wanton insult; that we can sleep without fear of being burnt in our beds, or travel without making our wills; that no Amy Robsarts are thrown down trap doors by Richard Varneys with impunity; that no Red Reiver of Westburn Flat sets fire to peaceful cottages; that no Claverhouse signs cold blooded death warrants in sport; that we have no Tristan the Hermit, or Petit Andre, crawling near us, like spiders, and making our flesh creep, and our hearts sicken within us at every movement of our lives ye who have produced this change in the face of nature and society, return to earth once more, and beg pardon of Sir Walter and his patrons, who sigh at not being able to undo all that you have done!

Leaving this question, there are two other remarks which we wished to make on the Novels. The one was, to express our admiration of the good nature of the mottos, in which the author has taken occasion to remember and quote almost every living author (whether illustrious or obscure) but himself an indirect argument in favour of the general opinion as to the source from which they spring and the other was, to hint our astonishment at the innumerable and incessant instances of bad and slovenly English in them, more, we believe, than in any other works now printed. We should think the writer could not possibly read the manuscript after he has once written it, or cverlook the press.

If there were a writer, who "born for the universe" , "Narrow'd his mind, And to party gave up what was meant for mankind" who, from the height of his genius looking abroad into nature, and scanning the recesses of the human heart, "winked and shut his apprehension up" to every thought and purpose that tended to the future good of mankind who, raised by affluence, the reward of successful industry, and by the voice of fame above the want of any but the most honourable patronage, stooped to the unworthy arts of adulation, and abetted the views of the great with the pettifogging feelings of the meanest dependant on office who, having secured the admiration of the public (with the probable reversion of immortality), showed no respect for himself, for that genius that had raised him to distinction, for that nature which he trampled under foot who, amiable, frank, friendly, manly in private life, was seized with the dotage of age and the fury of a woman, the instant politics were concerned who reserved all his candour and comprehensiveness of view for history, and vented his littleness, pique, resentment, bigotry, and intolerance on his contemporaries who took the wrong side, and defended it by unfair means who, the moment his own interest or the prejudices of others interfered, seemed to forget all that was due to the pride of intellect, to the sense of manhood who, praised, admired by men of all parties alike, repaid the public liberality by striking a secret and envenomed blow at the reputation of every one who was not the ready tool of power who strewed the slime of rankling malice and mercenary scorn over the bud and promise of genius, because it was not fostered in the hot bed of corruption, or warped by the trammels of servility who supported the worst abuses of authority in the worst spirit who joined a gang of desperadoes to spread calumny, contempt, infamy, wherever they were merited by honesty or talent on a different side who officiously undertook to decide public questions by private insinuations, to prop the throne by nicknames, and the altar by lies who being (by common consent), the finest, the most humane and accomplished writer of his age, associated himself with and encouraged the lowest panders of a venal press; deluging, nauseating the public mind with the offal and garbage of Billingsgate abuse and vulgar slang; showing no remorse, no relenting or compassion towards the victims of this nefarious and organised system of partyproscription, carried on under the mask of literary criticism and fair discussion, insulting the misfortunes of some, and trampling on the early grave of others:

"Who would not grieve if such a man there be? Who would not weep if Atticus were he?"

But we believe there is no other age or country in the world (but ours), in which such genius could have been so degraded!

12

Lord Byron

Lord Byron and Sir Walter Scott are among writers now living the two, who would carry away a majority of suffrages as the greatest geniuses of the age. The former would, perhaps, obtain the preference with fine gentlemen and ladies (squeamishness apart) the latter with the critics and the vulgar. We shall treat of them in the same connection, partly on account of their distinguished preeminence, and partly because they afford a complete contrast to each other. In their poetry, in their prose, in their politics, and in their tempers, no two men can be more unlike.

If Sir Walter Scott may be thought by some to have been, "Born universal heir to all humanity," it is plain Lord Byron can set up no such pretension. He is, in a striking degree, the creature of his own will. He holds no communion with his kind; but stands alone, without mate or fellow: "As if a man were author of himself,And owned no other kin."

He is like a solitary peak, all access to which is cut off not more by elevation than distance. He is seated on a lofty eminence, "cloud capt," or reflecting the last rays of setting suns; and in his poetical moods reminds us of the fabled Titans, retired to a ridgy steep, playing on their Pan's pipes, and taking up ordinary men and things in their hands with haughty indifference. He raises his subject to himself, or tramples on it; he neither stoops to, nor loses himself in it.

He exists not by sympathy, but by antipathy. He scorns all things, even himself. Nature must come to him to sit for her picture he does not go to her. She must consult his time, his convenience, and his humour; and wear a sombre or a fantastic garb, or his Lordship turns his back upon her. There is no ease, no unaffected simplicity of manner, no "golden mean."

All is strained, or petulant in the extreme. His thoughts are sphered and crystalline; his style "prouder than when blue

Iris bends; "his spirit fiery, impatient, wayward, indefatigable. Instead of taking his impressions from without, in entire and almost unimpaired masses, he moulds them according to his own temperament, and heats the materials of his imagination in the furnace of his passions.

Lord Byron's verse glows like a flame, consuming everything in its way; Sir Walter Scott's glides like a river, clear, gentle, harmless. The poetry of the first scorches, that of the last scarcely warms. The light of the one proceeds from an internal source, ensanguined, sullen, fixed; the other reflects the hues of Heaven, or the face of nature, glancing vivid and various. The productions of the Northern Bard have the rust and the freshness of antiquity about them; those of the Noble Poet cease to startle from their extreme ambition of novelty, both in style and matter. Sir Walter's rhymes are "silly sooth".

"And dally with the innocence of thought,Like the old age" his Lordship's Muse spurns the olden time, and affects all the supercilious airs of a modern fine lady and an upstart.

The object of the one writer is to restore us to truth and nature: the other chiefly thinks how he shall display his own power, or vent his spleen, or astonish the reader either by starting new subjects and trains of speculation, or by expressing old ones in a more striking and emphatic manner than they have been expressed before. He cares little what it is he says, so that he can say it differently from others.

This may account for the charges of plagiarism which have been repeatedly brought against the Noble Poet if he can borrow an image or sentiment from another, and heighten it by an epithet or an allusion of greater force and beauty than is to be found in the original passage, he thinks he shows his superiority of execution in this in a more marked manner than if the first suggestion had been his own. It is not the value of the observation itself he is solicitous about; but he wishes to shine by contrast even nature only serves as a foil to set off his style.

He therefore takes the thoughts of others (whether contemporaries or not) out of their mouths, and is content to make them his own, to set his stamp upon them, by imparting to them a more meretricious gloss, a higher relief, a greater loftiness of tone, and a characteristic inveteracy of purpose. Even in those collateral ornaments of modern style, sloveuliness, abruptness, and eccentricity (as well as in terseness and significance), Lord Byron, when he pleases, defies competition and surpasses all his contemporaries. Whatever he does, he must do in a more decided and daring manner than any one else he lounges with extravagance, and yawns so as to alarm the reader! Self will, passion, the love of singularity, a disdain of himself and of others (with a conscious sense that this is among the ways and means of procuring admiration) are the proper categories of his mind: he is a lordly writer, is above his own reputation, and condescends to the Muses with a scornful grace!

Lord Byron, who in his politics is a liberal, in his genius is haughty and aristocratic: Walter Scott, who is an aristocrat in principle, is popular in his writings, and is (as it were) equally servile to nature and to opinion. The genius of Sir Walter is essentially imitative, or "denotes a foregone conclusion:" that of Lord Byron is self dependent; or at least requires no aid, is governed by no law, but the impulses of its own will. We confess, however much we may admire independence of feeling and erectness of spirit in general or practical questions, yet in works of genius we prefer him who bows to the authority of nature, who appeals to actual objects, to mouldering superstitions, to history, observation, and tradition, before him who only consults the pragmatical and restless workings of his own breast, and gives them out as oracles to the world.

We like a writer (whether poet or prose writer) who takes in (or is willing to take in) the range of half the universe in feeling, character, description, much better than we do one who obstinately and invariably shuts himself up in the Bastile of his own ruling passions. In short, we had rather be Sir Walter Scott (meaning thereby the Author of Waverley) than Lord Byron, a hundred times over. And for the reason just given, namely, that he casts his descriptions in the mould of nature, ever varying, never tiresome, always interesting and always instructive, instead of casting them constantly in the mould of his own individual impressions. He gives us man as he is, or as he was, in almost every variety of situation, action, and feeling.

Lord Byron makes man after his own image, woman after his own heart; the one is a capricious tyrant, the other a yielding slave; lie gives us the misanthrope and the voluptuary by turns; and with these two characters, burning or melting in their own fires, he makes out everlasting centos of himself. He hangs the cloud, the film of his existence over all out ward things sits in the centre of his thoughts, and enjoys dark night, bright day, the glitter and the gloom "in cell monastic" we see the mournful pall, the crucifix, the deathes heads, the faded chaplet of flowers, the gleaming tapers, the agonised brow of genius, the wasted form of beauty but we are still imprisoned in a dungeon, a curtain intercepts our view, we do not breathe freely the air of nature or of our own thoughts the other admired author draws aside the curtain, and the veil of egotism is rent, and he shows us the crowd of living men and women, the endless groups, the landscape background, the cloud and the rainbow, and enriches our imaginations and relieves one passion by another, and expands and lightens reflection, and takes away that tightness at the breast which arises from thinking or wishing to think that there is nothing in the world out of a man's self!

In this point of view, the Author of Waverley is one of the greatest teachers of morality that ever lived, by emancipating the mind from petty, narrow, and bigotted prejudices: Lord Byron is the greatest pamperer of those prejudices, by seeming to think there is nothing else worth encouraging but the seeds or the full luxuriant growth of dogmatism and self conceit.

In reading the Scotch Novels, we never think about the author, except from a feeling of curiosity respecting our unknown benefactor: in reading Lord Byron's works, he himself is never absent from our minds. The colouring of Lord Byron's style, however rich and dipped in Tyrian dyes, is nevertheless opaque, is in itself an object of delight and wonder: Sir Walter Scott's is perfectly transparent. In studying the one, you seem to gaze at the figures cut in stained glass, which exclude the view beyond, and where the pure light of Heaven is only a means of setting off the gorgeousness of art: in reading the other, you look through a noble window at the clear and varied landscape without. Or to sum up the distinction in one word,

Sir Walter Scott is the most dramatic writer now living; and Lord Byron is the least so.

It would be difficult to imagine that the Author of Waverley is in the smallest degree a pedant; as it would be hard to persuade ourselves that the Author of Childe Harold and Don Juan is not a coxcomb, though a provoking and sublime one. In this decided preference given to Sir Walter Scott over Lord Byron, we distinctly include the prose works of the former; for we do not think his poetry alone by any means entitles him to that precedence. Sir Walter in his poetry, though pleasing and natural, is a comparative trifler: it is in his anonymous productions that he has shown himself for what he is!

Intensity is the great and prominent distinction of Lord Byron's writings. He seldom gets beyond force of style, nor has he produced any regular work or masterly whole. He does not prepare any plan beforehand, nor revise and retouch what he has written with polished accuracy. His only object seems to be to stimulate himself and his readers for the moment to keep both alive, to drive away ennui, to substitute a feverish and irritable state of excitement for listless indolence or even calm enjoyment. For this purpose he pitches on any subject at random without much thought or delicacy he is only impatient to begin and takes care to adorn and enrich it as he proceeds with "thoughts that breathe and words that burn." He composes (as he himself has said) whether he is in the bath, in his study, or on horseback he writes as habitually as others talk or think and whether we have the inspiration of the Muse or not, we always find the spirit of the man of genius breathing from his verse.

He grapples with his subject, and moves, penetrates, and animates it by the electric force of his own feelings. He is often monotonous, extravagant, offensive; but he is never dull, or tedious, but when he writes prose. Lord Byron does not exhibit a new view of nature, or raise insignificant objects into importance by the romantic associations with which he surrounds them; but generally (at least) takes common place thoughts and events and endeavours to express them in stronger and statelier language than others. His poetry stands like a Martello tower by the side of his subject. He does not, like Mr. Wordsworth, lift poetry from the ground, or create a sentiment out of nothing. He does not describe a daisy or a periwinkle, but the cedar or the cypress: not "poor men's cottages, but princes' palaces." His Childe Harold contains a lofty and impassioned review of the great events of history, of the mighty objects left as wrecks of time, but he dwells chiefly on what is familiar to the mind of every schoolboy; has brought out few new traits of feeling or thought; and has done no more than justice to the reader's preconceptions by the sustained force and brilliancy of his style and imagery.

Lord Byron's earlier productions, Lara, the Corsair, *etc.* were wild and gloomy romances, put into rapid and shining verse. They discover the madness of poetry, together with the inspiration: sullen, moody, capricious, fierce, inexorable, gloating on beauty, thirsting for revenge, hurrying from the extremes of pleasure to pain, but with nothing permanent, nothing healthy or natural. The gaudy decorations and the morbid sentiments remind one of flowers strewed over the face of death! In his Childe Harold (as has been just observed) he assumes a lofty and philosophic tone, and "reasons high of providence, fore knowledge, will, and fate." He takes the highest points in the history of the world, and comments on them from a more commanding eminence: he shows us the crumbling monuments of time, he invokes the great names, the mighty spirit of antiquity.

The universe is changed into a stately mausoleum: in solemn measures he chaunts a hymn to fame. Lord Byron has strength and elevation enough to fill up the moulds of our classical and time hallowed recollections, and to rekindle the earliest aspirations of the mind after greatness and true glory with a pen of fire. The names of Tasso, of Ariosto, of Dante, of Cincinnatus, of Cæsar, of Scipio, lose nothing of their pomp or their lustre in his hands, and when he begins and continues a strain of panegyric on such subjects, we indeed sit down with him to a banquet of rich praise, brooding over imperishable glories, Lord Byron seems to cast himself indignantly from "this bank and shoal of time," or the frail tottering bark that bears up modern reputation, into the huge sea of ancient renown, and to revel there with untired, outspread plume. Even this in him is spleen his contempt of his contemporaries makes him turn back to the lustrous past, or project himself forward to the dim future! Lord Byron's tragedies, Faliero, Sardanapalus, *etc.* are not equal to his other works. They want the essence of the drama.

They abound in speeches and descriptions, such as he himself might make either to himself or others, lolling on his couch of a morning, but do not carry the reader out of the poet's mind to the scenes and events recorded. They have neither action, character, nor interest, but are a sort of gossamer tragedies, spun out, and glittering, and spreading a flimsy veil over the face of nature.

Yet he spins them on. Of all that he has done in this way, the Heaven and Earth (the same subject as Mr. Moore Loves of the Angels) is the laugh, the public will not. In like manner, in the controversy about Pope, he claps Mr. Bowles on the back with a coarse facetious familiarity, as if he were his chaplain whom he had invited to dine with him, or was about to present to a benefice. The reverend divine might submit to the obligation, but he has no occasion to subscribe to the jest. If it is a jest that Mr. Bowles should be a parson, and Lord Byron a peer, the world knew this before; there was no need to write a pamphlet to prove it.

The Don Juan indeed has great power; but its power is owing to the force of the serious writing, and to the oddity of the contrast between that and the flashy passages with which it is interlarded. From the sublime to the ridiculous there is but one step. You laugh and are surprised that any one should turn round and travestie himself: the drollery is in the utter discontinuity of ideas and feelings. He makes virtue serve as a foil to vice; dandyism is (for want of any other) a variety of genius. A classical intoxication is followed by the splashing of soda water, by frothy effusions of ordinary bile. After the lightning and the hurricane, we are introduced to the interior of the cabin and the contents of the wash hand basins. The solemn hero of tragedy plays Scrub in the farce. This is "very tolerable and not to be endured." The Noble Lord is almost the only writer who has prostituted his talents in this way.

He hallows in order to desecrate; takes a pleasure in defacing the images of beauty his hands have wrought; and raises our hopes and our belief in goodness to Heaven only to dash them to the earth again, and break them in pieces the more effectually from the very height they have fallen. Our enthusiasm for genius or virtue is thus turned into a jest by the very person who has kindled it, and who thus fatally quenches the spark of both. It is not that Lord Byron is sometimes serious and sometimes trifling, sometimes profligate, and sometimes moral but when he is most serious and most moral, he is only preparing to mortify the unsuspecting reader by putting a pitiful hoax upon him. This is a most unaccountable anomaly. It is as if the eagle were to build its eyry in a common sewer, or the owl were seen soaring to the mid day sun. Such a sight might make one laugh, but one would not wish or expect it to occur more than once!

In fact, Lord Byron is the spoiled child of fame as well as fortune. He has taken a surfeit of popularity, and is not contented to delight, unless he can shock the public. He would force them to admire in spite of decency and common sense he would have them read what they would read in no one but himself, or he would not give a rush for their applause. He is to be "a chartered libertine," from whom insults are favours, whose contempt is to be a new incentive to admiration.

His Lordship is hard to please: he is equally averse to notice or neglect, enraged at censure and scorning praise. He tries the patience of the town to the very utmost, and when they show signs of weariness or disgust, threatens to discard them. He says he will write on, whether he is read or not. He would never write another page, if it were not to court popular applause, or to affect a superiority over it. In this respect also, Lord Byron presents a striking contrast to Sir Walter Scott. The latter takes what part of the public favour falls to his share, without grumbling (to be sure, he has no reason to complain); the former is always quarrelling with the world about his modicum of applause, the spolia opima of vanity, and ungraciously throwing the offerings of incense heaped on his shrine back in the faces of his admirers. Again, there is no taint in the writings of the Author of Waverley, all is fair and natural and above board: he never outrages the public mind. He introduces no anomalous character: broaches no staggering opinion. If he goes back to old prejudices and superstitions as a relief to the modern reader, while Lord Byron floats on swelling paradoxes:

Like proud seas under him; if the one defers too much to the spirit of antiquity, the other panders to the spirit of the age, goes to the very edge of extreme and licentious speculation, and breaks his neck over it. Grossness and levity are the playthings of his pen.

It is a ludicrous circumstance that he should have dedicated his Cain to the worthy Baronet! Did the latter ever acknowledge the obligation? We are not nice, not very nice; but we do not particularly approve those subjects that shine chiefly from their rottenness: nor do we wish to see the Muses dressed out in the flounces of a false or questionable philosophy, like Portia and Nerissa in the garb of Doctors of Law.

We like metaphysics as well as Lord Byron; but not to see them making flowery speeches, nor dancing a measure in the fetters of verse. We have as good as hinted, that his Lordship's poetry consists mostly of a tissue of superb common places; even his paradoxes are common place. They are familiar in the schools: they are only new and striking in his dramas and stanzas, by being out of place. In a word, we think that poetry moves best within the circle of nature and received opinion: speculative theory and subtle casuistry are forbidden ground to it. But Lord Byron often wanders into this ground wantonly, wilfully, and unwarrantably. The only apology we can conceive for the spirit of some of Lord Byron's writings, is the spirit of some of those opposed to him. They would provoke a man to write anything. "Farthest from them is best." The extravagance and license of the one seems a proper antidote to the bigotry and narrowness of the other. The first Vision of Judgment was a set off to the second, though: "None but itself could be its parallel."

Perhaps the chief cause of most of Lord Byron's errors is, that he is that anomaly in letters and in society, a Noble Poet. It is a double privilege, almost too much for humanity. He has all the pride of birth and genius. The strength of his imagination leads him to indulge in fantastic opinions; the elevation of his rank sets censure at defiance. He becomes a pampered egotist. He has a seat in the House of Lords, a niche in the Temple of Fame.

Everyday mortals, opinions, things, are not good enough for him to touch or think of. A mere nobleman is, in his estimation, but "the tenth transmitter of a foolish face:" a mere man of genius is no better than a worm. His Muse is also a lady of quality. The people are not polite enough for him: the Court is not sufficiently intellectual. He hates the one and despises the other.

By hating and despising others, he does not learn to be satisfied with himself. A fastidious man soon grows querulous and splenetic. If there is nobody but ourselves to come up to our idea of fancied perfection, we easily get tired of our idol. When a man is tired of what he is, by a natural perversity he sets up for what he is not.

If, he is a poet, he pretends to be a metaphysician: if he is a patrician in rank and feeling, he would fain be one of the people. His ruling motive is not the love of the people, but of distinction; not of truth, but of singularity. He patronises men of letters out of vanity, and deserts them from caprice, or from the advice of friends. He embarks in an obnoxious publication to provoke censure, and leaves it to shift for itself for fear of scandal. We do not like.

Sir Walter's gratuitous servility: we like Lord Byron's preposterous liberalism little better. He may affect the principles of equality, but he resumes his privilege of peerage, upon occasion. His Lordship has made great offers of service to the Greeks money and horses. He is at present in Cephalonia, waiting the event!

We had written thus far when news came of the death of Lord Byron, and put an end at once to a strain of somewhat peevish invective, which was intended to meet his eye, not to insult his memory. Had we known that we were writing his epitaph, we must have done it with a different feeling. As it is, we think it better and more like himself, to let what we had written stand, than to take up our leaden shafts, and try to melt them into "tears of sensibility," or mould them into dull praise, and an affected show of candour. We were not silent during the author's life time, either for his reproof or encouragement (such as we could give, and he did not disdain to accept) nor can we now turn undertakers' men to fix the glittering plate upon his coffin, or fall into the procession of popular woe. Death cancels every thing but truth; and strips a man of every thing but genius and virtue. It is a sort of natural canonisation.

It makes the meanest of us sacred it installs the poet in his immortality, and lifts him to the skies. Death is the great assayer of the sterling ore of talent. At his touch the drossy particles fall off, the irritable, the personal, the gross, and mingle with the dust the finer and more ethereal part mounts with the winged spirit to watch over our latest memory, and protect our bones from insult. We consign the least worthy qualities to oblivion, and cherish the nobler and imperishable nature with double pride and fondness. Nothing could show the real superiority of genius in a more striking point of view than the idle contests and the public indifference about the place of Lord Byron's interment, whether in Westminster Abbey or his own family vault. A king must have a coronation a nobleman a funeral procession. The man is nothing without the pageant. The poet's cemetery is the human mind, in which he sows the seeds of never ending thought his monument is to be found in his works:

"Nothing can cover his high fame but Heaven; No pyramids set off his memory, But the eternal substance of his greatness."

Lord Byron is dead: he also died a martyr to his zeal in the cause of freedom, for the last, best hopes of man. Let that be his excuse and his epitaph! tests and the public indifference about the place of Lord Byron's interment, whether in Westminster Abbey or his own family vault. A king must have a coronation a nobleman a funeral procession. The man is nothing without the pageant. The poet's cemetery is the human mind, in which he sows the seeds of never ending thought his monument is to be found in his works:

"Nothing can cover his high fame but Heaven; No pyramids set off his memory, But the eternal substance of his greatness."

Lord Byron is dead: he also died a martyr to his zeal in the cause of freedom, for the last, best hopes of man. Let that be his excuse and his epitaph! there is poetry, in its birth. If history is a grave study, poetry may be said to be a graver: its materials lie deeper, and are spread wider. History treats, for the most part, of the cumbrous and unwieldy masses of things, the empty cases in which the affairs of the world are packed, under the heads of intrigue or war, in different states, and from century to century: but there is no thought or feeling that call have entered into the mind of man, which he would be eager to communicate to others, or which they would listen to with delight, that is not a fit subject for poetry. It is not a branch of authorship: it is "the stuff of which our life is made." The rest is "mere oblivion," a dead letter: for all that is worth remembering in life, is the poetry of it. Fear is poetry, hope is poetry, love is poetry, hatred is poetry; contempt, jealousy, remorse, admiration, wonder, pity, despair, or madness, are all poetry.

Poetry is that fine particle within us, that expands, rarefies, refines, raises our whole being: without it "man's life is poor as beast's." Man is a poetical animal: and those of us who do not study the principles of poetry, act upon them all our lives, like Molière Bourgeois Gentilhomme, who had always spoken prose without knowing it.

The child is a poet in fact, when he first plays at hide and seek, or repeats the story of Jack the Giant killer; the shepherd boy is a poet, when he first crowns his mistress with a garland of flowers; the countryman, when he stops to look at the rainbow; the city apprentice, when he gazes after the LordMayor's show; the miser, when he hugs his gold; the courtier, who builds his hopes upon a smile; the savage, who paints his idol with blood; the slave, who worships a tyrant, or the tyrant, who fancies himself a god; the vain, the ambitious, the proud, the choleric man, the hero and the coward, the beggar and the king, the rich and the poor, the young and the old, all live in a world of their own making; and the poet does no more than describe what all the others think and act. If his art is folly and madness, it is folly and madness at second hand. "There is warrant for it." Poets alone have not "such seething brains, such shaping fantasies, that apprehend more than cooler reason can.

The lunatic, the lover, and the poet are of imagination all compact. One sees more devils than vast hell can hold; The madman. While the lover, all as frantic, Sees Helen's beauty in a brow of Egypt. The poet's eye in a fine frenzy rolling, Doth glance from heav'n to earth, from earth to heav'n; And as imagination bodies forth, The forms of things unknown, the poet's pen, Turns them to shape, and gives to airy nothing A local habitation and a name. Such tricks hath strong imagination."

If poetry is a dream, the business of life is much the same. If it is a fiction, made up of what we wish things to be, and fancy that they are, because we wish them so, there is no other nor better reality. Ariosto has described the loves of Angelica and Medoro: but was not Medoro, who carved the name of his mistress on the barks of trees, as much enamoured of her charms as he?

Homer has celebrated the anger of Achilles: but was not the hero as mad as the poet? Plato banished the poets from his Commonwealth, lest their descriptions of the natural man should spoil his mathematical man, who was to be without passions and affections, who was neither to laugh nor weep, to feel sorrow nor anger, to be cast down nor elated by any thing. This was a chimera, however, which never existed but in the brain of the inventor; and Homer's poetical world has outlived Plato's philosophical Republic.

Poetry then is an imitation of nature, but the imagination and the passions are a part of man's nature. We shape things according to our wishes and fancies, without poetry; but poetry is the most emphatical language that can be found for those creations of the mind "which ecstacy is very cunning in." Neither a mere description of natural objects, nor a mere delineation of natural feelings, however distinct or forcible, constitutes the ultimate end and aim of poetry, without the heightenings of the imagination. The light of poetry is not only a direct but also a reflected light, that while it shows us the object, throws a sparkling radiance on all around it: the flame of the passions, communicated to the imagination, reveals to us, as with a flash of lightning, the inmost recesses of thought, and penetrates our whole being. Poetry represents forms chiefly as they suggest other forms; feelings, as they suggest forms or other feelings. Poetry puts a spirit of life and motion into the universe. It describes the flowing, not the fixed. It does not define the limits of sense, or analyse the distinctions of the understanding, but signifies the excess; of the imagination beyond the actual or ordinary impression of any object or feeling.

The poetical impression of any object is that uneasy, exquisite sense of beauty or power that cannot be contained within itself; that is impatient of all limit; that (as flame bends to flame) strives to link itself to some other image of kindred beauty or grandeur; to enshrine itself, as it were, in the highest forms of fancy, and to relieve the aching sense of pleasure by expressing it in the boldest manner, and by the most striking examples of the same quality in other instances. Poetry, according to Lord Bacon, for this reason "has something divine in it, because it raises the mind and hurries it into sublimity, by conforming the shows of things to the desires of the soul, instead of subjecting the soul to external things, as reason and history do." It is strictly the language of the imagination; and the imagination is that faculty which represents objects, not as they are in themselves, but as they are moulded by other thoughts and feelings, into an infinite variety of shapes and combinations of power. This language is not the less true to nature, because it is false

in point of fact; but so much the more true and natural, if it conveys the impression which the object under the influence of passion makes on the mind. Let an object, for instance, be presented to the senses in a state of agitation or fear and the imagination will distort or magnify the object, and convert it into the likeness of whatever is most proper to encourage the fear. "Our eyes are made the fools" of our other faculties. This is the universal law of the imagination,

"That if it would but apprehend some joy, It comprehends some bringer of that joy: Or in the night imagining some fear, How easy is a bush suppos'd a bear!"

When Iachimo says of Imogen,

"The flame o' the taper Bows toward her, and would under peep her lids, To see the enclosed lights" this passionate interpretation of the motion of the flame to accord with the speaker's own feelings, is true poetry. The lover, equally with the poet, speaks of the auburn tresses of his mistress as locks of shining gold, because the least tinge of yellow in the hair has, from novelty and a sense of personal beauty, a more lustrous effect to the imagination than the purest gold. We compare a man of gigantic stature to a tower: not that he is any thing like so large, but because the excess of his size beyond what we are accustomed to expect, or the usual size of things of the same class, produces by contrast a greater feeling of magnitude and ponderous strength than another object of ten times the same dimensions.

The intensity of the feeling makes up for the disproportion of the objects. Things are equal to the imagination, which have the power of affecting the mind with an equal degree of terror, admiration, delight, or love. When Lear calls upon the heavens to avenge his cause, "for they are old like him," there is nothing extravagant or impious in this sublime identification of his age with theirs; for there is no other image which could do justice to the agonising sense of his wrongs and his despair!

Poetry is the high wrought enthusiasm of fancy and feeling. As in describing natural objects, it impregnates sensible impressions with the forms of fancy, so it describes the feelings of pleasure or pain, by blending them with the strongest movements of passion, and the most striking forms of nature. Tragic poetry, which is the most impassioned species of it, strives to carry on the feeling to the utmost point of sublimity or pathos, by all the force of comparison or contrast; loses the sense of present stiffering in the imaginary exaggeration of it; exhausts the terror or pity by an unlimited indulgence of it; grapples with impossibilities in its desperate impatience of restraint; throws us back upon the past, forward into the future; brings every moment of our being or object of nature in startling review before us; and in the rapid whirl of events, lifts us from the depths of woe to the highest contemplations on human life. When Lear says, of Edgar, "Nothing but his unkind daughters could have brought him to this;" what a bewildered amazement, what a wrench of the imagination, that cannot be brought to conceive of any other cause of misery than that which has bowed it down, and absorbs all other sorrow in its own! His sorrow, like a flood, supplies the sources of all other sorrow.

Again, when he exclaims in the mad scene, "The little dogs and all, Tray, Blanche, and Sweetheart, see, they bark at me!" it is passion lending occasion to imagination to make every creature in league against him, conjuring up ingratitude and insult in their least looked for and most galling shapes, searching every thread and fibre of his heart, and finding out the last remaining image of respect or attachment in the bottom of his breast, only to torture and kill it!

In like manner the "So I am" of Cordelia gushes from her heart like a torrent of tears, relieving it of a weight of love and of supposed ingratitude, which had pressed upon it for years. What a fine return of the passion upon itself is that in Othello with what a mingled agony of regret and despair he clings to the last traces of deparfed happiness when he exclaims, "Oh now, for ever Farewel the tranquil mind. Farewel content; Farewel the plumed troops and the big wars, That make ambition virtue!

Oh farewel! Farewel the neighing steed, and the shrill trump, The spirit stirring drum, the ear piercing fife, The royal banner, and all quality, Pride, pomp, and circumstance of glorious war: And O you mortal engines, whose rude throats The immortal Jove's dread clarnours counterfeit, Farewel! Othello's occupation's gone!"

How his passion lashes itself up and swells and rages like a tide in its sounding course, when, in answer to the doubts expressed of his returning love, he says, "Never, Iago. Like to the Pontic sea, Whose icy current and compulsive course Ne'er feels retiring ebb, but keeps due on To the Propontic and the Hellespont: Even so my bloody thoughts, with violent pace, Shall ne'er look back, ne'er ebb to humble love, Till that a capable and wide revenge Swallow them up."

The climax of his expostulation afterwards with Desdemona is at that line, "But there where I had garner'd up my heart,To be discarded thence!

One mode in which the dramatic exhibition of passion excites our sympathy without raising our disgust is, that in proportion as it sharpens the edge of calamity and disappointment, it strengthens the desire of good. It enhances our consciousness of the blessing, by making us sensible of the magnitude of the loss. The storm of passion lays bare and shews us the rich depths of the human soul: the whole of our existence, the sum total of our passions and pursuits, of that which we desire and that which we dread, is brought before us by contrast; the action and reaction are equal; the keenness of immediate suffering only gives us a more intense aspiration after, and a more intimate participation with the antagonist world of good; makes us drink deeper of the cup of human life; tugs at the heart strings; loosens the pressure about them; and calls the springs of thought and feeling into play with tenfold force.

Impassioned poetry is an emanation of the moral and intellectual part of our nature, as well as of the sensitive of the desire to know, the will to act, and the power to feel; and ought to appeal to these different parts of our constitution, in order to be perfect. The domestic or prose tragedy, which is thought to be the most natural, is in this sense the least so, because it appeals almost exclusively to one of these faculties, our sensibility.

The tragedies of Moore and Lillo, for this reason, however affecting at the time, oppress and lie like a dead weight upon the mind, a load of misery which it is unable to throw off: the tragedy of Shakspeare, which is true poetry, stirs our inmost af fections; abstracts evil from itself by combining it with all the forms of imagination, and with the deepest workings of the heart, and rouses the whole man within us.

The pleasure, however, derived from tragic poetry, is not anything peculiar to it as poetry, as a fictitious and fanciful thing. It is not an anomaly of the imagination. It has its source and ground work in the common love of strong excitement. As Mr. Burke observes, people flock to see a tragedy; but if there were a public execution in the next street, the theatre would very soon be empty. It is not then the difference between fiction and reality that solves the difficulty. Children are satisfied with the stories of ghosts and witches in plain prose: nor do the hawkers of full, true, and particular accounts of murders and executions about the streets, find it necessary to have them turned into penny ballads, before they can dispose of these interesting and authentic documents. The grave politician drives a thriving trade of abuse and calumnies poured out against those whom he makes his enemies for no other end than that he may live by them.

The popular preacher makes less frequent mention of heaven than of hell. Oaths and nicknames are only a more vulgar sort of poetry or rhetoric. We are as fond of indulging our violent passions as of reading a description of those of others. We are as prone to make a torment of our fears, as to luxuriate in our hopes of good. If it be asked, Why we do so? the best answer will be, Because we cannot help it. The sense of power is as strong a principle in the mind as the love of pleasure. Objects of terror and pity exercise the same despotic control over it as those of love or beauty. It is as natural to hate as to love, to despise as to admire, to express our hatred or contempt, as our love or admiration.

"Masterless passion sways us to the moodOf what it likes or loathes."

Not that we like what we loathe; but we like to indulge our hatred and scorn of it; to dwell upon it, to exasperate our idea of it by every refinement of ingenuity and extravagance of illustration; to make it a bugbear to ourselves, to point it out to others in all the splendour of deformity, to embody it to the senses, to stigmatise it by name, to grapple with it in thought, in action, to sharpen our intellect, to arm our will against it, to know the worst we have to contend with, and to contend with it to the utmost.

Poetry is only the highest eloquence of passion, the most vivid form of expression that can be given to our conception of any thing, whether pleasurable or painful, mean or dignified, delightful or distressing. It is the perfect coincidence of the image and the words with the feeling we have, and of which we cannot get rid in any other way, that gives an instant "satisfaction to the thought." This is equally the origin of wit and fancy, of comedy and tragedy, of the sublime and pathetic.

When Pope says of the Lord Mayor's shew, "Now night descending, the proud scene is o'er, But lives in Settle's numbers one day more!" when Collins makes Danger, with "limbs of giant mould," "Throw him on the steep, Of some loose hanging rock asleep: when Lear calls out in extreme anguish, "Ingratitude, thou marble hearted fiend, How much more hideous shew'st in a child, Than the sea monster!" the passion of contempt in the one case, of terror in the other, and of indignation in the last, is perfectly satisfied. We see the thing ourselves, and shew it to others as we feel it to exist, and as, in spite of ourselves, we are compelled to think of it. The imagination, by thus embodying and turning them to shape, gives an obvious relief to the indistinct and importunate cravings of the will. We do not wish the thing to be so; but we wish it to appear such as it is. For knowledge is conscious power; and the mind is no longer, in this case, the dupe, though it may be the victim of vice or folly.

Poetry is in all its shapes the language of the imagination and the passions, of fancy and will. Nothing, therefore, can be more absurd than the outcry which has been sometimes raised by frigid and pedantic critics, for reducing the language of poetry to the standard of common sense and reason: for the end and use of pqetry, "both at the first and now, was and is to hold the mirror up to nature," seen through the medium of passion and imagination, not divested of that medium by means of literal truth or abstract reason.

The painter of history might as well be required to represent the face of a person who has just trod upon a serpent with the still life expression of a common portrait, as the poet to describe the most striking and vivid impressions which things can be supposed to make upon the mind, in the language of common conversation. Let who will strip nature of the colours and the shapes of fancy, the poet is not bound to do so; the impressions of common sense and strong imagination, that is, of passion and indifference, cannot be the same, and they must have a separate language to do justice to either. Objects must strike differently upon the mind, independently of what they are in themselves, as long as we have a different interest in them, as we see them in a different point of view, nearer or at a greater distance (morally or physically speaking) from novelty, from old acquaintance, from our ignorance of them, from our fear of their consequences, from contrast, from unexpected likeness. We can no more take away the faculty of the imagination, than we can see all objects without light or shade. Some things must dazzle us by their preternatural light; others must hold us in suspense, and tempt our curiosity to explore their obscurity.

Those who would dispel these various illusions, to give us their drab coloured creation in their stead, are not very wise. Let the naturalist, if he will, catch the glow worm, carry it home with him in a box, and find it next morning nothing but a little grey worm; let the poet or the lover of poetry visit it at evening, when beneath the scented hawthorn and the crescent moon it has built itself a palace of emerald light.

This is also one part of nature, one appearance which the glow worm presents, and that not the least interesting; so poetry is one part of the history of the human mind, though it is neither science nor philosophy. It cannot be concealed, however, that the progress of knowledge and refinement has a tendency to circumscribe the limits of the imagination, and to clip the wings of poetry.

The province of the imagination is principally visionary, the unknown and undefined: the understanding restores things to their natural boundaries, and strips them of their fanciful pretensions. Hence the history of religious and poetical enthusiasm is much the same; and both have received a sensible shock from the progress of experimental philosophy. It is the undefined and uncommon that gives birth and scope to the imagination: we can only fancy what we do not know. As in looking into the mazes of a tangled wood we fill them with what shapes we please, with ravenous beasts, with caverns vast, and drear enchantments, so, in our ignorance of the world about us, we make gods or devils of the first object we see, and set no bounds to the wilful suggestions of our hopes and fears.

"And visions, as poetic eyes avow, Hang on each leaf and cling to every bough."

There can never be another Jacob's dream. Since that time, the heavens have gone farther off, and grown astronomical.

They have become averse to the imagination, nor will they return to us on the squares of the distances, or on Doctor Chalmers's Discourses. Rembrandt's picture brings the matter nearer to us. It is not only the progress of mechanical knowledge, but the necessary advances of civilisation that are unfavourable to the spirit of poetry. We not only stand in less awe of the preternatural world, but we can calculate more surely, and look with more indifference, upon the regular routine of this.

The heroes of the fabulous ages rid the world of monsters and giants. At present we are less exposed to the vicissitudes of good or evil, to the incursions of wild beasts or "bandit fierce," or to the unmitigated fury of the elements. The time has been that "our fell of hair would at a dismal treatise rouse and stir as life were in it." But the police spoils all; and we now hardly so much as dream of a midnight murder. Macbeth is only tolerated in this country for the sake of the music; and in the United States of America, where the philosophical principles of government are carried still farther in theory and practice, we find that the Beggar's Opera is hooted from the stage. Society, by degrees, is constructed into a machine that carries us safely and insipidly from one end of life to the other, in a very comfortable prose style.

"Obscurity her curtain round them drew, And siren Sloth a dull quietus sung."

The remarks which have been here made, would, in some measure, lead to a solution of the question of the comparative merits of painting and poetry. I do not mean to give any preference, but it should seem that the argument which has been sometimes set up, that painting must affect the imagination more strongly, because it represents the image more distinctly, is not well founded. We may assume without much temerity, that poetry is more poetical than painting. When artists or connoisseurs talk on stilts about the poetry of painting, they shew that they know little about poetry, and have little love for the art. Painting gives the object itself; poetry what it implies. Painting embodies what a thing contains in itself: poetry suggests what exists out of it, in any manner connected with it. But this last is the proper province of the imagination.

Again, as it relates to passion, painting gives the event, poetry the progress of events: but it is during the progress, in the interval of expectation and suspense, while our hopes and fears are strained to the highest pitch of breathless agony, that the pinch of the interest lies:

"Between the acting of a dreadful thing And the first motion, all the interim is Like a phantasma or a hideous dream. The mortal instruments are then in council; And the state of man, like to a little kingdom, Suffers then the nature of an insurrection."

But by the time that the picture is painted, all is over. Faces are the best part of a picture; but even faces are not what we chiefly remember in what interests us most. But it may be asked then, Is there any thing better than Claude Lorraine's landscapes, than Titian's portraits, than Raphael's cartoons, or the Greek statues? Of the two first I shall say nothing, as they are evidently picturesque, rather than imaginative. Raphael's cartoons are certainly the finest comments that ever were made on the Scriptures. Would their effect be the same if we were not acquainted with the text? But the New Testament existed before the cartoons. There is one subject of which there is no cartoon, Christ washing the feet of the disciples the night before his death. But that chapter does not need a commentary! It is for want of some such resting place for the imagination that the Greek statues are little else than specious forms. They are marble to the touch and to the heart. They have not an informing principle within them. In their faultless excellence they appear sufficient to themselves. By their beauty they are raised above the frailties of passion or suffering. By their beauty they are deified. But they are not objects of religious faith to us, and their forms are a reproach to common humanity. They seem to have no sympathy with us, and not to want our admiration.

Poetry in its matter and form is natural imagery or feeling, combined with passion and fancy. In its mode of conveyance, it combines the ordinary use of language, with musical expression. There is a question of long standing in what the essence of poetry consists; or what it is that determines why one set of ideas should be expressed in prose, another in verse.

Milton has told us his idea of poetry in a single line, "Thoughts that voluntary moveHarmonious numbers."

As there are certain sounds that excite certain movements, and the song and dance go together, so there are, no doubt, certain thoughts that lead to certain tones of voice, or modulations of sound, and change "the words of Mercury into the songs of Apollo." There is a striking instance of this adaptation of the movement of sound and rhythm to the subject, in Spenser's description of the Satyrs accompanying Una to the cave of Sylvanus.

So from the ground she fearless doth arise, And walketh forth without suspect of crime.

But that chapter does not need a commentary! It is for want of some such resting place for the imagination that the Greek statues are little else than specious forms. They are marble to the touch and to the heart. They have not an informing principle within them. In their faultless excellence they appear sufficient to themselves. By their beauty they are raised above the frailties of passion or suffering. By their beauty they are deified. But they are not objects of religious faith to us, and their forms are a reproach to common humanity. They seem to have no sympathy with us, and not to want our admiration.

Poetry in its matter and form is natural imagery or feeling, combined with passion and fancy. In its mode of conveyance, it combines the ordinary use of language, with musical expression. There is a question of long standing in what the essence of poetry consists; or what it is that determines why one set of ideas should be expressed in prose, another in verse. Milton has told us his idea of poetry in a single line, "Thoughts that voluntary moveHarmonious numbers."

As there are certain sounds that excite certain movements, and the song and dance go together, so there are, no doubt, certain thoughts that lead to certain tones of voice, or modulations of sound, and change "the words of Mercury into the songs of Apollo." There is a striking instance of this adaptation of the movement of sound and rhythm to the subject, in Spenser's description of the Satyrs accompanying Una to the cave of Sylvanus.

So from the ground she fearless doth ariseAnd walketh forth without suspect of crime.

There is a near connection between music and deep rooted passion. Mad people sing. As often as articulation passes naturally into intonation, there poetry begins. Where one idea gives a tone and colour to others, where one feeling melts others into it, there can be no reason why the same principle should not be extended to the sounds by which the voice utters these emotions of the soul, and blends syllables and lines into each other. It is to supply the inherent defect of harmony in the customary mechanism of language, to make the sound an echo to the sense, when the sense becomes a sort of echo to itself to mingle the tide of verse, "the golden cadences of poetry," with the tide of feeling, flowing and murmuring as it flows in short, to take the language of the imagination from off the ground, and enable it to spread its wings where it may indulge its own impulses: "Sailing with supreme dominion, Through the azure deep of air" without being stopped, or fretted, or diverted with the abruptnesses and petty obstacles, and discordant flats and sharps of prose, that poetry was invented.

It is to common language, what springs are to a carriage, or wings to feet. In ordinary speech we arrive at a certain harmony by the modulations of voice: in poetry the same thing is done systematically by a regular collocation of syllables. It has been well observed, that every one who declaims warmly, or grows intent upon a subject, rises into a sort of blank verse or measured prose. The merchant, as described in Chaucer, went on his way "sounding always the increase of his winning." Every prose writer has more or less of rhythmical adaptation, except poets, who, when deprived of the regular mechanism of verse, seem to have no principle of-modulation left in their writings.

An excuse might be made for rhyme in the same manner. It is but fair that the ear should linger on the sounds that delight it, or avail itself of the same brilliant coincidence and unexpected recurrence of syllables, that have been displayed in the invention and collocation of images. It is allowed that rhyme assists the memory; and a man of wit and shrewdness has been heard to say, that the only four good lines of poetry are the well known ones which tell the number of days in the months of the year.

Thirty days hath September, *etc.* But if the jingle of names assists the memory, may it not also quicken the fancy? and there are other things worth having at our fingers' ends, besides the contents of the aliiianac. Pope's versification is tiresome, from its excessive sweetness and uniformity. Shakspeare's blank verse is the perfection of dramatic dialogue.

All is not poetry that passes for such: nor does verse make the whole difference between poetry and prose. The Iliad does not cease to be poetry in a literal translation; and Addison's Campaign has been very properly denominated a Gazette in rhyme. Common prose differs from poetry, as treating for the most part either of such trite, familiar, and irksome matters of fact, as convey no extraordinary impulse to the imagination, or else of such difficult and laborious processes of the understanding, as do not admit of the wayward or violent movements either of the imagination or the passions.

I will mention three works which come as near to poetry as possible without absolutely being so, namely, the Pilgrim's Progress, Robinson Crusoe, and the Tales of Boccaccio. Chaucer and Dryden have translated some of the last into English rhyme, but the essence and the power of poetry was there before. That which lifts the spirit above the earth, which draws the soul out of itself with indescribable longings, is poetry in kind, and generally fit to become so in name, by being "married to immortal verse." If it is of the essence of poetry to strike and fix the imagination, whether we will or no, to make the eye of childhood glisten with the starting tear, to be never thought of afterwards with indifference, John Bunyan and Daniel Defoe may be permitted to pass for poets in their way. The mixture of fancy and reality in the Pilgrim's Progress was never equalled in any allegory.

His pilgrims walk above the earth, and yet are on it. What zeal, what beauty, what truth of fiction! What deep feeling in the description of Christian's swimming across the water at last, and in the picture of the Shining Ones within the gates, with wings at their backs and garlands on their heads, who are to wipe all tears from his eyes! The writer's genius, though not "dipped in dews of Castalie," was baptised with the Holy Spirit and with fire.

The prints in this book are no small part of it. If the confinement of Philoctetes in the island of Lemnos was a subject for the most beautiful of all the Greek tragedies, what shall we say to Robinson Crusoe in his? Take the speech of the Greek hero on leaving his cave, beautiful as it is, and compare it with the reflections of the English adventurer in his solitary place of confinement. The thoughts of home, and of all from which he is for ever cut off, swell and press against his bosom, as the heaving ocean rolls its ceaseless tide against the rocky shore, and the very beatings of his heart become audible in the eternal silence that surrounds him. Thus he says,

"As I walked about, either in my hunting, or for viewing the country, the anguish of my soul at my condition would break out upon me on a sudden, and my very heart would die within me to think of the woods, the mountains, the deserts I was in; and how I was a prisoner, locked up with the eternal bars and bolts of the ocean, in an uninhabited wilderness, without redemption. In the midst of the greatest composures of my mind, this would break out upon me like a storm, and make me wring my hands, and weep like a child. Sometimes it would take me in the middle of my work, and I would immediately sit down and sigh, and look upon the ground for an hour or two together, and this was still worse to me, for if I could burst out into tears, or vent myself in words, it would go off, and the grief having exhausted itself would abate."

The story of his adventures would not make a poem like the Odyssey, it is true; but the relator had the true genius of a poet. It has been made a question whether Richardson's romances are poetry; and the answer perhaps is, that they are not poetry, because they are not romance. The interest is worked up to an inconceivable height; but it is by an infinite number of little things, by incessant labour and calls upon the attention, by a repetition of blows that have no rebound in them.

The sympathy excited is not a voluntary contribution, but a tax. Nothing is unforced and spontaneous. There is a want of elasticity and motion. The story does not "give an echo to the scat where love is throned." The heart does not answer of itself like a chord in music. The fancy does not run on before the writer with breathless expectation, but is dragged along with an infinite number of pins and wheels, like those with which the Lilliputians dragged Gulliver pinioned to the royal palace. Sir Charles Grandison is a coxcomb.

What sort of a figure would he cut, translated into an epic poem, by the side of Achilles? Clarissa, the divine Clarissa, is too interesting by half. She is interesting in her ruffles, in her gloves, her samplers, her aunts and uncles she is interesting in all that is uninteresting. Such things, however intensely they may be brought home to us, are not conductors to the imagination. There is infinite truth and feeling in Richardson; but it is extracted from a caput mortuum of circumstances: it does not evaporate of itself. His poetical genius is like Ariel confined in a pine tree, and requires an artificial process to let it out. Shakspeare says, Our poesy is as a gum Which issues whence 'tis nourished, our gentle flame Provokes itself, and like the current flies Each bound it chafes.

I shall conclude this general account with some remarks on four of the principal works of poetry in the world, at different periods of history: Homer, the Bible, Dante, and let me add, Ossian. In Homer, the principle of action or life is predominant; in the Bible, the principle of faith and the idea of Providence; Dante is a personification of blind will; and in Ossian we see the decay of life, and the lag end of the world. Homer's poetry is the heroic: it is full of life and action: it is bright as the day, strong as a river. In the vigour of his intellect, he grapples with all the objects of nature, and enters into all the relations of social life.

He saw many countries, and the manners of many men; and he has brought them all together in his poem. He describes his heroes going to battle with a prodigality of life, arising from an exuberance of animal spirits: we see them before us, their number, and their order of battle, poured out upon the plain, "all plumed like estriches, like eagles newly bathed, wanton as goats, wild as young bulls, youthful as May, and gorgeous as the sun at midsummer," covered with glittering armour, with dust and blood; while the Gods quaff their nectar in golden cups, or mingle in the fray; and the old men assembled on the walls of Troy rise up with reverence as Helen passes by them. The multitude of things in Homer is wonderful; their splendour, their truth, their force, and variety. His poetry is, like his religion, the poetry of number and form: he describes the bodies as well as the souls of men.

The poetry of the Bible is that of imagination and of faith: it is abstract and disembodied: it is not the poetry of form, but of power; not of multitude, but of immensity. It does not divide into many, but aggrandises into one. Its ideas of nature are like its ideas of God. It is not the poetry of social life, but of solitude: each man seems alone in the world with the original forms of nature, the rocks, the earth, and the sky.

It is not the poetry of action or heroic enterprise, but of faith in a supreme Providence, and resignation to the power that governs the universe. As the idea of God was removed farther from humanity, and a scattered polytheism, it became more profound and intense as it became more universal, for the Infinite is present to every thing: "If we fly into the uttermost parts of the earth, it is there also; if we turn to the cast or the west, we cannot escape from it." Man is thus aggrandised in the image of his Maker. The history of the patriarchs is of this kind; they are founders of the chosen race of people, the inheritors of the earth; they exist in the generations which are to come after them. Their poetry, like their religious creed, is vast, unformed, obscure, and infinite; a vision is upon it an invisible hand is suspended over it.

The spirit of the Christian religion consists in the glory hereafter to be revealed; but in the Hebrew dispensation, Providence took an immediate share in the affairs of this life. Jacob's dream arose out of this intimate communion between heaven and earth: it was this that let down, in the sight of the youthful patriarch, a golden ladder from the sky to the earth, with angels ascending and descending upon it, and shed a light upon the lonely place, which can never pass away. The story of Ruth, again, is as if all the depth of natural affection in the human race was involved in her breast. There are descriptions in the book of Job more prodigal of imagery, more intense in passion, than anything in Homer, as that of the state of his prosperity, and of the vision that came upon him by night. The metaphors in the Old Testament are more boldly figurative. Things were collected more into masses, and gave a greater momentum to the imagination.

Dante was the father of modern poetry, and he may therefore claim a place in this connection. His poem is the first great step from Gothic darkness and barbarism; and the struggle of thought in it to burst the thraldom in which the human mind had been so long held, is felt in every page. He stood bewildered, not appalled, on that dark shore which separates the ancient and the modern world; and saw the glories of antiquity dawning through the abyss of time, while revelation opened its passage to the other world. He was lost in wonder at what had been done before him, and he dared to emulate it.

Dante seems to have been indebted to the Bible for the gloomy tone of his mind, as well as for the prophetic fury which exalts and kindles his poetry; but he is utterly unlike Homer. His genius is not a sparkling flame, but the sullen heat of a furnace. He is power, passion, self will personified. In all that relates to the descriptive or fanciful part of poetry, he bears no comparison to many who had gone before, or who have come after him; but there is a gloomy abstraction in his conceptions, which lies like a dead weight upon the mind; a benumbing stupor, a breathless awe, from the intensity of the impression; a terrible obscurity, like that which oppresses us in dreams; an identity of interest, which moulds every object to its own purposes, and clothes all things with the passions and imaginations of the human soul, that make amends for all other deficiencies.

The immediate objects he presents to the mind are not much in themselves, they want grandeur, beauty, and order; but they become every thing by the force of the character he impresses upon them. His mind lends its own power to the objects which it contemplates, instead of borrowing it from them. He takes advantage even of the nakedness and dreary vacuity of his subject. His imagination peoples the shades of death, and broods over the silent air. He is the severest of all writers, the most hard and impenetrable, the most opposite to the flowery and glittering; who relies most on his own power, and the sense of it in others, and who leaves most room to the imagination of his readers. Dante's only endeavour is to interest; and he interests by exciting our sympathy with the emotion by which he is himself possessed. He does not place before us the objects by which that emotion has been created; but he seizes on the attention, by sliewing us the effect they produce on his feelings; and his poetry accordingly gives the same thrilling and overwhelming sensation, which is caught by gasing on the face of a person who has seen some object of horror.

The improbability of the events, the abruptness and monotony in the Inferno, are excessive: but the interest never flags, from the continued earnestness of the author's mind. Dante's great power is in combining internal feelings with external objects. Thus the gate of hell, on which that withering inscription is written, seems to be endowed with speech and consciousness, and to utter its dread warning, not without a sense of mortal woes. This author habitually unites the absolutely local and individual with the greatest wildness and mysticism. In the midst of the obscure and shadowy regions of the lower world, a tomb suddenly rises up with the inscription, "I am the tomb of Pope Anastasius the Sixth": and half the personages whom he has crowded into the Inferno are his own acquaintance. All this, perhaps, tends to heighten the effect by the bold intermixture of realities, and by an appeal, as it were, to the individual knowledge and experience of the reader. He affords few subjects for picture. There is, indeed, one gigantic one, that of Count Ugolino, of which Michael Angelo made a bas relief, and which Sir Joshua Reynolds ought not to have painted.

Another writer whom I shall mention last, and whom I cannot persuade myself to think a mere modern in the groundwork, is Ossian. He is a feeling and a name that can never be destroyed in the minds of his readers. As Homer is the first vigour and lustihed, Ossian is the decay and old age of poetry. He lives only in the recollection and regret of the past. There is one impression which he conveys more entirely than all other poets, namely, the sense of privation, the loss of all things, of friends, of good name, of country he is even without God in the world. He converses only with the spirits of the departed; with the motionless and silent clouds. The cold moonlight sheds its faint lustre on his head; the fox peeps out of the ruined tower; the thistle waves its beard to the wandering gale; and the strings of his harp seem, as the hand of age, as the tale of other times, passes over them, to sigh and rustle like the dry reeds in the winter's wind!

The feeling of cheerless desolation, of the loss of the pith and sap of existence, of the annihilation of the substance, and the clinging to the shadow of all things as in a mock embrace, is here perfect. In this way the lamentation of Selma for the loss of Salgar is the finest of all. If it were indeed possible to shew that this writer was nothing, it would only be another instance of mutability, another blank made, another void left in the heart, another confirmation of that feeling which makes him so often complain, "Roll on, ye dark brown years, ye bring nos joy on your wing to Ossian!"

13

18th Century in Literature

History of the Period

The most striking political feature of the times was the rise of constitutional and party government. The Revolution of 1688, which banished the Stuarts, had settled the king question by making Parliament supreme in England, but not all Englishmen were content with the settlement. No sooner were the people in control of the government than they divided into hostile parties: the liberal Whigs, who were determined to safeguard popular liberty, and the conservative Tories, with tender memories of kingcraft, who would leave as much authority as possible in the royal hands. On the extreme of Toryism was a third party of zealots, called the Jacobites, who aimed to bring the Stuarts back to the throne, and who for fifty years filled Britain with plots and rebellion. The literature of the age was at times dominated by the interests of these contending factions.

The two main parties were so well balanced that power shifted easily from one to the other. To overturn a Tory or a Whig cabinet only a few votes were necessary, and to influence such votes London was flooded with pamphlets. Even before the great newspapers appeared, the press had become a mighty power in England, and any writer with a talent for argument or satire was almost certain to be hired by party leaders. Addison, Steele, Defoe, Swift,—most of the great writers of the age were, on occasion, the willing servants of the Whigs or Tories. So the new politician replaced the old nobleman as a patron of letters.

Another feature of the age was the rapid development of social life. In earlier ages the typical Englishman had lived much by himself; his home was his castle, and in it he developed his intense individualism; but in the first half of the eighteenth century some three thousand public coffeehouses and a large number of private clubs appeared in London alone; and the sociability of which these clubs were an expression was typical of all English cities. Meanwhile country life was in sore need of refinement.

The influence of this social life on literature was inevitable. Nearly all writers frequented the coffeehouses, and matters discussed there became subjects of literature; hence the enormous amount of eighteenth-century writing devoted to transient affairs, to politics, fashions, gossip. Moreover, as the club leaders set the fashion in manners or dress, in the correct way of taking snuff or of wearing wigs and ruffles, so the literary leaders emphasised formality or correctness of style, and to write prose like Addison, or verse like Pope, became the ambition of aspiring young authors.

There are certain books of the period (seldom studied amongst its masterpieces) which are the best possible expression of its thought and manners. The Letters of Lord Chesterfield, for example, especially those written to his son, are more significant, and more readable, than anything produced by Johnson. Even better are the Memoirs of Horace Walpole, and his gossipy Letters, of which Thackeray wrote:

"Fiddles sing all through them; wax lights, fine dresses, fine jokes, fine plate, fine equipages glitter and sparkle; never was such a brilliant, smirking Vanity Fair as that through which he leads us."

Two other significant features of the age were the large part played by England in Continental wars, and the rapid expansion of the British empire. These Continental wars, which have ever since influenced British policy, seem to have originated (aside from the important matter of self-interest) in a double motive: to prevent any one nation from gaining overwhelming superiority by force of arms, and to save the smaller "buffer" states from being absorbed by their powerful neighbors.

Thus the War of the Spanish Succession (1711) prevented the union of the French and Spanish monarchies, and preserved the smaller states of Holland and Germany. As Addison then wrote, at least half truthfully:

'T is Britain's care to watch o'er Europe's fate,
And hold in balance each contending state:
To threaten bold, presumptuous kings with war,
And answer her afflicted neighbors' prayer.

The expansion of the empire, on the whole the most marvelous feature of English history, received a tremendous impetus in this age when India, Australia and the greater part of North America were added to the British dominions, and when Captain Cook opened the way for a belt of colonies around the whole world.

The influence of the last-named movement hardly appears in the books which we ordinarily read as typical of the age. There are other books, however, which one may well read for his own unhampered enjoyment: such expansive books as Hawkesworth's *Voyages* (1773), corresponding to Hakluyt's famous record of Elizabethan exploration, and especially the Voyages of Captain Cook, (The first of Cook's fateful voyages appears in Hawkesworth's collection.

The second was recorded by Cook himself (1777), and the third by Cook and Captain King (1784). See Synge, *Captain Cook's Voyages Around the World* (London, 1897).) which take us from the drawing-room chatter of politics or fashion or criticism into a world of adventure and great achievement. In such works, which make no profession of literary style, we feel the lure of the sea and of lands beyond the horizon, which is as the mighty background of English literature from Anglo-Saxon times to the present day.

It is difficult to summarise the literature of this age, or to group such antagonistic writers as Swift and Addison, Pope and Burns, Defoe and Johnson, Goldsmith and Fielding, with any fine discrimination.

It is simply for convenience, therefore, that we study eighteenth-century writings in three main divisions: the reign of so-called classicism, the revival of romantic poetry, and the beginnings of the modern novel. As a whole, it is an age of prose rather than of poetry, and in this respect it differs from all preceding ages of English literature.

EIGHTEENTH-CENTURY CLASSICISM

The above title is an unfortunate one, but since it is widely used we must try to understand it as best we can. Yet when one begins to define "classicism" one is reminded of that old bore Polonius, who tells how Hamlet is affected:

Your noble son is mad:
Mad, call I it; for to define true madness,
What is't but to be nothing else but mad?

In our literature the word "classic" was probably first used in connection with the writers of Greece and Rome, and any English work which showed the influence of such writers was said to have a classic style. If we seek to the root of the word, we shall find that it refers to the *classici*, that is, to the highest of the classes into which the census divided the Roman people; hence the proper use of "classic" to designate the writings that have won first rank in any nation. As Goethe said, "Everything that is good in literature is classical."

Gradually, however, the word "classic" came to have a different meaning, a meaning now expressed by the word "formal." In the Elizabethan age, as we have seen, critics insisted that English plays should conform to the rules or "unities" of the Greek drama, and plays written according to such rules were called classic. Again, in the eighteenth century, English poets took to studying ancient authors, especially Horace, to find out how poetry should be written. Having discovered, as they thought, the rules of composition, they insisted on following such rules rather than individual genius or inspiration. It is largely because of this adherence to rules, this slavery to a fashion of the time, that so much of eighteenth-century verse seems cold and artificial, a thing made to order rather than the natural expression of human feeling. The writers themselves were well satisfied with their formality, however, and called their own the Classic or Augustan age of English letters.

ALEXANDER POPE (1688-1744)

It was in 1819 that a controversy arose over the question, Was Pope a poet? To have asked that in 1719 would have indicated that the questioner was ignorant; to have asked it a half century later might have raised a doubt as to his sanity, for by that time Pope was acclaimed as a master by the great majority of poets in England and America. We judge now, looking at him in perspective and comparing him with Chaucer or Burns, that he was not a great poet but simply the kind of poet that the age demanded. He belongs to eighteenth-century London exclusively, and herein he differs from the master poets who are at home in all places and expressive of all time.

LIFE. Pope is an interesting but not a lovable figure. Against the petty details of his life we should place, as a background, these amasing achievements: that this poor cripple, weak of body and spiteful of mind, was the supreme literary figure of his age; that he demonstrated how an English poet could live by his pen, instead of depending on patrons; that he won greater fame and fortune than Shakespeare or Milton received from their contemporaries; that he dominated the fashion of English poetry during his lifetime, and for many years after his death. Such are the important facts of Pope's career.

For the rest: he was born in London, in the year of the Revolution (1688). Soon after that date his father, having gained a modest fortune in the linen business, retired to Binfield, on the fringe of Windsor Forest. There Pope passed his boyhood, studying a little under private tutors, forming a pleasurable acquaintance with Latin and Greek poets. From fourteen to twenty, he tells us, he read for amusement; but from twenty to twenty-seven he read for "improvement and instruction."

The most significant traits of these early years were his determination to be a poet and his talent for imitating any writer who pleased him. Dryden was his first master, from whom he inherited the couplet, then he imitated the French critic Boileau and the Roman poet Horace. By the time he was twenty four the publication of his *Essay on Criticism* and The Rape of the Lock had made him the foremost poet of England. By his translation of Homer he made a fortune, with which he bought a villa at Twickenham. There he lived in the pale sunshine of literary success, and there he quarreled with every writer who failed to appreciate his verses, his jealousy overflowing at last in *The Dunciad* (Iliad of Dunces), a witty but venomous lampoon, in which he took revenge on all who had angered him.

Next to his desire for glory and revenge, Pope loved to be considered a man of high character, a teacher of moral philosophy. His ethical teaching appears in his *Moral Epistles*, his desire for a good reputation is written large in his Letters, which he secretly printed, and then alleged that they had been made public against his wish. These Letters might impress us as the utterances of a man of noble ideals, magnanimous with his friends, patient with his enemies, until we reflect that they were published by the author for the purpose of giving precisely that impression.

Another side of Pope's nature is revealed in this: that to some of his friends, to Swift and Bolingbroke for example, he showed gratitude, and that to his parents he was ever a dutiful son. He came perhaps as near as he could to a real rather than an artificial sentiment when he wrote of his old mother:

> Me let the tender office long engage,
> To rock the cradle of reposing age.

Works of Pope

Pope's first important work, *An Essay on Criticism* (1711), is an echo of the rules which Horace had formulated in his Ars Poetica, more than seventeen centuries before Pope was born. The French critic Boileau made an alleged improvement of Horace in his L'Art Poétique, and Pope imitated both writers with his rimed *Essay*, in which he attempted to sum up the rules by which poetry should be judged. And he did it, while still under the age of twenty-five, so brilliantly that his characterisation of the critic is unmatched in our literature. A few selections will serve to show the character of the work:

> First follow nature, and your judgment frame
> By her just standard, which is still the same:
> Unerring nature, still divinely bright,
> One clear, unchanged and universal light,
> Life, force and beauty must to all impart,
> At once the source and end and test of Art.

Poets, like painters, thus unskilled to trace
The naked nature and the living grace,
With gold and jewels cover every part,
And hide with ornaments their want of art.
True wit is nature to advantage dressed,
What oft was thought, but ne'er so well expressed.
Expression is the dress of thought, and still
Appears more decent, as more suitable.

Pope's next important poem, *The Rape of the Lock* (1712), is his most original and readable work. The occasion of the poem was that a fop stole a lock of hair from a young lady, and the theft plunged two families into a quarrel which was taken up by the fashionable set of London. Pope made a mock-heroic poem on the subject, in which he satirised the fads and fashions of Queen Anne's age.

Ordinarily Pope's fancy is of small range, and proceeds jerkily, like the flight of a woodpecker, from couplet to couplet; but here he attempts to soar like the eagle. He introduces dainty aerial creatures, gnomes, sprites, sylphs, to combat for the belles and fops in their trivial concerns; and herein we see a clever burlesque of the old epic poems, in which gods or goddesses entered into the serious affairs of mortals. The craftsmanship of the poem is above praise; it is not only a neatly pointed satire on eighteenth-century fashions but is one of the most graceful works in English verse.

An excellent supplement to *The Rape of the Lock*, which pictures the superficial elegance of the age, is *An Essay on Man*, which reflects its philosophy. That philosophy under the general name of Deism, had fancied to abolish the Church and all revealed religion, and had set up a new-old standard of natural faith and morals. Of this philosophy Pope had small knowledge; but he was well acquainted with the discredited Bolingbroke, his "guide, philosopher and friend," who was a fluent exponent of the new doctrine, and from Bolingbroke came the general scheme of the *Essay on Man*.

The poem appears in the form of four epistles, dealing with man's place in the universe, with his moral nature, with social and political ethics, and with the problem of happiness.

These were discussed from a common-sense viewpoint, and with feet always on solid earth. As Pope declares:

> Know then thyself, presume not God to scan;
> The proper study of mankind is man....
> Created half to rise, and half to fall;
> Great lord of all things, yet a prey to all;
> Sole judge of truth, in endless error hurled;
> The glory, jest and riddle of the world.

Throughout the poem these two doctrines of Deism are kept in sight: that there is a God, a Mystery, who dwells apart from the world; and that man ought to be contented, even happy, in his ignorance of matters beyond his horizon:

> All nature is but art, unknown to thee;
> All chance, direction which thou canst not see;
> All discord, harmony not understood;
> All partial evil, universal good;
> And, spite of pride, in erring reason's spite,
> One truth is clear: whatever is, is right.

The result is rubbish, so far as philosophy is concerned, but in the heap of incongruous statements which Pope brings together are a large number of quotable lines, such as:

> Honor and shame from no condition rise;
> Act well your part, there all the honor lies.

It is because of such lines, the care with which the whole poem is polished, and the occasional appearance of real beauty (such as the passage beginning, "Lo, the poor Indian") that the *Essay on Man* occupies such a high place in eighteenth-century literature.

It is hardly necessary to examine other works of Pope, since the poems already named give us the full measure of his strength and weakness. His talent is to formulate rules of poetry, to satirise fashionable society, to make brilliant epigrams in faultless couplets. His failure to move or even to interest us greatly is due to his second-hand philosophy, his inability to feel or express emotion, his artificial life apart from nature and humanity. When we read Chaucer or Shakespeare, we have the impression that they would have been at home in any age or place, since they deal with human interests that are the same yesterday, to-day and forever; but we can hardly imagine Pope feeling at ease anywhere save in his own set and in his own generation. He is the poet of one period, which set great store by formality, and in that period alone he is supreme.

JONATHAN SWIFT (1667-1745)

In the history of literature Swift occupies a large place as the most powerful of English satirists; that is, writers who search out the faults of society in order to hold them up to ridicule. To most readers, however, he is known as the author of *Gulliver's Travels*, a book which young people still read with pleasure, as they read *Robinson Crusoe* or any other story of adventure. In the fate of that book, which was intended to scourge humanity but which has become a source of innocent entertainment, is a commentary on the colossal failure of Swift's ambition.

LIFE. Little need be recorded of Swift's life beyond the few facts which help us to understand his satires. He was born in Dublin, of English parents, and was so "bantered by fortune" that he was compelled to spend the greater part of his life in Ireland, a country which he detested. He was very poor, very proud; and even in youth he railed at a mocking fate which compelled him to accept aid from others. For his education he was dependent on a relative, who helped him grudgingly. After leaving Trinity College, Dublin, the only employment he could find was with another relative, Sir William Temple, a retired statesman, who hired Swift as a secretary and treated him as a servant.

Galled by his position and by his feeling of superiority (for he was a man of physical and mental power, who longed to be a master of great affairs) he took orders in the Anglican Church; but the only appointment he could obtain was in a village buried, as he said, in a forsaken district of Ireland. There his bitterness overflowed in *A Tale of a Tub* and a few pamphlets of such satiric power that certain political leaders recognised Swift's value and summoned him to their assistance.

To understand his success in London one must remember the times. Politics were rampant; the city was the battleground of Whigs and Tories, whose best weapon was the printed pamphlet that justified one party by heaping abuse or ridicule on the other. Swift was a master of satire, and he was soon the most feared author in England. He seems to have had no fixed principles, for he was ready to join the Tories when that party came into power and to turn his literary cannon on the Whigs, whom he had recently supported. In truth, he despised both parties; his chief object was to win for himself the masterful position in Church or state for which, he believed, his talents had fitted him.

For several years Swift was the literary champion of the victorious Tories; then, when his keen eye detected signs of tottering in the party, he asked for his reward. He obtained, not the great bishopric which he expected, but an appointment as Dean of St. Patrick's Cathedral in Dublin. Small and bitter fruit this seemed to Swift, after his years of service, but even so, it was given grudgingly.

When the Tories went out of power Swift's political occupation was gone. The last thirty years of his life were spent largely in Dublin. There in a living grave, as he regarded it, the scorn which he had hitherto felt for individuals or institutions widened until it included humanity. Such is the meaning of his Gulliver's Travels. His only pleasure during these years was to expose the gullibility of men, and a hundred good stories are current of his practical jokes,—such as his getting rid of a crowd which had gathered to watch an eclipse by sending a solemn messenger to announce that, by the Dean's orders, the eclipse was postponed till the next day. A brain disease fastened upon him gradually, and his last years were passed in a state of alternate stupor or madness from which death was a blessed deliverance.

Works of Swift

The poems of Swift, though they show undoubted power (every smallest thing he wrote bears that stamp), may be passed over with the comment of his relative Dryden, who wrote: "Cousin Swift, you will never be a poet." The criticism was right, but thereafter Swift jeered at Dryden's poetry. We may pass over also the *Battle of the Books*, the *Drapier's Letters* and a score more of satires and lampoons. Of all these minor works the *Bickerstaff Papers*, which record Swift's practical joke on the astrologers, are most amusing.

Swift's fame now rests largely upon his *Gulliver's Travels*, which appeared in 1726 under the title, "Travels into Several Remote Nations of the World, by Lemuel Gulliver, first a Surgeon and then a Captain of Several Ships." In the first voyage we are taken to Lilliput, a country inhabited by human beings about six inches tall, with minds in proportion. The capers of these midgets are a satire on human society, as seen through Swift's scornful eyes.

In the second voyage we go to Brobdingnag, where the people are of gigantic stature, and by contrast we are reminded of the petty "human insects" whom Gulliver represents. The third voyage, to the Island of Laputa, is a burlesque of the scientists and philosophers of Swift's day. The fourth leads to the land of the Houyhnhnms, where intelligent horses are the ruling creatures, and humanity is represented by the Yahoos, a horribly degraded race, having the forms of men and the bestial habits of monkeys.

Such is the ferocious satire on the elegant society of Queen Anne's day. Fortunately for our peace of mind we can read the book for its grim humor and adventurous action, as we read any other good story. Indeed, it surprises most readers of *Gulliver* to be told that the work was intended to wreck our faith in humanity.

In all his satires Swift's power lies in his prose style—a convincing style, clear, graphic, straightforward—and in his marvelous ability to make every scene, however distant or grotesque, as natural as life itself. As Emerson said, he describes his characters as if for the police. His weakness is twofold: he has a fondness for coarse or malodorous references, and he is so beclouded in his own soul that he cannot see his fellows in a true light. In one of his early works he announced the purpose of all his writing: My hate, whose lash just Heaven has long decreed, Shall on a day make Sin and Folly bleed. That was written at twenty-six, before he took orders in the Church. As a theological student it was certainly impressed upon the young man that Heaven keeps its own prerogatives, and that sin and folly have never been effectually reformed by lashing. But Swift had a scorn of all judgment except his own. As the eyes of fishes are so arranged that they see only their prey and their enemies, so Swift had eyes only for the vices of men and for the lash that scourges them. When he wrote, therefore, he was not an observer, or even a judge; he was a criminal lawyer prosecuting humanity on the charge of being a sham. A tendency to insanity may possibly account both for his spleen against others and for the self-tortures which made him, as Archbishop King said, "the most unhappy man on earth."

There is one oasis in the bitter desert of Swift's writings, namely, his *Journal to Stella.* While in the employ of Temple he was the daily companion of a young girl, Esther Johnson, who was an inmate of the same household. Her love for Swift was pure and constant; wherever he went she followed and lived near him, bringing a ray of sunshine into his life, in a spirit which reminds us of the sublime expression of another woman: "For whither thou goest, I will go; and where thou lodgest, I will lodge; thy people shall be my people, and thy God my God." She was probably married to Swift, but his pride kept him from openly acknowledging the union. While he was at London he wrote a private journal for Esther (Stella) in which he recorded his impressions of the men and women he met, and of the political battles in which he took part.

That journal, filled with strange abbreviations to which only he and Stella had the key, can hardly be called literature, but it is of profound interest. It gives us glimpses of a woman who chose to live in the shadow; it shows the better side of Swift's nature, in contrast with his arrogance toward men and his brutal treatment of women; and finally, it often takes us behind the scenes of a stage on which was played a mixed comedy of politics and society.

JOSEPH ADDISON (1672-1719)

In Addison we have a pleasant reflection of the new social life of England. Select almost any feature of that life, and you shall find some account of it in the papers of Addison: its party politics in his Whig Examiner; its "grand tour," as part of a gentleman's education, in his *Remarks on Italy*; its adventure on foreign soil in such poems as "The Campaign"; its new drama of decency in his *Cato*; its classic delusions in his *Account of the Greatest English Poets*; its frills, fashions and similar matters in his *Spectator* essays. He tried almost every type of literature, from hymns to librettos, and in each he succeeded well enough to be loudly applauded. In his own day he was accounted a master poet, but now he is remembered as a writer of prose essays.

Life

Addison's career offers an interesting contrast to that of Swift, who lived in the same age. He was the son of an English clergyman, settled in the deanery of Lichfield, and his early training left upon him the stamp of good taste and good breeding. In school he was always the model boy; in Oxford he wrote Latin verses on safe subjects, in the approved fashion; in politics he was content to "oil the machine" as he found it; in society he was shy and silent (though naturally a brilliant talker) because he feared to make some slip which might mar his prospects or the dignity of his position.

A very discreet man was Addison, and the only failure he made of discretion was when he married the Dowager Countess of Warwick, went to live in her elegant Holland House, and lived unhappily ever afterwards. The last is a mere formal expression. Addison had not depth enough to be really unhappy. From the cold comfort of the Dowager's palace he would slip off to his club or to Will's Coffee house. There, with a pipe and a bottle, he would loosen his eloquent tongue and proceed to "make discreetly merry with a few old friends."

His characteristic quality appears in the literary work which followed his Latin verses. He began with a flattering "Address to Dryden," which pleased the old poet and brought Addison to the attention of literary celebrities. His next effort was "The Peace of Ryswick," which flattered King William's statesmen and brought the author a chance to serve the Whig party. Also it brought a pension, with a suggestion that Addison should travel abroad and learn French and diplomacy, which he did, to his great content, for the space of three years. The death of the king brought Addison back to England. His pension stopped, and for a time he lived poorly "in a garret," as one may read in Thackeray's *Henry Esmond*. Then came news of an English victory on the Continent (Marlborough's victory at Blenheim), and the Whigs wanted to make political capital out of the event. Addison was hunted up and engaged to write a poem. He responded with "The Campaign," which made him famous. Patriots and politicians ascribed to the poem undying glory, and their judgment was accepted by fashionable folk of London. To read it now is to meet a formal, uninspired production, containing a few stock quotations and, incidentally, a sad commentary on the union of Whiggery and poetry.

From that moment Addison's success was assured. He was given various offices of increasing importance; he entered Parliament; he wrote a classic tragedy, *Cato*, which took London by storm (his friend Steele had carefully "packed the house" for the first performance); his essays in *The Spectator* were discussed in every fashionable club or drawing-room; he married a rich countess; he was appointed Secretary of State. The path of politics, which others find so narrow and slippery, was for Addison a broad road through pleasant gardens. Meanwhile Swift, who could not follow the Addisonian way of kindness and courtesy, was eating bitter bread and railing at humanity.

After a brief experience as Secretary of State, finding that he could not make the speeches expected of him, Addison retired on a pension. His unwavering allegiance to good form in all matters appears even in his last remark, "See how a Christian can die." That was in 1719. He had sought the easiest, pleasantest way through life, and had found it. Thackeray, who was in sympathy with such a career, summed it up in a glowing panegyric:

"A life prosperous and beautiful, a calm death; an immense fame and affection afterwards for his happy and spotless name."

Works of Addison

Addison's great reputation was won chiefly by his poetry; but with the exception of a few hymns, simple and devout, his poetical works no longer appeal to us. He was not a poet but a verse-maker. His classic tragedy *Cato*, for example (which met with such amasing success in London that it was taken over to the Continent, where it was acclaimed "a masterpiece of regularity and elegance"), has some good passages, but one who reads the context is apt to find the elegant lines running together somewhat drowsily. Nor need that reflect on our taste or intelligence. Even the cultured Greeks, as if in anticipation of classic poems, built two adjoining temples, one dedicated to the Muses and the other to Sleep.

The *Essays* of Addison give us the full measure of his literary talent. In his verse, as in his political works, he seems to be speaking to strangers; he is on guard over his dignity as a poet, as Secretary of State, as husband of a countess; but in his *Essays* we meet the man at his ease, fluent, witty, light-hearted but not frivolous,—just as he talked to his friends in Will's Coffeehouse. The conversational quality of these *Essays* has influenced all subsequent works of the same type,—a type hard to define, but which leaves the impression of pleasant talk about a subject, as distinct from any learned discussion.

The *Essays* cover a wide range: fashions, dress, manners, character sketches, letters of travel, ghost stories, satires on common vices, week-end sermons on moral subjects. They are never profound, but they are always pleasant, and their graceful style made such a lasting impression that, half a century later, Dr. Johnson summed up a general judgment when he said:

"Whoever wishes to attain an English style, familiar but not coarse, and elegant but not ostentatious, must give his days and nights to the volumes of Addison."

Addison and Steele

Of these two associates Richard Steele (1672-1729) had the more original mind, and his writings reveal a warm, human sympathy that is lacking in the work of his more famous contemporary. But while Addison cultivated his one talent of writing, Steele was like Defoe in that he always had some new project in his head, and some old debt urging him to put the project into immediate execution. He was in turn poet, political pamphleteer, soldier, dramatist, member of Parliament, publisher, manager of a theater, following each occupation eagerly for a brief season, then abandoning it cheerfully for another,—much like a boy picking blueberries in a good place, who moves on and on to find a better bush, eats his berries on the way, and comes home at last with an empty pail.

While holding the political office of "gazetteer" (one who had a monopoly of official news) the idea came to Steele of publishing a literary magazine. The inventive Defoe had already issued *The Review* (1704), but that had a political origin. With the first number of *The Tatler* (1709) the modern magazine made its bow to the public.

This little sheet, published thrice a week and sold at a penny a copy, contained more or less politics, to be sure, but the fact that it reflected the gossip of coffeehouses made it instantly popular. After less than two years of triumph Steele lost his official position, and *The Tatler* was discontinued. The idea remained, however, and a few months later appeared *The Spectator* (1711), a daily magazine which eschewed politics and devoted itself to essays, reviews, letters, criticisms,—in short, to "polite" literature. Addison, who had been a contributor to The Tatler entered heartily into the new venture, which had a brief but glorious career. He became known as "Mr. Spectator," and the famous Spectator Essays are still commonly attributed to him, though in truth Steele furnished a large part of them.

Because of their cultivated prose style, Steele and Addison were long regarded as models, and we are still influenced by them in the direction of clearness and grace of expression. How wide their influence extended may be seen in American literature.

Hardly had *The Spectator* appeared when it crossed the Atlantic and began to dominate our English style on both sides of the ocean. Franklin, in Boston, studied it by night in order to imitate it in the essay which he slipped under the printing-house door next morning; and Boyd, in Virginia, reflects its influence in his charming Journal of exploration. Half a century later, the Hartford Wits were writing clever sketches that seemed like the work of a new "Spectator"; another half century, and Irving, the greatest master of English prose in his day, was still writing in the Addisonian manner, and regretting as he wrote that the leisurely style showed signs, in a bustling age, "of becoming a little old-fashioned."

DR. JOHNSON AND HIS CIRCLE

Since Caxton established the king's English as a literary language our prose style has often followed the changing fashion of London. Thus, Lyly made it fantastic, Dryden simplified it, Addison gave it grace; and each leader set a fashion which was followed by a host of young writers. Hardly had the Addisonian style crossed the Atlantic, to be the model for American writers for a century, when London acclaimed a new prose fashion—a ponderous, grandiloquent fashion, characterised by mouth-filling words, antithetical sentences, rounded periods, sonorous commonplaces—which was eagerly adopted by orators and historians especially. The man who did more than any other to set this new oratorical fashion in motion was the same Dr. Samuel Johnson who advised young writers to study Addison as a model. And that was only one of his amusing inconsistencies.

Johnson was a man of power, who won a commanding place in English letters by his hard work and his downright sincerity. He won his name of "the great lexicographer" by his *Dictionary*, which we no longer consult, but which we remember as the first attempt at a complete English lexicon. If one asks what else he wrote, with the idea of going to the library and getting a book for pleasure, the answer must be that Johnson's voluminous works are now as dead as his dictionary. One student of literature may be interested in such a melancholy poem as "The Vanity of Human Wishes"; another will be entertained by the anecdotes or blunt criticisms of the *Lives of the Poets*; a third may be uplifted by the Rambler Essays, which are well called "majestically moral productions"; but we shall content ourselves here by recording Johnson's own refreshing criticism of certain ancient authors, that "it is idle to criticise what nobody reads."

Perhaps the best thing he wrote was a minor work, which he did not know would ever be published. This was his manly Letter to Lord Chesterfield, a nobleman who had treated Johnson with discourtesy when the poor author was making a heroic struggle, but who offered his patronage when the Dictionary was announced as an epoch-making work. In his noble refusal of all extraneous help Johnson unconsciously voiced Literature's declaration of independence: that henceforth a book must stand or fall on its own merits, and that the day of the literary patron was gone forever.

Life

The story of Johnson's life (1709-1784) has been so well told that one is loath to attempt a summary of it. We note, therefore, a few plain facts: that he was the son of a poor bookseller; that despite poverty and disease he obtained his classic education; that at twenty-six he came to London, and, after an experience with patrons, rebelled against them; that he did every kind of hackwork to earn his bread honestly, living in the very cellar of Grub Street, where he was often cold and more often hungry; that after nearly thirty years of labor his services to literature were rewarded by a pension, which he shared with the poor; that he then formed the Literary Club (including Reynolds, Pitt, Gibbon, Goldsmith, Burke, and almost every other prominent man in London) and indulged nightly in his famous "conversations," which were either monologues or knockdown arguments; and that in his old age he was regarded as the king of letters, the oracle of literary taste in England.

Such is the bare outline of Johnson's career. To his character, his rough exterior and his kind heart, his vast learning and his Tory prejudices, his piety, his melancholy, his virtues, his frailty, his "mass of genuine manhood," only a volume could do justice. Happily that volume is at hand. It is Boswell's Life of Johnson, a famous book that deserves its fame.

BOSWELL'S JOHNSON

Boswell was an inquisitive barrister who came from Edinburgh to London and thrust himself into the company of great men. To Johnson, then at the summit of his fame, "Bozzy" was devotion itself, following his master about by day or night, refusing to be rebuffed, jotting down notes of what he saw and heard. After Johnson's death he gathered these notes together and, after seven years of labor, produced his incomparable *Life of Johnson* (1791).

The greatness of Boswell's work may be traced to two causes. First, he had a great subject. The story of any human life is interesting, if truthfully told, and Johnson's heroic life of labor and pain and reward was passed in a capital city, among famous men, at a time which witnessed the rapid expansion of a mighty empire. Second, Boswell was as faithful as a man could be to his subject, for whom he had such admiration that even the dictator's frailties seemed more impressive than the virtues of ordinary humanity. So Boswell concealed nothing, and felt no necessity to distribute either praise or blame. He portrayed a man just as that man was, recorded the word just as the word was spoken; and facing the man we may see his enraptured audience,—at a distance, indeed, but marvelously clear, as when we look through the larger end of a field glass at a landscape dominated by a mountain. One who reads this matchless biography will know Johnson better than he knows his own neighbor; he will gain, moreover, a better understanding of humanity, to reflect which clearly and truthfully is the prime object of all good literature.

EDMUND BURKE (1729-1797)

This brilliant Irishman came up to London as a young man of twenty-one. Within a few years—such was his character, his education, his genius—he had won a reputation among old statesmen as a political philosopher. Then he entered Parliament, where for twenty years the House listened with growing amazement to his rhythmic periods, and he was acclaimed the most eloquent of orators.

Among Burke's numerous works those on America, India and France are deservedly the most famous. Of his orations on American subjects a student of literature or history may profitably read "On Taxation" (1774) and "On Conciliation" (1775), in which Burke presents the Whig argument in favour of a liberal colonial policy. The Tory view of the same question was bluntly presented by Johnson in his essay "Taxation No Tyranny"; while like a reverberation from America, powerful enough to carry across the Atlantic, came Thomas Paine's "Common Sense," which was a ringing plea for colonial independence.

Of Burke's works pertaining to India "The Nabob of Arcot's Debts" (1785) and the "Impeachment of Warren Hastings" (1786) are interesting to those who can enjoy a long flight of sustained eloquence. Here again Burke presents the liberal, the humane view of what was then largely a political question; but in his *Reflections on the French Revolution* (1790) he goes over to the Tories, thunders against the revolutionists or their English sympathisers, and exalts the undying glories of the British constitution. The *Reflections* is the most brilliant of all Burke's works, and is admired for its superb rhetorical style.

To examine any of these works is to discover the author's characteristic method: first, his framework or argument is carefully constructed so as to appeal to reason; then this framework is buried out of sight and memory by a mass of description, digression, emotional appeal, allusions, illustrative matter from the author's wide reading or from his prolific imagination. Note this passage from the *French Revolution*:

"It is now sixteen or seventeen years since I saw the Queen of France, then the Dauphiness, at Versailles; and surely never lighted on this orb, which she hardly seemed to touch, a more delightful vision. I saw her just above the horizon, decorating and cheering the elevated sphere she had just begun to move in, glittering like the morning star, full of life and splendor and joy. Oh, what a revolution! And what a heart must I have to contemplate without emotion that elevation and that fall! Little did I dream, when she added titles of veneration to those of distant, enthusiastic, respectful love, that she should ever be obliged to carry the sharp antidote against disgrace concealed in that bosom; little did I dream that I should have lived to see such disasters fallen upon her in a nation of gallant men, in a nation of men of honour and of cavaliers. I thought ten thousand swords must have leaped from their scabbards to avenge even a look that threatened her with insult. But the age of chivalry is gone.

That of sophisters, economists and calculators has succeeded; and the glory of Europe is extinguished for ever.

Never, never more shall we behold that generous loyalty to rank and sex, that proud submission, that dignified obedience, that subordination of the heart, which kept alive, even in servitude itself, the spirit of an exalted freedom. The unbought grace of life, the cheap defence of nations, the nurse of manly sentiment and heroic enterprise is gone! It is gone, that sensibility of principle, that chastity of honour, which felt a stain like a wound, which inspired courage whilst it mitigated ferocity, which ennobled whatever it touched, and under which vice itself lost half its evil by losing all its grossness."

That is finely expressed, but it has no bearing on the political matter in question; namely, whether the sympathy of England should be extended to the French revolutionists in their struggle for liberty. This irrelevancy of Burke suggests our first criticism: that he is always eloquent, and usually right; but he is seldom convincing, and his eloquence is a hindrance rather than a help to his main purpose.

So we are not surprised to hear that his eloquent speech on Conciliation emptied the benches; or that after his supreme effort in the impeachment of Hastings—an effort so tremendously dramatic that spectators sobbed, screamed, were carried out in fits—the object of all this invective was acquitted by his judges. Reading the works now, they seem to us praiseworthy not for their sustained eloquence, which is wearisome, but for the brilliancy of certain detached passages which catch the eye like sparkling raindrops after a drenching shower. It was the splendor of such passages, their vivid imagery and harmonious rhythm, which led Matthew Arnold to assert that Burke was the greatest master of prose style in our literature. Anybody can make such an assertion; nobody can prove or disprove it.

The Historians

Perhaps it was the rapid expansion of the empire in the latter, part of the eighteenth century which aroused such interest in historical subjects that works of history were then more eagerly welcomed than poetry or fiction. Gibbon says in his *Memoirs* that in his day "history was the most popular species of composition." It was also the best rewarded; for while

Johnson, the most renowned author of his time, wrote a romance (Rasselas) hoping to sell it for enough to pay for his mother's funeral, Robertson easily disposed of his History of the Emperor Charles V for £4500; and there were others who were even better paid for popular histories, the very titles of which are now forgotten.

Of all the historical works of the age, and their name was legion, only one survives with something of its original vitality, standing the double test of time and scholarship. This is The Decline and Fall of the Roman Empire (1776), a work which remained famous for a century, and which still has its admiring readers. It was written by Edward Gibbon (1737-1794), who belonged to the Literary Club that gathered about Johnson, and who cultivated his style, he tells us, first by adopting the dictator's rounded periods, and then practicing them "till they moved to flutes and hautboys."

The scope of Gibbon's work is enormous. It begins with the Emperor Trajan (A.D. 98) and carries us through the convulsions of a dying civilisation, the descent of the Barbarians on Rome, the spread of Christianity, the Crusades, the rise of Mohammedanism,—through all the confused history of thirteen centuries, ending with the capture of Constantinople by the Turks, in 1453. The mind that could grasp such vast and chaotic materials, arrange them in orderly sequence and resent them as in a gorgeous panorama, moves us to wonder.

To be sure, there are many things to criticise in Gibbon's masterpiece,—the author's love of mere pageants; his materialism; his inability to understand religious movements, or even religious motives; his lifeless figures, which move as if by mechanical springs,—but one who reads the *Decline and Fall* may be too much impressed by the evidences of scholarship, of vast labor, of genius even, to linger over faults. It is a "monumental" work, most interesting to those who admire monuments; and its style is the perfection of that oratorical, Johnsonese style which was popular in England in 1776, and which, half a century later, found its best American mouthpiece in Daniel Webster. The influence of Gibbon may still be seen in the orators and historians who, lacking the charm of simplicity, clothe even their platitudes in high-sounding phrases.

THE REVIVAL OF ROMANTIC POETRY

Every age has had its romantic poets—that is, poets who sing the dreams and ideals of life, and whose songs seem to be written naturally, spontaneously, as from a full heart—but in the eighteenth century they were completely overshadowed by formal versifiers who made poetry by rule. At that time the imaginative verse which had delighted an earlier age was regarded much as we now regard an old beaver hat; Shakespeare and Milton were neglected, Spenser was but a name, Chaucer was clean forgotten. If a poet aspired to fame, he imitated the couplets of Dryden or Pope, who, as Cowper said,

Made poetry a mere mechanic art,
And every warbler has his tune by heart.

Among those who made vigorous protest against the precise and dreary formalism of the age were Collins and Gray, whose names are commonly associated in poetry, as are the names of Addison and Steele in prose. They had the same tastes, the same gentle melancholy, the same freedom from the bondage of literary fashion. Of the two, William Collins (1721-1759) was perhaps the more gifted poet. His exquisite "Ode to Evening" is without a rival in its own field, and his brief elegy beginning, "How sleep the brave," is a worthy commemoration of a soldier's death and a nation's gratitude. It has, says Andrew Lang, the magic of an elder day and of all time.

Thomas Gray (1716-1771) is more widely known than his fellow poet, largely because of one fortunate poem which "returned to men's bosoms" as if sure of its place and welcome. This is the "Elegy Written in a Country Churchyard" (1750), which has been translated into all civilised tongues, and wnich is known, loved, quoted wherever English is spoken.

To criticise this favourite of a million readers seems almost ruthless, as if one were pulling a flower to pieces for the sake of giving it a botanical name. A pleasanter task is to explain, if one can, the immense popularity of the "Elegy." The theme is of profound interest to every man who reveres the last resting place of his parents, to the nation which cherishes every monument of its founders, and even to primitive peoples, like the Indians, who refuse to leave the place where their fathers are buried, and who make the grave a symbol of patriotism. With this great theme our poet is in perfect sympathy. His attitude is simple and reverent; he treads softly, as if on holy ground. The natural setting or atmosphere of his poem, the peace of evening falling on the old churchyard at Stoke Poges, the curfew bell, the cessation of daily toil, the hush which falls upon the twilight landscape like a summons to prayer,—all this is exactly as it should be. Finally, Gray's craftsmanship, his choice of words, his simple figures, his careful fitting of every line to its place and context, is as near perfection as human skill could make it.

Other poems of Gray, which make his little book precious, are the four odes: "To Spring," "On a Distant Prospect of Eton College," "The Progress of Poesy" and "The Bard," the last named being a description of the dramatic end of an old Welsh minstrel, who chants a wild prophecy as he goes to his death. These romantic odes, together with certain translations which Gray made from Norse mythology, mark the end of "classic" domination in English poetry.

OLIVER GOLDSMITH (1728-1774)

Most versatile of eighteenth-century writers was "poor Noll," a most improvident kind of man in all worldly ways, but so skillful with his pen that Johnson wrote a sincere epitaph to the effect that Goldsmith attempted every form of literature, and adorned everything which he attempted. The form of his verse suggests the formal school, and his polished couplets rival those of Pope; but there the resemblance ceases. In his tenderness and humor, in his homely subjects and the warm human sympathy with which he describes them, Goldsmith belongs to the new romantic school of poetry.

Life

The life of Goldsmith has inspired many pens; but the subject, far from being exhausted, is still awaiting the right biographer. The poet's youthful escapades in the Irish country, his classical education at Trinity College, Dublin, and his vagabond studies among gypsies and peddlers, his childish attempts at various professions, his wanderings over Europe, his shifts and makeshifts to earn a living in London, his tilts with Johnson at the Literary Club, his love of gorgeous raiment, his indiscriminate charity, his poverty, his simplicity, his success in the art of writing and his total failure in the art of living,—such kaleidoscopic elements make a brief biography impossible. The character of the man appears in a single incident. Landing one day on the Continent with a flute, a spare shirt and a guinea as his sole outward possessions, the guinea went for a feast and a game of cards at the nearest inn, and the shirt to the first beggar that asked for it. There remained only the flute, and with that Goldsmith fared forth confidently, like the gleeman of old with his harp, delighted at seeing the world, utterly forgetful of the fact that he had crossed the Channel in search of a medical education.

That aimless, happy-go-lucky journey was typical of Goldsmith's whole life of forty-odd years. Those who knew him loved but despaired of him. When he passed away (1774) Johnson summed up the feeling of the English literary world in the sentence, "He was a very great man, let not his frailties be remembered."

GOLDSMITH'S PROSE AND VERSE

Among the forgotten works of Goldsmith we note with interest several that he wrote for children: a fanciful History of England, an entertaining but most unreliable *Animated Nature,* and probably also the tale of "Little Goody Twoshoes." These were written (as were all his other works) to satisfy the demands of his landlady, or to pay an old debt, or to buy a new cloak,—a plum-coloured velvet cloak, wherewith to appear at the opera or to dazzle the Literary Club. From among his works we select four, as illustrative of Goldsmith's versatility.

The Citizen of the World, a series of letters from an alleged Chinese visitor, invites comparison with the essays of Addison or Steele. All three writers are satirical, all have a high moral purpose, all are masters of a graceful style, but where the

"Spectator" touches the surface of life, Goldsmith often goes deeper and probes the very spirit of the eighteenth century. Here is a paragraph from the first letter, in which the alleged visitor, who has heard much of the wealth and culture of London, sets down his first impressions:

> "From these circumstances in their buildings, and from the dismal looks of the inhabitants, I am induced to conclude that the nation is actually poor, and that, like the Persians, they make a splendid figure everywhere but at home. The proverb of Xixofou is, that a man's riches may be seen in his eyes if we judge of the English by this rule, there is not a poorer nation under the sun."

The Deserted Village (1770) is the best remembered of Goldsmith's poems, or perhaps one should say "verses" in deference to critics like Matthew Arnold who classify the work with Pope's *Essay on Man*, as a rimed dissertation rather than a true poem. To compare the two works just mentioned is to discover how far Goldsmith is from his formal model. In Pope's "Essay" we find common sense, moral maxims and some alleged philosophy, but no emotion, no romance, no men or women. The "Village," on the other hand, is romantic even in desolation; it awakens our interest, our sympathy; and it gives us two characters, the Parson and the Schoolmaster, who live in our memories with the best of Chaucer's creations. Moreover, it makes the commonplace life of man ideal and beautiful, and so appeals to readers of widely different tastes or nationalities. Of the many ambitious poems written in the eighteenth century, the two most widely read (aside from the songs of Burns) are Goldsmith's "Village," which portrays the life of simple country people, and Gray's "Elegy," which laments their death.

Goldsmith's one novel, *The Vicar of Wakefield* (1766), has been well called "the Prince Charming" of our early works of fiction. This work has a threefold distinction: its style alone is enough to make it pleasant reading; as a story it retains much of its original charm, after a century and a half of proving; by its moral purity it offered the best kind of rebuke to the vulgar tendency of the early English novel, and influenced subsequent fiction in the direction of cleanness and decency.

The story is that of a certain vicar, or clergyman, Dr. Primrose and his family, who pass through heavy trials and misfortunes. These might crush or embitter an ordinary man, but they only serve to make the Vicar's love for his children, his trust in God, his tenderness for humanity, shine out more clearly, like star's after a tempest. Mingled with these affecting trials are many droll situations which probably reflect something of the author's personal escapades; for Goldsmith was the son of a clergyman, and brought himself and his father into his tale. As a novel, that is, a reflection of human life in the form of a story, it contains many weaknesses; but despite its faults of moralising and sentimentality, the impression which the story leaves is one of "sweetness and light." Swinburne says that, of all novels he had seen rise and fall in three generations, The Vicar of Wakefield alone had retained the same high level in the opinion of its readers.

Another notable work is Goldsmith's comedy *She Stoops to Conquer*. The date of that comedy (1773) recalls the fact that, though it has been played for nearly a century and a half, during which a thousand popular plays have been forgotten, it is still a prime favourite on the amateur stage. Perhaps the only other comedies of which the same can be said with approximate truth are *The Rivals* (1775) and *The School for Scandal* (1777) of Richard Brinsley Sheridan.

The plot of *She Stoops to Conquer* is said to have been suggested by one of Goldsmith's queer adventures. He arrived one day at a village, riding a borrowed nag, and with the air of a lordly traveler asked a stranger to direct him "to the best house in the place." The stranger misunderstood, or else was a rare wag, for he showed the way to the abode of a wealthy gentleman. There Goldsmith made himself at home, ordered the servants about, invited his host to share a bottle of wine,—in short, made a great fool of himself. Evidently the host was also a wag, for he let the joke run on till the victim was ready to ride away. (There is some doubt as to the source of Goldsmith's plot. It may have been suggested by an earlier French comedy by Marivaux.)

From some such crazy escapade Goldsmith made his comedy of manners, a lively, rollicking comedy of topsy-turvy scenes, all hinging upon the incident of mistaking a private house for a public inn. We have called *She Stoops to Conquer* a comedy of eighteenth-century manners, but our continued interest in its absurdities would seem to indicate that it is a comedy of human nature in all ages.

ROBERT BURNS (1759-1796)

Burns is everywhere acclaimed the poet of Scotland, and for two good reasons: because he reflects better than any other the emotions of the Scottish people, and because his book is a summary of the best verse of his native land. Practically all his songs, such as "Bonnie Boon" and "Auld Lang Syne," are late echoes of much older verses; his more ambitious poems borrow their ideas, their satire or sentiment, their form even, from Ferguson, Allan Ramsay and other poets, all of whom aimed (as Scott aimed in "Lochinvar") to preserve the work of unnamed minstrels whose lines had been repeated in Highlands or Lowlands for two centuries. Burns may be regarded, therefore, as a treasury of all that is best in Scottish song. His genius was to take this old material, dear to the heart of the native, and give it final expression.

Life

The life of Burns is one to discourage a biographer who does not relish the alternative of either concealing the facts or apologising for his subject. We shall record here only a few personal matters which may help us to understand Burns's poetry. Perhaps the most potent influence in his life was that which came from his labor in the field. He was born in a clay biggin, or cottage, in the parish of Alloway, near the little town of Ayr.

Auld Ayr, wham ne'er a town surpasses
For honest men and bonnie lasses.

His father was a poor crofter, a hard working, God fearing man of the Covenanter type, who labored unceasingly to earn a living from the soil of a rented farm. The children went barefoot in all seasons, almost from the time they could walk they were expected to labor and at thirteen Bobbie was doing a man's work at the plow or the reaping. The toil was severe, the reward, at best, was to escape dire poverty or disgraceful debt, but there was yet a nobility in the life which is finely reflected in "The Cotter's Saturday Night," a poem which ranks with Whittier's "Snow Bound" among the best that labor has ever inspired.

As a farmer's boy Burns worked in the open, in close contact with nature, and the result is evident in all his verse. Sunshine or storm, bird song or winter wind, the flowers, the stars, the dew of the morning,—open Burns where you will, and you are face to face with these elemental realities. Sometimes his reflection of nature is exquisitely tender, as in "To a Mouse" or "To a Mountain Daisy"; but for the most part he regards nature not sentimentally, like Gray, or religiously, like Wordsworth and Bryant, but in a breezy, companionable way which suggests the song of "Under the Greenwood Tree" in *As You Like It*. Another influence in Burns's life came from his elementary education.

There were no ancient classics studied in the school which he attended,—fortunately, perhaps, for his best work is free from the outworn classical allusions which decorate the bulk of eighteenth-century verse. In the evening he listened to tales from Scottish history, which stirred him deeply and made him live in a present world rather than in the misty region of Greek mythology. One result of this education was the downright honesty of Burns's poems. Here is no echo from a vanished world of gods and goddesses, but the voice of a man, living, working, feeling joy or sorrow in the presence of everyday nature and humanity.

For another formative influence Burns was indebted to Betty Davidson, a relative and an inmate of the household, who carried such a stock of old wives' tales as would scare any child into fits on a dark night. Hear Burns speak of her:

"She had, I suppose, the largest collection in the country of tales and songs concerning devils, ghosts, fairies, brownies, witches, warlocks, spunkies, kelpies, elf-candles, dead-lights, wraiths, apparitions, cantrips, giants, enchanted towers, dragons, and other trumpery. This cultivated the latent seeds of poetry, but had so strong an effect upon my imagination that to this hour, in my nocturnal rambles, I sometimes keep a sharp look-out in suspicious places." Reflections of these grotesque superstitions appear in such poems as the "Address to the Deil" and "Tam o' Shanter." The latter is commonly named as one of the few original works of Burns, but it is probably a retelling of some old witch-tale of Betty Davidson. The evil influence in Burns's life may be only suggested. It leads first to the tavern, to roistering and dissipation, to entanglements in vulgar love affairs; then swiftly to the loss of a splendid poetic gift, to hopeless debts, to degrading poverty, to an untimely death. Burns had his chance, if ever poet had it, after the publication of his first book (the famous Kilmarnock edition of 1786) when he was called in triumph to Edinburgh.

There he sold another edition of his poems for a sum that seemed fabulous to a poor crofter; whereupon he bought a farm and married his Jean Armour. He was acclaimed throughout the length and breadth of his native land, his poems were read by the wise and by the ignorant, he was the poet of Scotland, and the nation, proud of its gifted son, stood ready to honor and follow him.

But the old habits were too strong, and Burns took the downhill road. To this element of dissipation we owe his occasional bitterness, railing and coarseness, which make an expurgated edition of his poems essential to one who would enjoy the reading.

There is another element, often emphasised for its alleged influence on Burns's poetry. During his lifetime the political world was shaken by the American and French revolutions, democracy was in the air, and the watchwords "Liberty, Equality, Fraternity" inspired many a song besides the *Marseillaise* and many a document besides the Declaration of Independence.

That Burns was aware of this political commotion is true, but he was not much influenced by it. He was at home only in his own Scottish field, and even there his interests were limited,—not to be compared with those of Walter Scott, for example. When the Bastille was stormed, and the world stood aghast, Burns was too much engrossed in personal matters to be greatly moved by distant affairs in France. Not to the Revolution, therefore, but to his Scottish blood do we owe the thrilling "Scots Wha Hae," one of the world's best battle songs, not to the new spirit of democracy abroad but to the old Covenanter spirit at home do we owe "A Man's a Man for a' That" with its assertion of elemental manhood.

The Songs of Burns

From such an analysis of Burns's life one may forecast his subject and his method. Living intensely in a small field, he must discover that there are just two poetic subjects of abiding interest. These are Nature and Humanity, and of these Burns must write from first-hand knowledge, simply, straight forwardly, and with sincerity. Moreover, as Burns lives in an intense way, reading himself rather than books, he must discover that the ordinary man is more swayed by strong feeling than by logical reasons. He will write, therefore, of the common emotions that lie between the extremes of laughter and tears, and his appeal will be to the heart rather than to the head of his reader. This emotional power of Burns, his masterful touch upon human heartstrings, is the first of his poetic qualities; and he has others which fairly force themselves upon the attention. For example, many of his lyrics ("Auld Lang Syne," "Banks o' Doon," "Flow Gently, Sweet Afton," "O Wert Thou in the Cauld Blast") have been repeatedly set to music; and the reason is that they were written to music, that in such poems Burns was refashioning some old material to the tune of a Scottish song. There is a singing quality in his poetry which not only makes it pleasant reading but which is apt to set the words tripping to melody. For a specific example take this stanza from "Of a' the Airts," a lyric which one can hardly read without making a tune to match it:

> I see her in the dewy flow'rs,
> I see her sweet and fair;
> I hear her in the tunefu' birds,
> I hear her charm the air:
> There's not a bonie flow'r that springs
> By fountain, shaw or green,
> There's not a bonie bird that sings,
> But minds me o' my Jean.

Sympathy is another marked characteristic of Burns, a wide, all-embracing sympathy that knows no limit save for hypocrites, at whom he pointed his keenest satire. His feeling for nature is reflected in "To a Mouse" and "To a Daisy"; his comradeship with noble men appears in "The Cotter's Saturday Night," with riotous and bibulous men in "The Jolly Beggars," with smugglers and their ilk in "The Deil's Awa' with the Exciseman," with patriots in "Bannockburn," with men who mourn in "To Mary in Heaven," and with all lovers in a score of famous lyrics.

Side by side with Burns's sympathy (for Smiles live next door to Tears) appears his keen sense of humor, a humor that is sometimes rollicking, as in "Contented wi' Little," and again too broad for decency. For the most part, however, Burns contents himself with dry, quiet sarcasm delivered with an air of great seriousness:

Ah, gentle dames, it gars me greet
To think how mony counsels sweet,
How mony lengthened sage advices
The husband frae the wife despises!

Why Burns is Read

Such qualities, appearing on almost every page of Burns's little book of poetry, show how widely he differs from the formal school of Pope and Dryden. They labor to compose poetry, while Burns gives the impression of singing, as naturally as a child sings from a full heart. Again, most eighteenth-century poets wrote for the favoured few, but Burns wrote for all his neighbors. His first book was bought farmers, plowboys, milkmaids,—by every Lowlander who could scrape together three shillings to buy a treasure. Then scholars got hold of it, taking it from humble hands, and Burns was called to Edinburgh to prepare a larger edition of his songs. For a half century Scotland kept him to herself, (Up to 1850 Burns was rarely mentioned in treatises on English literature. One reason for his late recognition was that the Lowland vocabulary employed in most of his poems was only half intelligible to the ordinary English reader) then his work went wide in the world, to be read again by plain men and women, by sailors on the sea, by soldiers round the campfire, by farmers, mechanics, tradesmen, who in their new homes in Australia or America warmed themselves at the divine fire which was kindled, long ago, in the little clay biggin at Alloway.

If one should ask, Why this world wide welcome to Burns, the while Pope remains a mark for literary criticism? the answer is that Burns has a most extraordinary power of touching the hearts of common men. He is one of the most democratic of poets, he takes for his subject a simple experience—a family gathering at eventide, a fair, a merrymaking, a joy, a grief, the finding of a flower, the love of a lad for a lass—and with rare simplicity reflects the emotion that such an experience awakens.

Seen through the poet's eyes, this simple emotion becomes radiant and lovely, a thing not of earth but of heaven. That is the genius of Burns, to ennoble human feeling, to reveal some hidden beauty in a commonplace experience. The luminous world of fine thought and fine emotion which we associate with the name of poetry he opened not to scholars alone but to all humble folk who toil and endure. As a shoemaker critic once said, "Burns confirms my former suspicion that the world was made for me as well as for Cæsar."

MINOR POETS OF ROMANTICISM

There were other poets who aided in the romantic revival, and among them William Cowper (1731-1800) is one of the most notable. His most ambitious works, such as *The Task* and the translation of Homer into blank verse, have fallen into neglect, and he is known to modern readers chiefly by a few familiar hymns and by the ballad of "John Gilpin."

Less gifted but more popular than Cowper was James Macpherson (1736-1796), who made a sensation that spread rapidly over Europe and America with his *Fingal* (1762) and other works of the same kind—wildly heroic poems which, he alleged, were translations from Celtic manuscripts written by an ancient bard named Ossian. Another and better literary forgery appeared in a series of ballads called *The Rowley Papers,* dealing with medieval themes.

These were written by "the marvelous boy" Thomas Chatterton (1752-1770), who professed to have found the poems in a chest of old manuscripts. The success of these forgeries, especially of the "Ossian" poems, is an indication of the awakened interest in medieval poetry and legend which characterised the whole romantic movement.

In this connection, Thomas Percy (1729-1811) did a notable work when he published, after years of research, his Reliques of Ancient English Poetry (1765). This was a collection of old ballads, which profoundly influenced Walter Scott, and which established a foundation for all later works of balladry.

Another interesting figure in the romantic revival is William Blake (1757-1827), a strange, mystic child, a veritable John o' Dreams, whom some call madman because of his huge, chaotic, unintelligible poems, but whom others regard as the supreme poetical genius of the eighteenth century. His only readable works are the boyish *Poetical Sketches* (1783) and two later volumes called *Songs of Innocence* and Songs of Experience (1794).

Even these contain much to make us question Blake's sanity; but they contain also a few lyrics that might have been written by an elf rather than a man,—beautiful, elusive lyrics that haunt us like a strain of gypsy music, a memory of childhood, a bird song in the night:

Can the eagle see what is in the pit,
Or wilt thou go ask the mole?
Can wisdom be put in a silver rod,
Or love in a golden bowl?

In the witchery of these lyrics eighteenth-century poetry appears commonplace; but they attracted no attention, even "Holy Thursday," the sweetest song of poor children ever written, passing unnoticed. That did not trouble Blake, however, who cared nothing for rewards. He was a childlike soul, well content,

To see the world in a grain of sand,
And a heaven in a wild flower;
Hold infinity in the palm of your hand,
And eternity in an hour.

THE EARLY ENGLISH NOVEL

An important literary event of the eighteenth century was the appearance of the modern novel. This invention, generally credited to the English, differs radically from the old romance, which was known to all civilised peoples. Walter Scott made the following distinction between the two types of fiction: the romance is a story in which our interest centers in marvelous incidents, brought to pass by extraordinary or superhuman characters; the novel is a story which is more natural, more in harmony with our experience of life. Such a definition, though faulty, is valuable in that it points to the element of imagination as the distinguishing mark between the romance and the true novel.

Take, for example, the romances of Arthur or Sindbad or the Green Knight. Here are heroes of more than human endurance, ladies of surpassing loveliness, giants, dragons, enchanters, marvelous adventures in the land of imagination. Such fanciful stories, valuable as a reflection of the ideals of different races, reached their highest point in the Middle Ages, when they were used to convey the ideals of chivalry and knightly duty.

They grew more fantastic as they ran to seed, till in the Elizabethan age they had degenerated into picaresque stories (from *picaro,* "a rogue") which recounted the adventures not of a noble knight but of some scoundrel or outcast. They were finally laughed out of literature in numerous burlesques, of which the most famous is *Don Quixote* (1605). In the humor of this story, in the hero's fighting windmills and meeting so many adventures that he had no time to breathe, we have an excellent criticism not of chivalry, as is sometimes alleged, but of extravagant popular romances on the subject.

Compare now these old romances with *Ivanhoe* or Robinson Crusoe or *Lorna Doone* or *A Tale of Two Cities*. In each of the last-named novels one may find three elements: a story, a study, and an exercise of the creative imagination. A modern work of fiction must still have a good story, if anybody is to read it; must contain also a study or observation of humanity, not of superhuman heroes but of men and women who work or play or worship in close relationship to their fellows. Finally, the story and the study must be fused by the imagination, which selects or creates various scenes, characters, incidents, and which orders or arranges its materials so as to make a harmonious work that appeals to our sense of truth and beauty; in other words, a work of art.

Such is the real novel, a well-told story in tune with human experience, holding true to life, exercising fancy but keeping it under control, arousing thought as well as feeling, and appealing to our intellect as well as to our imagination. (This convenient division of prose fiction into romances and novels is open to challenge. Some critics use the name "novel" for any work of prose fiction. They divide novels into two classes, stories (or short stories) and romances. The story relates simple or detached incidents; the romance deals with life in complex relations, dominated by strong emotions, especially by the emotion of love.

Other critics arrange prose fiction in the following classes: novels of adventure (Robinson Crusoe, The Last of the Mohicans), historical novels (Ivanhoe, The Spy), romantic novels (Lorna Doone, The Heart of Midlothian), novels of manners (Cranford, Pride and Prejudice), novels of personality (Silas Marner, The Scarlet Letter), novels of purpose (Oliver Twist, Uncle Tom's Cabin). Still another classification arranges fiction under two heads, romance and realism. In the romance, which portrays unusual incidents or characters, we see the ideal, the poetic side of humanity; in the realistic novel, dealing with ordinary men and women, the prosaic element of life is emphasised.)

DEFOE (1661-1731)

Among the forerunners of the modern novel is Daniel Foe, author of *Robinson Crusoe,* who began to call himself "Defoe" after he attained fame. He produced an amasing variety of wares: newspapers, magazines, ghost stories, biographies, journals, memoirs, satires, picaresque romances, essays on religion, reform, trade, projects,—in all more than two hundred works. These were written in a picturesque style and with such a wealth of detail that, though barefaced inventions for the most part, they passed for veracious chronicles. One critic, thinking of the vividly realistic *Journal of the Plague Year* and Memoirs of a Cavalier, says that "Defoe wrote history, but invented the facts"; another declares that "the one little art of which Defoe was past master was the art of forging a story and imposing it on the world as truth." The long list of his works ends with a *History of the Devil*, in 1726.

DeFoe's career was an extraordinary one. By nature and training he seems to have preferred devious ways to straight, and to have concealed his chief motive whether he appeared as reformer or politician, tradesman or writer, police-spy or friend of outcasts. His education, which he picked up from men and circumstance, was more varied than any university could have given him. Perhaps the chief factor in this practical education was his ability to turn every experience to profitable account. As a journalist he invented the modern magazine (his *Review* appeared in 1704, five years before Steele's *Tatler*); also he projected the interview, the editorial, the "scoop," and other features which still figure in our newspapers.

As a hired pamphleteer, writing satires against Whigs or Tories, he learned so many political secrets that when one party fell he was the best possible man to be employed by the other. While sitting in the stocks (in punishment for writing a satirical pamphlet that set Tories and Churchmen by the ears) he made such a hit with his doggerel verses against the authorities that crowds came to the pillory to cheer him and to buy his poem. While in durance vile, in the old Newgate Prison, he mingled freely with all sorts of criminals (there were no separate cells in those days), won their secrets, and used them to advantage in his picaresque romances. He learned also so much of the shady side of London life that no sooner was he released than he was employed as a secret service agent, or spy, by the government which had jailed him.

It is as difficult to find the real Foe amidst such devious trails as to determine where a caribou is from the maze of footprints which he leaves behind him. He seems to have been untiring in his effort to secure better treatment of outcast folk, he speaks of himself with apparent sincerity, as having received his message from the Divine Spirit, but the impression which he made upon the upper classes was reflected by Swift, who called him "a grave, dogmatical rogue".

For many years he was a popular hero, trusted not only by the poor but by the criminal classes (ordinarily keen judges of honesty in other men), until his secret connection with the government became known. Then suspicion fell upon him, his popularity was destroyed and he fled from London. The last few years of his life were spent in hiding from real or imaginary enemies.

Defoe was approaching his sixtieth year when he wrote Robinson Crusoe (1719), a story which has been read thrcugh out the civilised world, and which, after two centuries of life, is still young and vigorous. The first charm of the book is in its moving adventures, which are surprising enough to carry us through the moralising passages. These also have their value; for who ever read them without asking, What would I have done or thought or felt under such circumstances? The work of society is now so comfortably divided that one seldom dreams of being his own mechanic, farmer, hunter, herdsman, cook and tailor, as Crusoe was. Thinking of his experience we are brought face to face with our dependence on others, with our debt to the countless, unnamed men whose labor made civilisation possible. We understand also the pioneers, who in the far, lonely places of the earth have won a home and country from the wilderness.

When the adventures are duly appreciated we discover another charm of *Robinson Crusoe,* namely, its intense reality. Defoe had that experience of many projects, and that vivid imagination, which enabled him to put himself in the place of his hero, (The basis of *Robinson Crusoe* was the experience of an English sailor, Alexander Selkirk, or Selcraig, who was marooned on the lonely island of Juan Fernandez, off the coast of Chile. There he lived in solitude for the space of five years before he was rescued. When Selkirk returned to England (1709) an account of his adventures appeared in the public press.) to anticipate his needs, his feelings, his labors and triumph.

That Crusoe was heroic none will deny; yet his heroism was of a different kind from that which we meet in the old romances. Here was no knight "without fear and without reproach," but a plain man with his strength and weakness. He despaired like other men; but instead of giving way to despair he drew up a list of his blessings and afflictions, "like debtor and creditor," found a reasonable balance in his favour, and straightway conquered himself,—which is the first task of all real heroes. Again, he had horrible fears; he beat his breast, cried out as one in mortal terror; then "I thought that would do little good, so I began to make a raft." So he overcame his fears, as he overcame the difficulties of the place, by setting himself to do alone what a whole race of men had done before him. *Robinson Crusoe* is therefore history as well as fiction; its subject is not Alexander Selkirk but Homo Sapiens; its lesson is the everlasting triumph of will and work.

RICHARDSON

One morning in 1740 the readers of London found a new work for sale in the bookshops. It was made up of alleged letters from a girl to her parents, a sentimental girl who opened her heart freely, explaining its hopes, fears, griefs, temptations, and especially its moral sensibilities. Such a work of fiction was unique at that time. Delighted readers waited for another and yet another volume of the same story, till more than a year had passed and *Pamela, or Virtue Rewarded* reached its happy ending. The book made a sensation in England; it was speedily translated, and repeated its triumph on the other side of the Channel. Comparatively few people could read it now without being bored, but it is famous in the history of literature as the first English novel; that is, a story of a human life under stress of emotion, told by one who understood the tastes of his own age, and who strove to keep his work true to human nature in all ages.

The author of *Pamela*, Samuel Richardson (1689—1761), was a very proper person, well satisfied with himself, who conducted a modest business as printer and bookseller. For years he had practiced writing, and had often been employed by sentimental young women who came to him for model love letters. Hence the extraordinary knowledge of feminine feelings which Richardson displayed; hence also the epistolary form in which his novels were written. His aim in all his work was to teach morality and correct deportment. His strength was in his power to analyse and portray emotions. His weakness lay in his vanity, which led him to shun masculine society and to foregather at tea tables with women who flattered him.

Led by the success of *Pamela,* which portrayed the feelings of a servant girl, the author began another series of letters which ended in the eight-volume novel *Clarissa, or The History of a Young Lady* (1748). The story appeared in installments, which were awaited with feverish impatience till the agony drew to an end, and the heroine died amid the sobs of ten thousand readers. Yet the story had power, and the central figure of Clarissa was impressive in its pathos and tragedy. The novel would still be readable if it were stripped of the stilted conversations and sentimental gush in which Richardson delighted; but that would leave precious little of the story.

Fielding

In vigorous contrast with the prim and priggish Richardson is Henry Fielding (1707-1754), a big, jovial, reckless man, full of animal spirits, who was ready to mitigate any man's troubles or forget his own by means of a punch bowl or a venison potpie. He was noble born, but seems to have been thrown on the world to shift for himself. After an excellent education he studied law, and was for some years a police magistrate, in which position he increased his large knowledge of the seamy side of life. He had a pen for vigorous writing, and after squandering two modest fortunes (his own and his wife's) he proceeded to earn his living by writing buffooneries for the stage. Then appeared Richardson's Pamela, or Virtue Rewarded, and in ridiculing its sentimental heroine Fielding found his vocation as a novelist.

He began *Joseph Andrews* (1742) as a joke, by taking for his hero an alleged brother of Pamela, who was also virtuous but whose reward was to be kicked out of doors. Then the story took to the open road, among the inns and highways of an age when traveling in rural England was almost as adventurous as campaigning in Flanders. In the joy of his story Fielding soon forgot his burlesque of Richardson, and attempted what he called a realistic novel; that is, a story of real life. The morality and decorum which Richardson exalted appeared to Fielding as hypocrisy; so he devoted himself to a portrayal of men and manners as he found them.

Undoubtedly there were plenty of good men and manners at that time, but Fielding had a vagabond taste that delighted in rough scenes, and of these also eighteenth-century England could furnish an abundance. Hence his *Joseph* Andrews is a picture not of English society, as is often alleged, but only of the least significant part of society. The same is true of *Tom Jones* (1749), which is the author's most vigorous work, and of *Amelia* (1751), in which, though he portrays one good woman, he repeats many of the questionable incidents of his earlier works.

There is power in all these novels, the power of keen observation, of rough humor, of downright sincerity; but unhappily the power often runs to waste in long speeches to the reader, in descriptions of brutal or degrading scenes, and in a wholly unnecessary coarseness of expression.

INFLUENCE OF THE EARLY NOVELS

The idea of the modern novel seems to have been developed by several English authors, each of whom, like pioneers in a new country, left his stamp on subsequent works in the same field. Richardson's governing motive may be summed up in the word "sensibility," which means "delicacy of feeling," and which was a fashion, almost a fetish, in eighteenth-century society. Because it was deemed essential to display proper or decorous feeling on all occasions, Richardson's heroines were always analysing their emotions; they talked like a book of etiquette; they indulged in tears, fainting, transports of joy, paroxysms of grief, apparently striving to make themselves as unlike a real woman as possible. It is astonishing how far and wide this fad of sensibility spread through the literary world, and how many gushing heroines of English and American fiction during the next seventy-five years were modeled on Pamela or Clarissa.

In view of this artificial fashion, the influence of Fielding was like the rush of crisp air into a hot house. His aim was realistic, that is, to portray real people in their accustomed ways. Unfortunately his aim was spoiled by the idea that to be realistic one must go to the gutter for material. And then appeared Goldsmith, too much influenced by the fad of sensibility, but aiming to depict human life as governed by high ideals, and helping to cleanse the English novel from brutality and indecency.

There were other early novelists, a host of them, but in Richardson, Fielding and Goldsmith we have enough. Richardson emphasised the analysis of human feeling or motive, and that of itself was excellent; but his exaggerated sentimentality set a bad fashion which our novelists were almost a century in overcoming. Fielding laid stress on realism, and that his influence was effective is shown in the work of his disciple Thackeray, who could be realistic without being coarse. And Goldsmith made all subsequent novelists his debtors by exalting that purity of domestic life to which every home worthy of the name forever strives or aspires.

If it be asked, What novels of the early type ought one to read? the answer is simple. Unless you want to curdle your blood by a tale of mystery and horror (in which case Mrs. Radcliffe's *Mysteries of Udolpho* will serve the purpose) there are only two that young readers will find satisfactory: the realistic *Robinson Crusoe* by Defoe, and the romantic *Vicar of Wakefield* by Goldsmith.

14

Romanticism

The changing landscape of Britain brought about by the steam engine has two major outcomes: the boom of industrialism with the expansion of the city, and the consequent depopulation of the countryside as a result of the enclosures, or privatisation of pastures. Most peasants poured into the city to work in the new factories.

This abrupt change is revealed by the change of meaning in five key words: industry (once meaning "creativity"), democracy (once disparagingly used as "mob rule"), class (from now also used with a social connotation), art (once just meaning "craft"), culture (once only belonging to farming).

But the poor condition of workers, the new class-conflicts and the pollution of the environment causes a reaction to urbanism and industrialisation prompting poets to rediscover the beauty and value of nature. Mother earth is seen as the only source of wisdom, the only solution to the ugliness caused by machines.

The superiority of nature and instinct over civilisation had been preached by Jean Jacques Rousseau and his message was picked by almost all European poets. The first in England were the Lake Poets, a small group of friends including William Wordsworth and Samuel Taylor Coleridge. These early Romantic Poets brought a new emotionalism and introspection, and their emergence is marked by the first romantic Manifesto in English literature, the "Preface to the Lyrical Ballads".

This collection was mostly contributed by Wordsworth, although Coleridge must be credited for his long and impressive *Rime of the Ancient Mariner*, a tragic ballad about the survival of one sailor through a series of supernatural events on his voyage through the south seas which involves the slaying of an albatross, the death of the rest of the crew, a visit from Death and his mate, Life-in-Death, and the eventual redemption of the Mariner. Coleridge and Wordsworth, however, understood romanticism in two entirely different ways: while Coleridge sought to make the supernatural "real" (much like sci-fi movies use special effects to make unlikely plots believable), Wordsworth sought to stir the imagination of readers through his down-to-earth characters taken from real life (in "The Idiot Boy", for example), or the beauty of the Lake District that largely inspired his production (as in "Lines Composed a Few Miles Above Tintern Abbey").

The "Second generation" of Romantic poets includes Lord Byron, Percy Bysshe Shelley and John Keats. Byron, however, was still influenced by 18th-century satirists and was, perhaps the least 'romantic' of the three. His amours with a number of prominent but married ladies was also a way to voice his dissent on the hypocrisy of a high society that was only apparently religious but in fact largely libertine, the same that had derided him for being physically impaired. His first trip to Europe resulted in the first two cantos of Childe Harold's Pilgrimage, a mock-heroic epic of a young man's adventures in Europe but also a sharp satire against London society. Despite *Childe Harold*'s success on his return to England, accompanied by the publication of *The Corsair* his alleged incestuous affair with his half-sister Augusta Leigh in 1816 actually forced him to leave England for good and seek asylum on the continent.

Here he joined Percy Bysshe Shelley, his wife Mary, with his secretary John William Polidori on the shores of Lake Geneva during the 'year without a summer' of 1816. Polidori's *The Vampyre* was published in 1819, creating the literary vampire genre. His short story was inspired by the life of Lord Byron and his poem *The Giaour*.

One of Percy Shelley's most prominent works is the *Ode to the West Wind*. Despite his apparent refusal to believe in God, this poem is considered a homage to pantheism, the recognition of a spiritual presence in nature. Shelley's groundbreaking poem *The Masque of Anarchy* calls for nonviolence in protest and political action. It is perhaps the first modern statement of the principle of nonviolent protest. Mahatma Gandhi's passive resistance was influenced and inspired by Shelley's verse, and

Gandhi would often quote the poem to vast audiences. The plot for Mary Shelley's *Frankenstein* is said to have come from a nightmare she had during stormy nights on Lake Geneva in the company of Percy Shelley, Lord Byron, and John Polidori. Her idea of making a body with human parts stolen from different corpses and then animating it with electricity was perhaps influenced by Alessandro Volta's invention and Luigi Galvani's experiments with dead frogs. Frankenstein's chilling tale also suggests modern organ transplants, tissue regeneration, reminding us of the moral issues raised by today's medicine. But the creature of Frankenstein is incredibly romantic as well. Although "the monster" is intelligent, good and loving, he is shunned by everyone because of his ugliness and deformity, and the desperation and envy that result from social exclusion turn him against the very man who created him.

John Keats did not share Byron's and Shelley's extremely revolutionary ideals, but his cult of pantheism is as important as Shelley's. Keats was in love with the ancient stones of the Parthenon that Lord Elgin had brought to England from Greece, also known as the Elgin Marbles).

He celebrates ancient Greece: the beauty of free, youthful love couples here with that of classical art. Keats's great attention to art, especially in his *Ode on a Grecian Urn* is quite new in romanticism, and it inspired Walter Pater's and then Oscar Wilde's belief in the absolute value of art as independent from aesthetics.

Some rightly think that the most popular novelist of the era was Sir Walter Scott, whose grand historical romances inspired a generation of painters, composers, and writers throughout Europe. Scott's novel-writing career was launched in 1814 with *Waverley*, often called the first historical novel, and was followed by *Ivanhoe*. His popularity in England and further abroad did much to form the modern stereotype of Scottish culture. Other novels by Scott which contributed to the image of him as a Scottish patriot include *Rob Roy*.

In retrospect, we now look back to Jane Austen, who wrote novels about the life of the landed gentry, seen from a woman's point of view, and wryly focused on practical social issues, especially marriage and choosing the right partner in life, with love being above all else. Austen's *Pride and Prejudice* would set the model for all Romance Novels to follow. Jane Austen created the ultimate hero and heroine in Darcy and Elizabeth, who must overcome their own stubborn pride and the prejudices they have toward each other, in order to come to a middle ground, where they finally realise their love for one another.

Austen's other most notable works include; *Sense and Sensibility, Mansfield Park, Persuasion* and *Emma*. In her novels, Austen brings to light the hardships women faced, who usually did not inherit money, could not work and where their only chance in life depended on the man they married. She brought to light not only the difficulties women faced in her day, but also what was expected of men and of the careers they had to follow. This she does with wit and humour and with endings where all characters, good or bad, receive exactly what they deserve. Poet, painter and printmaker William Blake is usually included among the English Romanticists, though his visionary work is much different from that of the others discussed in this section.

In America, with the essays and poetry of Ralph Waldo Emerson began an explosion of American English literature, which included the publication of Herman Melville's *Moby Dick* and the poetry of Walt Whitman and Emily Dickinson.

ROMANTIC POETRY

Romanticism largely began as a reaction against the prevailing Enlightenment ideals of the day. Inevitably, the characterisation of a broad range of contemporaneous poets and poetry under the single unifying name can be viewed more as an exercise in historical compartmentalisation than an attempt to capture the essence of the actual 'movement'.

Indeed, the term "Romanticism" did not arise until the Victorian period. Nonetheless, poets such as William Wordsworth were actively engaged in trying to create a new kind of poetry that emphasised intuition over reason and the pastoral over the urban, often eschewing consciously poetic language in an effort to use more everyday or "real" language. Wordsworth himself in the Preface to his and Coleridge's *Lyrical*

Ballads defined good poetry as "the spontaneous overflow of powerful feelings," though in the same sentence he goes on to clarify this statement by asserting that nonetheless any poem of value must still be composed by a man "possessed of more than usual organic sensibility (who has) also thought long and deeply;" he also emphasises the importance of the use of meter in poetry (which he views as one of the key features that differentiates poetry from prose). Although many people seize unfairly upon the notion of spontaneity in Romantic Poetry, one must realise that the movement was still greatly concerned with the pain of composition, of translating these emotive responses into the form of Poetry. Indeed, Samuel Taylor Coleridge, another prominent Romantic poet and critic in his *On Poesy or Art* sees art as "the mediatress between, and reconciler of nature and man". Such an attitude reflects what might be called the dominant theme of Romantic Poetry: the filtering of natural emotion through the human mind in order to create art, coupled with an awareness of the duality created by such a process.

Leigh Hunt. Although chronologically earliest among these writers, William Blake was a relatively late addition to the list; prior to the 1970s, romanticism was known for its "Big Five."

For some critics, the term establishes an artificial context for disparate work and removing that work from its real historical context" at the expense of equally valid themes (particularly those related to politics.)

The six most well-known authors are, in order of birth and with an example of their work:

- William Blake—The Marria ge of Heaven and Hell
- William Wordsworth—The Prelude
- Samuel Taylor Coleridge—Rime of the Ancient Mariner
- George Gordon, Lord Byron—Don Juan "· Childe Harold's Pilgrimage"
- Percy Bysshe Shelley—Prometheus Unbound "Adonais" "Ode to the West Wind" "Ozymandias"
- John Keats—Great Odes "· Hyperion" "Endymion"

The "Three Bards"

The term "Three Bards" (*Trzej Wieszczowie*) pertains to the three major poets of Romanticism in Polish literature. The word *Wieszcz* in English means *a prophet* and is according to a figure of legendary Ukrainian bard Wernyhora, so The "Three Bards" were considered as Ralph Waldo Emerson called it to be "Representative Men" of nations. Moreover, their verses for a long time were considered to be a moral typified, historiosophical and Metaphysical prophecy according to Christianity and ideals of Freedom, Love and Faith. It was heavy influenced by 1 Corinthians 14: "But everyone who prophesies speaks to men for their strengthening, encouragement and comfort" (1 Cor 14:3).

His memory was
Written upon, and deeply, but, because
It had long rotted in the dark, my friend
Could not read what was written: "We'd better send
For God. He will remember and tell us all."
(Adam Mickiewicz)

- Adam Mickiewicz, *Pan Tadeusz*
- Juliusz SBowacki, *Kordian*
- Zygmunt KrasiDski, *Irydion*

Sometimes Cyprian Kamil Norwid or Kornel Ujejski is called The "Fourth Bard".

Notable Females

Although the "Big Six" male poets remain the principal figures in English romantic literature, some of the best-regarded poets of the time were in fact women. Notable Female poets include: Mary Shelley, Anna Laetitia Barbauld, Charlotte Turner Smith, Mary Robinson, Hannah More and Joanna Baillie.

Characteristics of Romantic Poets

Beauty of the Supernatural: British Romantics believed something existed beyond the physical world. The Spirit world, according to Romantics, had unleashed its power and inspiration to overthrow tyranny in government and in literature. Unlike the American Romantics who wrote of ghosts, demonic cats, and rope-gnawing rats, British Romanticism's treatment of the supernatural excluded horror and the macabre and focused on supernatural energy and beauty.

Championing of the Individual: Revolution in Europe brought to light the importance of the individual. Ordinary people now became the subject of lofty language. British Romanticism attempted to free itself from traditional forms and subjects.

The Importance of Nature: The poet, according to the Romantics, is only at peace when in nature; moreover, while in nature, the poet intervened with the great Universal Mind. Romantic poets made frequent use of personification with nature, ascribing human traits to daffodils, fields, streams, and lakes. Nature, in essence, became emotionally expressive.

The Dangers of Technology: A natural consequence of celebrating nature was a disdain for technology and industrialism.

Major Early Romantic Poets

The following share characteristics of Romantic poets:

William Blake (1757-1827): Blake's poetry dwelt upon his divine vision and rebelled against traditional poetic forms and techniques. He created his own mythological world with man as the central figure. His more famous poems include *The Lamb,The Tyger, The Chimney Sweeper,* and *The Clod and the Pebble.* What makes Blake's poem especially attractive for teaching in high school is he often wrote two poems with the same title—one poem negative and one poem positive, excellent for compare and contrast writing.

William Wordsworth (1770-1850): The most famous of the British Romantics, Wordsworth is considered the nature poet. He revolutionised poetic subjects, focusing on ordinary people in rustic settings. He, in addition, wrote about and considered the poet as superior to all other writers. His most famous poems include *I Wandered Lonely as a Cloud, We are Seven,*and *I Travelled Among Unknown Men.* Most high school literature textbooks have at least one poem by Wordsworth.

Samuel Taylor Coleridge (1772-1834): Coleridge and Wordsworth are often grouped together as The Lake Poets, and for good reason. Together they are credited as the founders of the Romantic movement. Coleridge's most famous poems, *RIme of the Ancient Mariner, Kubla Kahn,* and *Christabel* have a distinct supernatural element and strongly influenced American Romantics such as Poe and Hawthorne.

Later Romantic Poets

The following share characteristics of Romantic poets:

Lord Byron (1788-1824): Lord Byron enjoyed unmatched popularity. Byron's most famous creations are his dark heroes, called Byronic heroes, who, in fact, were not heroes at all, but stood out from ordinary humans as larger than life. The Byronic hero brooded, possessed insatiable appetites and incredible strength, rebelled against societal norms, and forced upon himself exile. Byron's most famous works include *Don Juan* and *Childe Harold's Pilgrimage.* Lord Byron is generally reserved for university level literature courses and is rarely found in high school anthologies.

Percy Bysshe Shelley (1792-1822): Like all Romantics, Shelley was a radical non conformist. He campaigned for social justice, even marrying the daughter of Mary Wollstonecraft, an English leader in the women's rights movement. His wife would later write *Frankenstein.* His most famous poems include *Mutability, Ozymandias,* and *Ode to the West Wind.*

John Keats (1795-1821): Perhaps the most popular Later Romantic poet, Keats accomplished great things during his short life. His *Ode to a Nightingale, Ode on a Grecian Urn, and Ode on Melancholy* find their way into anthologies throughout the English speaking world. Keats considered contact with poets as a threat to his independence and therefore shunned his contemporaries.

15

Victorian Literature

Victorian literature is the literature produced during the reign of Queen Victoria (1837–1901) (the Victorian era). It forms a link and transition between the writers of the romantic period and the very different literature of the 20th century.

The 19th century saw the novel become the leading form of literature in English. The works by pre-Victorian writers such as Jane Austen and Walter Scott had perfected both closely-observed social satire and adventure stories. Popular works opened a market for the novel amongst a reading public. The 19th century is often regarded as a high point in British literature as well as in other countries such as France, the United States and Russia. Books, and novels in particular, became ubiquitous, and the "Victorian novelist" created legacy works with continuing appeal.

Novelists

Charles Dickens is a prime exemplar of Victorian novelist. Extraordinarily popular in his day with his characters taking on a life of their own beyond the page, Dickens is still one of the most popular and read authors of that time. His first real novel, *The Pickwick Papers*, written at only twenty-five, was an overnight success, and all his subsequent works sold extremely well.

He worked diligently and prolifically to produce entertaining writing the public wanted, but also to offer commentary on social challenges of the era. The comedy of his first novel has a satirical edge which pervades his writings. These deal with the plight of the poor and oppressed and end with a ghost story cut short by his death. The slow trend in his fiction towards darker themes is mirrored in much of the writing of the century, and literature after his death in 1870 is notably different from that at the start of the era.

William Thackeray was Dickens's great rival at the time. With a similar style but a slightly more detached, acerbic and barbed satirical view of his characters, he also tended to depict situations of a more middle class flavour than Dickens. He is best known for his novel *Vanity Fair*, subtitled *A Novel without a Hero*, which is also an example of a form popular in Victorian literature: the historical novel, in which very recent history is depicted.

Anthony Trollope tended to write about a slightly different part of the structure, namely the landowning and professional classes. Away from the big cities and the literary society, Haworth in West Yorkshire held a powerhouse of novel writing: the home of the Brontë family. Anne, Charlotte and Emily Brontë had time in their short lives to produce masterpieces of fiction although these were not immediately appreciated by Victorian critics. *Wuthering Heights*, Emily's only work, in particular has violence, passion, the supernatural, heightened emotion and emotional distance, an unusual mix for any novel but particularly at this time. It is a prime example of Gothic Romanticism from a woman's point of view during this period of time, examining class, myth, and gender. Another important writer of the period was George Eliot, a pseudonym which concealed a woman, Mary Ann Evans, who wished to write novels which would be taken seriously rather than the romances which women of the time were supposed to write.

The style of the Victorian novel

Victorian novels tend to be idealised portraits of difficult lives in which hard work, perseverance, love and luck win out in the end; virtue would be rewarded and wrongdoers are suitably punished. They tended to be of an improving nature with a central moral lesson at heart. While this formula was the basis for much of earlier Victorian fiction, the situation became more complex as the century progressed.

Other Literature

Children's Literature

The Victorians are sometimes credited with 'inventing childhood', partly via their efforts to stop child labour and the introduction of compulsory education. As children began to be able to read, literature for young people became a growth industry, with not only established writers producing works for children (such as Dickens' *A Child's History of England*) but also a new group of dedicated children's authors. Writers like Lewis Carroll, R. M. Ballantyne and Anna Sewell wrote mainly for children, although they had an adult following. Other authors such as Anthony Hope and Robert Louis Stevenson wrote mainly for adults, but their adventure novels are now generally classified as for children. Other genres include nonsense verse, poetry which required a child-like interest (*e.g.*, Lewis Carroll). School stories flourished: Thomas Hughes' Tom Brown's Schooldays and Kipling's Stalky and Co. are classics.

Poetry and Drama

Poetry in a sense settled down from the upheavals of the romantic era and much of the work of the time is seen as a bridge between this earlier era and the modernist poetry of the next century. Alfred Lord Tennyson held the poet laureateship for over forty years. Some Victorian poetry highly regarded at the time, such as William Ernest Henley's *Invictus,* is now seen as jingoistic and bombastic, but Tennyson's Charge of the Light Brigade was a fierce criticism of a famous military blunder; a pillar of the establishment not failing to attack the establishment. Comic verse abounded in the Victorian era. Magazines such as *Punch magazine* and *Fun magazine* teemed with humorous invention and were aimed at a well-educated readership. The most famous collection of Victorian comic verse is the Bab Ballads.

The husband and wife poetry team of Elizabeth Barrett Browning and Robert Browning conducted their love affair through verse and produced many tender and passionate poems. Both Matthew Arnold and Gerard Manley Hopkins wrote poems which sit somewhere in between the exultation of nature of the romantic Poetry and the Georgian Poetry of the early 20th century. Arnold's works hearken forward to some of the themes of these later poets, while Hopkins drew inspiration from verse forms of Old English poetry such as *Beowulf*. The reclaiming of the past was a major part of Victorian literature with an interest in both classical literature but also the medieval literature of England. The Victorians loved the heroic, chivalrous stories of knights of old and they hoped to regain some of that noble, courtly behaviour and impress it upon the people both at home and in the wider empire.

The best example of this is Alfred Tennyson's *Idylls of the King*, which blended the stories of King Arthur, particularly those by Thomas Malory, with contemporary concerns and ideas. The Pre-Raphaelite Brotherhood also drew on myth and folklore for their art, with Dante Gabriel Rossetti contemporaneously regarded as the chief poet amongst them, although his sister Christina is now held by scholars to be a stronger poet.

In dramatic, farces, musical burlesques, extravaganzas and comic operas competed with Shakespeare productions and serious drama by the likes of James Planché and Thomas William Robertson. In 1855, the German Reed Entertainments began a process of elevating the level of (formerly risqué) musical theatre in Britain that culminated in the famous series of comic operas by Gilbert and Sullivan and were followed by the 1890s with the first Edwardian musical comedies. The first play to achieve 500 consecutive performances was the London comedy *Our Boys* by H. J. Byron, opening in 1875. Its astonishing new record of 1,362 performances was bested in 1892 by *Charley's Aunt* by Brandon Thomas. After W. S. Gilbert, Oscar Wilde became the leading poet and dramatist of the late Victorian period. Wilde's plays, in particular, stand apart from the many now forgotten plays of Victorian times and have a much closer relationship to those of the Edwardian dramatists such as George Bernard Shaw, many of whose most important works were written in the 20th century. Wilde's 1895 comic masterpiece, *The Importance of Being Earnest*, was the greatest of the plays in which he held an ironic mirror to the aristocracy while displaying virtuosic mastery of wit and paradoxical wisdom. It has remained extremely popular.

Science, Philosophy and Discovery

The Victorian era was an important time for the development of science and the Victorians had a mission to describe and classify the entire natural world. Much of this writing does not rise to the level of being regarded as literature but one book in particular, Charles Darwin's *On the Origin of Species,* remains famous. The theory of evolution contained within the work shook many of the ideas the Victorians had about themselves and their place in the world. Although it took a long time to be widely accepted, it would dramatically change subsequent thought and literature. Other important non-fiction works of the time are the philosophical writings of John Stuart Mill covering logic, economics, liberty and utilitarianism. The large and influential histories of Thomas Carlyle: *The French Revolution, A History, On Heroes and Hero Worship* and Thomas Babington Macaulay: *The History of England from the Accession of James II.* The greater number of novels that contained overt criticism of religion did not stifle a vigorous list of publications on the subject of religion.

Two of the most important of these are John Henry Newman and Henry Edward Manning who both wished to revitalise Anglicanism with a return to the Roman Catholic Church. In a somewhat opposite direction, the ideas of socialism were permeating political thought at the time with Friedrich Engels writing his *Condition of the Working Classes in England* and William Morris writing the early socialist utopian novel *News from Nowhere.* One other important and monumental work begun in this era was the *Oxford English Dictionary* which would eventually become the most important historical dictionary of the English language.

Nature writing

In the U.S.A., Henry David Thoreau's works and Susan Fenimore Cooper's *Rural Hours* (1850) were canonical influences on Victorian nature writing. In the U.K., Philip Gosse and Sarah Bowdich Lee were two of the most popular nature writers in the early part of the Victorian era. The Illustrated London News, founded in 1842, was the world's first illustrated weekly newspaper and often published articles and illustrations dealing with nature; in the second half of the 19th century, books, articles, and illustrations on nature became widespread and popular among an increasingly urbanised reading public.

Supernatural and Fantastic Literature

The old Gothic tales that came out of the late 19th century are the first examples of the genre of fantastic fiction. These tales often centered on larger-than-life characters such as Sherlock Holmes, famous detective of the times, Barry Lee, big time gang leader, Sexton Blake, Phileas Fogg, and other fictional characters of the era, such as Dracula, Edward Hyde, The Invisible Man, and many other fictional characters who often had exotic enemies to foil. Spanning the 18th and 19th centuries, there was a particular type of story-writing known as gothic. Gothic literature combines romance and horror in attempt to thrill and terrify the reader.

Possible features in a gothic novel are foreign monsters, ghosts, curses, hidden rooms and witchcraft. Gothic tales usually take place in locations such as castles, monasteries, and cemeteries, although the gothic monsters sometimes cross over into the real world, making appearances in cities such as London and Paris. The problem with the classification of Victorian literature is great difference between the early works of the period and the later works which had more in common with the writers of the Edwardian period and many writers straddle this divide. People such as Arthur Conan Doyle, Rudyard Kipling, H. G. Wells, Bram Stoker, H. Rider Haggard, Jerome K. Jerome and Joseph Conrad all wrote some of their important works during Victoria's reign but the sensibility of their writing is frequently regarded as Edwardian.

The persistent popular embrace of Victorian literature has had a profound influence on modern literature and media. Writers such as Dickens and the Brontë sisters still sell robustly on most book resellers' lists and are frequently adapted into films and television productions, both directly and in modernised retellings. In addition, many modern novels such as *A Great and Terrible Beauty* demonstrate that the intricate cultural mores of the Victorian era finds a home in the modern cultural psyche.

16

Modern Literature

Modernist literature is the literary expression of the tendencies of modernism, especially high modernism. Modernistic literature tends to revolve around the themes of individualism, mistrust of institutions (government, religion) and the disbelief in any absolute truths, and to involve a literary structure that departs from conventionality and realism.

Modernism as a literary movement reached its height in Europe between 1900 and the middle 1920s. Modernist literature addressed aesthetic problems similar to those examined in non-literary forms of contemporaneous Modernist art, such as Modernist painting. Gertrude Stein's abstract writings, for example, have often been compared to the fragmentary and multi-perspectival Cubism of her friend Pablo Picasso. "The deepest problems of modern life derive from the claim of the individual to preserve the autonomy and individuality of his existence in the face of overwhelming social forces, of historical heritage, of external culture, and of the technique of life." The Modernist emphasis on a radical individualism can be seen in the many literary manifestos issued by various groups within the movement. The concerns expressed by Simmel above are echoed in Richard Huelsenbeck's "First German Dada Manifesto" of 1918: "Art in its execution and direction is dependent on the time in which it lives, and artists are creatures of their epoch.

The highest art will be that which in its conscious content presents the thousandfold problems of the day, the art which has been visibly shattered by the explosions of last week ... The best and most extraordinary artists will be those who every hour snatch the tatters of their bodies out of the frenzied cataract of life, who, with bleeding hands and hearts, hold fast to the intelligence of their time." The cultural history of humanity creates a unique common history that connects previous generations with the current generation of humans. The Modernist re-contextualisation of the individual within the fabric of this received social heritage can be seen in the "mythic method" which T.S. Eliot expounded in his discussion of James Joyce's *Ulysses*:

> "In using the myth, in manipulating a continuous parallel between contemporaneity and antiquity, Mr. Joyce is pursuing a method which others must pursue after him ... It is simply a way of controlling, of ordering, of giving a shape and a significance to the immense panorama of futility and anarchy which is contemporary history."

Modernist literature attempted to move from the bonds of Realist literature and to introduce concepts such as disjointed timelines. In the wake of Modernism, and post-enlightenment, metanarratives tended to be emancipatory, whereas before hand this was not a consistent characteristic. Contemporary metanarratives were becoming less relevant in light of the events of World War I, the rise of trade unionism, a general social discontent, and the emergence of psychoanalysis. The consequent need for a unifying function brought about a growth in the political importance of culture.

Modernist literature can be viewed largely in terms of its formal, stylistic and semantic movement away from Romanticism, examining subject matter that is traditionally mundane—a prime example being *The Love Song of J. Alfred Prufrock* by T. S. Eliot. Modernist literature often features a marked pessimism, a clear rejection of the optimism apparent in Victorian literature.

But the questioning spirit of modernism could also be seen, less elegiacally, as part of a necessary search for ways to make sense of a broken world. An example is *A Drunk Man Looks at the Thistle* by Hugh MacDiarmid, in which the individual artist applies Eliot's techniques to respond (in this case) to a historically fractured nationalism, using a more comic, parodic and "optimistic" (though no less "hopeless") modernist expression in which the artist as "hero" seeks to embrace complexity and locate new meanings. However, many Modernist works like Eliot's *The Waste Land* are marked by the absence of a central, unifying figure. In rejecting the solipsism of Romantics like Shelley and Byron, such works also reject the association of the subject with Cartesian dualism, collapsing narrative and narrator into a collection of disjointed fragments and overlapping voices.

Modernist literature often moves beyond the limitations of the Realist novel with a concern for larger factors such as social or historical change. These themes are prominent in "stream of consciousness" writing, notably in *Ulysses* by James Joyce, whose novel has been called "a demonstration and summation of the entire movement". Other examples can be seen in Virginia Woolf's *Kew Gardens* and *Mrs Dalloway*, Katherine Anne Porter's *Flowering Judas*, Jean Toomer's *Cane*, William Faulkner's *The Sound and the Fury*, and others.

Modernism as a literary movement is seen, in large part, as a reaction to the emergence of city life as a central force in society. Furthermore, an early attention to the object as freestanding became in later Modernism a preoccupation with form. The dyadic collapse of the distance between subject and object represented a movement from *means* to *is*. Where Romanticism stressed the subjectivity of experience, Modernist writers were more acutely conscious of the objectivity of their surroundings. In Modernism the object *is*; the language doesn't mean it *is*. This is a shift from an epistemological aesthetic to an ontological aesthetic or, in simpler terms, a shift from a knowledge-based aesthetic to a *being*-based aesthetic. This shift is central to Modernism.

Modernist Movement Development

Modernism is a literary style that emerged after the First World War. At this point, people began to doubt everything they were supposed to believe in surrounding ideas associated with the government, politics, religion, and everyday societal norms. Trust in higher powers and authority figures began to falter, and the inability to sort through the chaos of these mixed emotions left people disheartened, confused, and angry. This feeling of betrayal and uncertainty towards tradition influenced the writing of British authors between 1914-1919 both stylistically and in form. The Modernism movement then reached America in the 1920's.

Characteristics of Modernity/Modernism

Formal/Stylistic Characteristics

Juxtaposition, irony, comparisons, and satire are elements found in modernist writing. The most obvious stylistic tool of the modernist writer is that it is often written in first person. Rather than a traditional story having a beginning, middle and end, modernist writing typically reads as a rant. This can leave the reader slightly confused as to what they are supposed to take away from the work. Juxtaposition could be used for example in a way to represent something that would be often times unseen, for example, a cat and a mouse as best friends. Irony and satire are important tools for the modernist writer in aiding them to make fun of and point out faults in what they are writing about, normally problems within their society, whether it is governmental, political, or social ideas.

Thematic Characteristics

For the first-time reader, modernist writing can seem frustrating to understand because of the fragmentation and lack of conciseness of the writing. The plot, characters and themes of the text are not always linear. The goal of modernist literature is not heavily focused on catering to one particular audience in a formal way. Modernist writing is more interested in getting the writers ideas, opinions, and thoughts out into the public at as high a volume as possible. Modernist literature often forcefully opposes or gives an opinion on a social concept.

The breaking down of social norms, rejection of standard social ideas and traditional thoughts and expectations, objection to religion and anger towards the effects of the world wars, and the rejection of the truth are topics widely seen in this literary era. A rejection of history, social systems, and a sense of loneliness are also common themes. In trying to get their text as high of traffic as possible, modernist literature also creates their text in a stylistic and artistic way, using different fonts, sizes, symbols and colours in the production of their writing.

Modernist Manifestos

The modernist manifesto is a public statement of artistic convictions, normally brief and aggressive. The modernist manifesto was one of the most popular and proclaimed of outcomes of the modernist movement and modernist writing. The word 'manifesto' in Latin is 'to make public'. These authors had no particular audience in mind so long as their manifestos made it into the public eye. Hostility and vulgarity were often styles used within manifestos, as a means of grabbing an audience.

Modernist Poetry

Modernist poetry refers to poetry written between 1890 and 1950 in the tradition of modernist literature in the English language, but the dates of the term depend upon a number of factors, including the nation of origin, the particular school in question, and the biases of the critic setting the dates. It is usually said to have begun with the French Symbolist movement and it artificially ends with the Second World War. The beginning and ending of the modernist period are of course arbitrary: poets like Yeats and Rilke started in a post-Romantic, Symbolist vein and modernised their poetic idiom under the impact of political and literary developments; other poets, like T.S. Eliot, Ezra Pound, or E.E.

Cummings went on to produce significant work after World War II. The questions of impersonality and objectivity seem to be crucial to Modernist poetry. Modernism developed out of a tradition of lyrical expression, emphasising the personal imagination, culture, emotions and memories of the poet. For the modernists, it was essential to move away from the merely personal towards an intellectual statement that poetry could make about the world. Even when they reverted to the personal, like Eliot in the *Four Quartets* or Pound in the *The Cantos,* they distilled the personal into a poetic texture that claimed universal human significance. After World War II, a new generation of poets sought to revoke the effort of their predecessors towards impersonality and objectivity. Modernism ends with the turn towards confessional poetry in the work of Robert Lowell and Sylvia Plath, among others.

Bibliography

Abrams, M.H., *Natural Supernaturalism: Tradition and Revolution in Romantic Literature*: New York: W.W. Norton, 1973.

Adams, Joseph Quincy *A Life of William Shakespeare,* Boston: Houghton Mifflin, 1993.

Arnold, Janet: *Queen Elizabeth's Wardrobe Unlock'd,* W S Maney and Son Ltd, Leeds 1988.

Baldwin, T. W. *William Shakspere's Small Latine & Lesse Greek,* 1, Urbana, Ill: University of Illinois Press, OCLC 359037 , 1944.

Barber, C. L. *Shakespearian Comedy in the Comedy of Errors,* England: College English 25.7 , 1964.

Bentley, G. E. *Shakespeare: A Biographical Handbook,* New Haven: Yale University Press, 1961.

Berlin, Isaiah. *The Roots of Romanticism*. London: Chatto & Windus, 1999.

Berry, Ralph, *Changing Styles in Shakespeare,* London: Routledge, 2005.

Bertolini, John Anthony, *Shaw and Other Playwrights,* Pennsylvania: Pennsylvania State University Press, 1993.

Breckman,, Warren, *European Romanticism: A Brief History with Documents*. New York: Bedford/St. Martin's, 2007.

Brusher, Joseph H. *Popes Through The Ages*. Princeton: D. Van Nostland Company, Inc., 1959.

Chamberlin, E.R. *The Bad Popes*. Reprint: Barnes and Noble, 1993.

Chambers, E. K. *William Shakespeare: A Study of Facts and Problems,* 2 vols., Oxford: Clarendon Press, 1930.

Ciofalo, John J. "The Ascent of Genius in the Court and Academy." *The Self-Portraits of Francisco Goya.* Cambridge University Press, 2001.

Cone, Carl B. *Burke and the Nature of Politics, a detailed modern biography of Burke; somewhat uncritical and sometimes superficial regarding politics,* 1957.

Conor Cruise O'Brien, *The Great Melody. A Thematic Biography of Edmund Burke,* 1992.

Crompton, Louis. *Byron and Greek Love: Homophobia in 19th-Century England*. Faber and Faber, 1985.

Crowe, Ian, ed. *An Imaginative Whig: Reassessing the Life and Thought of Edmund Burke*. 247 pp. essays by scholars, 2005.

Digby, George Wingfield. *Elizabethan Embroidery*. New York: Thomas Yoseloff, 1964.

Dollison, John *Pope-pourri*. New York: Simon & Schuster, 1994.

Fay, Elizabeth, *Romantic Medievalism. History and the Romantic Literary Ideal*. Houndsmills, Basingstoke: Palgrave, 2002.

Frederick Dreyer, 'The Genesis of Burke's Reflections', *The Journal of Modern History*, Vol. 50, No. 3, pp. 462–479, 1978.

Garrett, Martin. 'Palgrave Literary Dictionary of Byron'. Palgrave, 2010.

Garrett, Martin: *George Gordon, Lord Byron*. (British Library Writers' Lives). London: British Library, 2000.

Gibbons, Luke. *Edmund Burke and Ireland: Aesthetics, Politics, and the Colonial Sublime*. 304 pp, 2003.

Grosskurth, Phyllis: *Byron: The Flawed Angel*. Hodder, 1997.

Guiccioli, Teresa, contessa di, *Lord Byron's Life in Italy*, transl. Michael Rees, ed. Peter Cochran, 2005.

Hibbert, Christopher. *King Mob: The Story of Lord George Gordon and the Riots*. Dorset Press, 1990.

Holmes, Richard. *The Age of Wonder: The Romantic Generation and the Discovery of the Beauty and Terror of Science*, 2009.

Hutton, Ronald: *The Stations of the Sun: A History of the Ritual Year in Britain*, 2001.

Hutton, Ronald:*The Rise and Fall of Merry England: The Ritual Year, 1400–1700*, 2001.

Ian Crowe, 'The career and political thought of Edmund Burke', *Journal of Liberal History*, Issue 40, Autumn 2003.

Jacob W. Grimm. *Selected Tales* pg 19. Penguin Classics, 1982.

Kelly, J.N.D. *The Oxford Dictionary of Popes*. Oxford: University Press, 1986.

Kirk, Russell. *Edmund Burke: A Genius Reconsidered* by a leader of American conservatism online edition, 1997.

Kramnick, Isaac. *The Rage of Edmund Burke: Portrait of an Ambivalent Conservative* online edition, 1977.

MacCarthy, Fiona: *Byron: Life and Legend*. John Murray, 2002.

Marcel, Brion. *Art of the Romantic Era*. Henry Holt & Company, Inc, 1996.

Marshall, P. J. *The Impeachment of Warren Hastings*, the standard history of the trial and Burke's role, 1965.

Masson, Scott, 'Romanticism', Ch.7 in *The Oxford Handbook of English Literature and Theology*, Oxford University Press, 2007.

Maxwell-Stuart, P.G. *Chronicle of the Popes: The Reign-by-Reign Record of the Papacy from St. Peter to the Present, with 308 Illustrations, 105 in Color*. London: Thames and Hudson, 1997.

McCalman, Iain, ed. *An Oxford Companion to the Romantic Age* online at Oxford Reference Online, 2009.

McGann, Jerome: *Byron and Romanticism*. Cambridge: Cambridge University Press, 2002.

Murray, Christopher, ed. *Encyclopedia of the romantic era*, (2 vol 2004); 850 articles by experts; 1600pp, 1850.

Norwich, John Julius. *The Popes: a History*. Chatto, 2011.

O'Gorman, Frank. *Edmund Burke: Edmund Burke: His Political Philosophy*, 153pp online edition, 2004.

Oueijan, Naji B. *A Compendium of Eastern Elements in Byron's Oriental Tales*. New York: Peter Lang Publishing, 1999.

Parkin, Charles. *The Moral Basis of Burke's Political Thought*, 1956.

Pocock, J.G.A. "Burke and the Ancient Constitution", *Historical Journal*, 125-43; shows Burke's debt to the Common Law tradition of the 17th century in JSTOR, 1960.

Prell, Donald: *Sailing with Byron from Genoa to Cephalonia*. Strand Publishing, 2009.

Robert Eccleshall, *English Conservatism since the Restoration*: London: Unwin Hyman, 1990.

Rosen, Fred: *Bentham, Byron and Greece*. Clarendon Press, Oxford, 1992.

Rosenblum, Robert, *Modern Painting and the Northern Romantic Tradition: Friedrich to Rothko*, (Harper & Row) 1975.

S. T. Coleridge: Anna Lætitia Barbauld first met Samuel Taylor Coleridge in August 179.

Schenk, H.G., *The Mind of the European Romantics: An Essay in Cultural History*, (Constable) 1966.

St Clair, William, *That Greece Might Still Be Free: The Philhellenes in the War of Independence*, 2008.

Steven Blakemore (ed.), *Burke and the French Revolution. Bicentennial Essays*: The University of Georgia Press, 1992.

Tekiner, Deniz, *Modern Art and the Romantic Vision*, (University Press of America) 2000.

Thiollet, Jean-Pierre: *Carré d'Art: Barbey d'Aurevilly, lord Byron, Salvador Dali, Jean-Edern Hallier*, Anagramme éditions, 2008.

Thomas Wellsted Copeland, 'Edmund Burke and the Book Reviews in Dodsley's Annual Register', *Publications of the Modern Language Association*, Vol. 57, No. 2. pp. 446–468, 1942.

Wilson, Derek. *The World Encompassed: Francis Drake and His Great Voyage*. New York, Harper & Row, 1977.

Yates, Frances A. *The Occult Philosophy in the Elizabethan Age*. London, Routledge & Kegan Paul, 1979.

Yates, Frances A. *Theatre of the World*. Chicago, University of Chicago Press, 1969.